B&T
24.95

RENAISSANCE DRAMA

New Series XIV ✑ 1983

Renaissance Drama

NEW SERIES XIV

Relations and Influences

Edited by Leonard Barkan

Northwestern University Press

EVANSTON 1983

The front cover illustration is "The Death of Lucretia" from Johann Ludwig Gottfried, *Historische Chronica* (Frankfurt, 1674).

The back cover illustration is "Salmacis and Hermaphroditus" from *Des vortrefflichlateinischen Poeten P. Ovidii Nasonis fünfzehn Verwandlungs-Bücher* (Nuremburg, n.d.). The illustrations are reprinted with the permission of Special Collections, Northwestern University Library.

Publication of this volume was made possible by a grant from the College of Arts and Sciences, Northwestern University.

Editorial Note

Renaissance Drama, an annual publication, provides a forum for scholars in various parts of the globe: wherever the drama of the Renaissance is studied. Coverage, so far as subject matter is concerned, is not restricted to any single national theater. The chronological limits of the Renaissance are interpreted liberally, and space is available for essays on precursors, as well as on the use of Renaissance themes by later writers. Editorial policy favors articles of some scope. Essays that are exploratory in nature, that are concerned with critical or scholarly methodology, that raise new questions or embody fresh approaches to perennial problems are particularly appropriate for a publication that originated from the proceedings of the Modern Language Association Conference on Research Opportunities in Renaissance Drama.

The Editor gratefully acknowledges his debt to the members of the Editorial Committee, and similar warm thanks are due to the editorial assistant, Cheri Peters, and to our administrative assistant, Marjorie Weiner. The efficient and expert help of the assistant editor, Janice Feldstein, has been absolutely indispensable.

Volume XV of *Renaissance Drama* will concern itself with Modes, Motifs, and Genres. Correspondence, submissions, and enquiries regarding future volumes should be addressed to Professor Leonard Barkan, Editor, *Renaissance Drama*, English Department, Northwestern University, Evanston, Illinois 60201.

Contents

RENAISSANCE DRAMA

New Series XIV ⚬ 1983

The Pharmacy of Machiavelli:
Roman Lucretia in Mandragola

RONALD L. MARTINEZ

I N A RECENT STUDY, Franco Fido treats critical views of Machiavelli's *Mandragola* under three implicit headings: (1) meritorious accounts that combine an awareness of the generic constraints on the play with a sense for specifically Machiavellian—hence political—concerns; (2) debatable interpretations that emphasize the resonances within the play of the author's personal difficulties after the Medici restoration in 1512; and (3) speculative readings that attempt to associate the events of the play with specific political agendas or with historical events contemporary with the play.[1] Fido concludes his survey by arguing for an understanding of *Mandragola* both as ironic valedictory, signaling the retreat

---

1. See Franco Fido, "Politica e teatro nel badalucco de Meser Nicia," now in *Le metamorfosi del centauro: Studi e letture da Boccaccio a Pirandello* (Rome, 1977), pp. 91–108. Giorgio Cavallini, *Interpretazione della Mandragola* (Milan, 1973), pp. 7–22, also gives a summary of critical thought on the play. For some accounts in English, see Marvin T. Herrick, *Italian Comedy in the Renaissance* (Urbana and London, 1960), pp. 80–85; Douglas Radcliffe-Umstead, *The Birth of Modern Comedy in Renaissance Italy* (Chicago and London, 1969), pp. 116–134; Leo Salingar, *Shakespeare and the Traditions of Comedy* (Cambridge, Eng., 1974), pp. 196–197, 199–200.

1

of political virtue from the *polis* to the bedroom, and as a plaything, "un badalucco," that serves to absorb the interest of an unemployed political genius.[2]

Fido's succinct study aims at imposing a measure of order on the disorderly house of *Mandragola* commentary: his lapidary summation argues the complete absorption of the play's complex tensions in the brilliant realization of the comic plot: "the imbalance between the end and the means is resolved, without apparent effort and without any residue, in the comic form."[3] In some respects, however, Fido may have done his work too well. A different approach to the play is that of Ezio Raimondi, who in a series of essays has taken soundings of the play's striking heterogeneity of inspiration and tonal register.[4] Raimondi's findings pose

2. Fido, pp. 107–108. For the convenience of the reader, Marvin T. Herrick's synopsis of the play follows:

Callimaco, a young Florentine who has been living in Paris for some years, has returned to his native city to see for himself a celebrated beauty, Madonna Lucrezia, wife of Messer Nicia Calfucci. The young woman has proved to be even more beautiful than reported, and he has fallen desperately in love with her. But what can he do? Lucrezia is as chaste as she is beautiful. Callimaco, who is no callow youth, perceives three weaknesses in the defense: the simplicity of the husband Nicia, the desire of the couple to have children, and the easygoing mother of the wife. Callimaco has reasoned soundly, and his campaign is successful, but not until he has engaged the help of the parasite Ligurio, who in turn has to call on a friar to win over the two women. It is Ligurio who devises the fraud that insures success: Callimaco poses as a learned physician from Paris who concocts a draught of mandragola guaranteed to make any woman conceive. There are complications, however, for it seems that the first man to cohabit with a patient who had drunk this potion will die within a week. Therefore it is necessary to kidnap some homeless young man to serve as the agent. This waif, of course, is Callimaco disguised as a strolling musician. Owing to the ready co-operation of the husband and mother-in-law, the arguments of the friar, and the expert timing of the parasite, everything runs like clockwork; the young man wins a beautiful mistress, the husband and his mother-in-law rejoice in the prospect of an heir, the parasite is sure of three meals a day for some time to come, and the father confessor is richer by 300 ducats [pp. 80-81].

3. Raimondi's important essays on Machiavelli are collected in *Politica e commedia dal Beroaldo al Machiavelli* (Bologna, 1972), pp. 141-286.

4. T. H. Sumberg, "*La mandragola,* An Interpretation," in *Journal of Politics,* XXIII (1961), 320-348; A. Parronchi, "La prima rappresentazione della *Mandragola*: Il modello per l'apparato. L'allegoria." in *La bibliofila,* LXIV (1962), 37-89. For Sumberg, Callimaco is generically the Prince, specifically a representation of the Medici, "patres patriae," who

the question of where we are to place *Mandragola* on a line that stretches from the Boccaccian *beffa* (trick) that inspires its comic situations to the learned context of Aristophanic satire to the political allegory that critics such as Sumberg, Parronchi, and Ridolfi claim to detect in the play.[5] If we are to see the play whole, we must be able to account both for the play's mocking tone—stridently in evidence from the acerbic prologue to the triumph of cuckoldry at play's end—and for its repeated invitations to judge the action in the context of Machiavelli's political thought. Once we have fully weighed both the play's levity and its gravity, we must come to terms with the undertone of pessimism and bitterness that many critics claim to detect in the apparently jocular events. The opinion of Nino Borsellino might be considered representative:[6]

The world of *Mandragola* is fervently anarchic, deprived of ideals, where the natural order of the instincts may be restored only through moral disorder. Machiavelli acknowledges this world with that sharp and lucid realism that does not conceal its bitterness: as if the "odd and spiteful bauble" of the comedy permitted him to relieve the oppressive malignity of fate [my translation].

---

will return to refertilize Florence, represented by Lucrezia, hitherto in the grasp of Nicia, who stands for political impotence. Ligurio might be Machiavelli himself. For Parronchi, the alignment of characters and historical personages is more exact: because, in his view, the first performance of *Mandragola* took place in September of 1518 as part of the celebrations commemorating the marriage of Lorenzo de Pierfrancesco de Medici to Marguerite de la Tour Angoulême, Callimaco must be Lorenzo returning "victorious" from France; Nicia is the ineffectual Piero Soderini, *gonfaloniere* for life of the Florentine republic (and whose wife was indeed sterile). Roberto Ridolfi, in his *Life of Niccolò Machiavelli*, 2d ed., trans. Cecil Grayson (Chicago, 1963), accepts the identification of Nicia with Soderini.

5. In *Commedie del Cinquecento,* ed. Nino Borsellino (Milan, 1962), I, xxvi. For substantially similar views, see G. D. Bonino, ed., *Il teatro Italiano,* II: *La commedia del 1500* (Turin, 1977), I, xliii–lii; and L. Russo, *Machiavelli* (Bari, 1957), p. 93. Raimondi, *Politica e commedia,* p. 162, merits citation: "Alla fine della commedia non si avverte liberazione alcuna, la parodia che si aggiunge al rito canonico della festa è come un veleno, un sospetto che non si placa nel trionfo gioioso e previsto della natura." The "dark" view of the play goes back at least to F. de Sanctis, *Storia della letteratura italiana,* ed. B. Croce (Bari, 1912), II, 94-102.

6. For the observation, see de Sanctis, *Storia,* p. 94. In many respects, my study vindicates de Sanctis's view of the play, if not his moral outrage and his anachronistic view that the play is superannuated.

With the intention of shedding some additional light on the problems raised by Machiavelli's play, I am proposing a detailed reconsideration of the textual relationship between *Mandragola* and Livy's account of Lucretia's suicide (*ab urbe condita*, I.57-59). Although the irony implicit in naming the (finally) pliable Florentine Lucrezia with the name of a Roman exemplar of chastity has been remarked, it has not served as a primary datum that might lead to a systematic view of the play.[7] Moreover, the consideration of Livy's text in conjunction with Machiavelli's addresses the principal critical problems outlined above; for the political result of the suicide in Livy's history plants for the critic the question of the political domain of Machiavelli's own text, while the somber events of Lucretia's death extend a dark background for the ribaldry and humor of Machiavelli's play. Let me first consider a few methodological questions.

Though topical allegories such as those of Sumberg and Parronchi have been attacked as unconvincing, it cannot be doubted that *Mandragola* invites some form of programmatic decoding. Felix Gilbert has defined Machiavelli's own brand of allegory as the discovery of general rules of political behavior in the events of classical antiquity.[8] Indeed, Machiavelli's argument that human nature is essentially invariable, and that states follow regular cycles of development (the Polybian thesis of *anakyklosis*) permits the construction of a transhistorical frame of interpretation within which the events of the present may be measured against those of antiquity.[9] The history of Rome and the history of contemporary Italy con-

---

7. One can do no better than quote de Sanctis: "La tragedia romana si trasforma nelle commedia fiorentina," *Storia*, p. 94. The idea that the play is at bottom tragic in mood is advanced by Benedetto Croce in "La commedia del rinascimento," reprinted in *Poesia popolare e poesia d'arte* (Bari, 1932), p. 247; the notion is developed by Russo, *Machiavelli*, p. 143. It has been restated recently by Ridolfi, *Studi sulla commedia del Machiavelli* (Pisa, 1968), pp. 65-66. Ian Donaldson's *The Rapes of Lucretia: A Myth and Its Transformations* (Oxford, 1982), appeared too late for me to exploit its rich inventory of literary and artistic treatments of Lucretia in the formulation of my own arguments. Donaldson addresses many of the issues I have considered in my own approach—the relation of political and sexual tyranny (p. 8) and the symbolism of Tarquin's knife (pp. 16-17), for example—but his own views of *Mandragola* are disappointingly conventional. His conclusion, that Machiavelli is *demythologizing* Lucretia (p. 93), could not be further from my own.

8. Felix Gilbert, *Machiavelli and Guicciardini* (Princeton, N.J., 1965), pp. 168-169.

9. For unchanging human nature, cf. Niccolò Machiavelli, *Discorsi sopra la prima deca di Tito Livio*, III, 43, in *Il principe e le opere politiche*, ed. Delio Cantimori (Milan, 1976), p. 451. English translations of the *Discorsi* are from *The Prince* and the *Discourses*, introd. Max

stitute two discourses that can be read in terms of one another—one way of defining allegory. The evidence for such an interpretive context may be found readily in *Mandragola,* from the references in the author's prologue to the corruption of the present age ("che per tutto traligna dall'antica virtù . . . il secolo presente") to the use of specifically Roman names (Lucrezia, Ligurio, Camillo) beyond the requirements of Plautine and Terentian example.[10] The comedy thus shares that comparative spirit that makes the juxtaposition of Roman and Italian events a reflex—indeed, a method—of the *Prince* and the *Discourses on the First Decade of Titus Livius.*[11] Nor is the play's political context merely general: readers have noted that Machiavelli situates Callimaco's departure from his native city in 1494, when the first French invasions of Italy, in Callimaco's words, destroyed the province of Italy (" ruinorno quella provincia").[12] As Luigi Russo observes, reflections on the effects of 1494 are uncharacteristic of the blandly apolitical Callimaco but typical of his author; Callimaco's

Lerner (New York, 1950) (translator of the *Discorsi* is Christine E. Detmold). Machiavelli's examples are the Gauls against the Romans and the hosts of Charles VIII against the Italians. For the "Polybian" thesis of cyclical history, see the *Discorsi,* I. For Machiavelli's use of Polybius, now generally accepted, see G. Sasso, *Niccolò Machiavelli, storia del suo pensiero politico* (Naples, 1958), pp. 308-315 (on the *anakyklosis*). As Sasso concludes, "La storia romana diviene dunque l'ideale criterio con cui il Machiavelli cerca di penetrare e di comprendere lo svolgimento della storia di Firenze." See also J.G.A. Pocock, *The Machiavellian Moment: Florentine Political Thought and the Atlantic Republican Tradition* (Princeton, N.J., 1975), pp. 186-194.

10. *Mandragola, prologo,* vv. 59-60. All citations to the play are to the edition of Franco Gaeta, in *Niccolò Machiavelli, Il teatro e tutti gli scritti letterari* (Milan, 1965), pp. 55-112; translations are mine. The language of the *prologo* also echoes the preface to Livy's *Ab urbe condita* (ed. R. S. Conway and C. F. Walters [Oxford, 1914]): "labente deinde paulatim disciplina velut desidentes primo mores sequatur animo, deinde ut magis magisque lapsi sint," etc., and Machiavelli's own adaptation of these ideas in the *Discorsi,* I, *proemio.* Hereafter *Ab urbe condita* is cited as *AUC.*

11. Gilbert, pp. 168-169; Sasso, p. 315. As in the prologue to the *Clizia* (Gaeta, p. 116), where Machiavelli explicitly describes the "translatio studii" from Greece to Rome to Italy, the names of the characters in *Mandragola* are both Greek (Sostrata, Timoteo, Siro, Callimaco, Nicia) and Roman (Lucrezia, Camillo, Ligurio).

12. Russo, p. 17. Machiavelli's idiom is a reference to the traditional designation of Italy as the "domina provinciarum." In *Discorsi* III.7 the revolt that expelled the Tarquins is compared with the expulsion of the Medici in 1494. See also I.48.

words in fact reiterate a phrase from the *Discourses*.[13] And the date does not simply dangle freely; Callimaco's opening soliloquy dates the action of the play to 1504, ten years after the first of the French invasions, establishing a mensuration by decades that recurs in the play and that corresponds to Machiavelli's division of political epochs in the allegorical *Decennali,* which begin in 1494.[14] In the context of Machiavelli's use of Livy both in *Mandragola* and in his commentary on the first *decade* of Livy's history, the ten-year segments in the play are linked to Livy's division of the books of his history into pentads and decades, which reflects the Roman practice of measuring years by *lustra*.[15] Though not necessarily coextensive, the measurement of time and of the articulations of narrative share common principles. Finally, as stated in the author's *prologo,* the *apparato* or stage set for *Mandragola* represents Florence, though the illusionism of the theater will permit, another day, the representation of Rome or Pisa.[16] For Parronchi, mention of Rome and Pisa helps to corroborate his view that the play celebrated the union of Lorenzo de Medici and his French bride.[17] But whether his hypothesis is proven or falsified, it remains suggestive that Machiavelli has chosen to mention both the illustrious model and parent of Florence—Rome—and Pisa, the city that was the most recalcitrant object of Florentine imperialism and

13. Russo, p. 17. For a parallel to "ruinorno quella provincia," see *Discorsi,* I.37. The political significance of *Mandragola* is acknowledged by Croce, p. 5, and L. Russo, *Commedie Fiorentine del '500* (Florence, 1939), pp. 15-16.

14. "Decennale primo," vv. 10-12 (ed. Gaeta, p. 236). For the importance of the ten-year interval in *Mandragola,* cf. Sumberg's list, pp. 40-41. Machiavelli's prefatory letter to the *Decennali,* addressed to Alamanno Salviato, refers to "transacti decenni labores Italicos" (Gaeta, p. 235). Verse 2 of the poem refers to the "duo passati lustri" and continues with "aveva il sol veloce sopra'l dorso / del nostro mondo ben termini mille / e quattrocento novanta quattro corso" (vv. 10-12).

15. For the division of the first 45 books of Livy's history, see T. R. Luce, *Livy: The Composition of His History* (Princeton, N.J., 1977), pp. 3-32, especially the last sentence on p. 32: "Scholars are agreed that in the extant books, including the missing decade 11-20, Livy blocked out his material according to pentads and decades." At Rome the closing of a *lustrum* entailed an official ceremony and included the taking of a census; cf. *AUC,* 47.1-7.

16. "Vedete l'apparato / quale or vi si dimostra: / questa è Firenze vostra; / un'altra volta sarà Roma o Pisa" (vv. 7-10).

17. Parronchi, pp. 71-79.

whose name dots the *Discourses* and the *Prince*.[18] Rome and Pisa frame
Florentine ambitions much as the French and the Turks (both also mentioned in *Mandragola*) mark the outer sphere of Italian influence in Europe
and the Mediterranean.[19] Thus the play's imagined spaces, as well as its
imagined setting in time, are set in terms of the structure of Machiavelli's
political vision.

My own argument, then, goes further than that of those who admit a
general relationship of *Mandragola* to the major political statements, but
remains distinct from the approaches of topical allegorists who discern a
specific, historical *dramatis personae* in the characters of the play. More
than a play with historical overtones, *Mandragola* is itself a form of
theorizing about, and interpreting, history and politics. Moreover, with
respect to the story of Lucretia in particular, Machiavelli is in an established Florentine humanist tradition, for it has been shown that for
early humanists and republicans alike, the iconography of the rape of
Lucretia was associated with anti-tyrannical and pro-republican views. At
the same time, the story of Lucretia appears in panels that mark the
progress of scientific perspective in the *scenografia* of the early Renaissance,
such that Machiavelli's choice of Lucretia as part of his subject occurs in a
context where a specific link between the Roman episode and the public
spectacle of the *commedia* had already been established. Some elaboration of
these points may be helpful.

Already in the late *trecento* the rape of Lucretia was the subject of a
pro-republican *declamatio* by Coluccio Salutati, and thus figures in the
complex debate, analyzed in detail by Hans Baron, over the relative
merits of tyrannies or republics that agitated humanists of the early
Renaissance.[20] To confirm the persistence of the Lucretia theme in the

18. For Pisa as the stumbling block of Florentine expansionist ambitions, see the
Discorsi, I, 38; I, 53; II, 1; III, 16; III, 43; III, 48; and *Il principe* (ed. Cantimori,) v, xx,
where the Pisans' tenacious love of their own freedoms is remarked.

19. For the Turkish threat in the Mediterranean, see the *Discorsi*, II, 1, where the
Turks are among the heirs of military empire; see also the "Decennale primo," vv.
205-207, and Machiavelli's letter of 18 May 1521 to Guicciardini (*Lettere,* ed. F. Gaeta
[Milan, 1961], p. 409). For Turks and the French compared, cf. *Il principe*, iv.

20. Hans Baron, *The Crisis of the Early Italian Renaissance* (Princeton, N.J., 1955). The
entire study is relevant to the question of Machiavelli's pro-republican attitudes, tracing
the progress and regress of republican enthusiasm in the early Humanist tradition. Co-

terms of the same debate, Guy Walton has shown that the Baltimore Lucretia panel, dated to 1504 or slightly after, caps a discernible tradition of representations of the rape of Lucretia and Brutus's subsequent oration over her body.[21] As Walton points out, the presence in the Baltimore Lucretia of the statues of David and Goliath and Judith and Holofernes make the anti-tyrannical polemic of the panel unmistakable, as these figures, once totems of Florentine resistance to Visconti tyranny, had come to signify the hostility of the Florentine republic to the continued dynastic pretensions of the Medici after their expulsion in 1494. The subject of Lucretia and Brutus (paired with the related episode of Appius and Virginia) is thus inscribed in a political iconography at the heart of Florentine civic concerns. In addition, as both Walton and Richard Krautheimer have shown, the Lucretia and Virginia panels, in their use of noble, classicizing architecture and their adoption of rigorous scientific perspective, are textbook examples of the so-called tragic scene. Krautheimer notes that the "tragic scene," whether devised for real or imaginary performances, evolves in close synchronization with the evolution of scientific perspective itself; its depiction of classical temples, arches, and plazas conform to canonical distinction, descending from Vitruvius through Alberti, between the archetypal "tragic" and "comic" scenes.[22] It is just such a "perspective," the famous Urbino panel, that

---

luccio Salutati refers to his declamation on Lucretia in a letter (*Epistolario di Coluccio Salutati*, ed. F. Novati, v. 4, [Rome, 1905] [Fonti per la storia d'Italia, v. 18], pp. 253-254); Novati gives in his note the passage to which Salutati refers, from Lucretia's answer to her father's and husband's pleas that she not commit suicide: "Nichil muliere mobilius: egritudinem animique motus nedum mollit sed extinguit tempus. si distulero, forsan incipient michi flagitiosa placere," etc. The passage is striking because it makes Lucretia's justification for suicide her fear of her own nature as a woman, "semper varium et mutabile."

21. Guy Walton, "The Lucretia Panel in the Isabella Stuart Gardner Museum in Boston," *Essays in Honor of Walter Freidlaender*, ed. by Marsyas, *Studies in the History of Art*, supplement II: a special volume, Institute of Fine Arts, New York University (1965), pp. 177-186. See figure I. The subject of Lucretia's rape and suicide is a popular subject of *cassoni* illustration throughout the quattrocento and cinquecento; Paul Schubring, *Cassoni*, (Leipzig, 1915) gives nineteen entries, of which eleven are illustrated. Of special interest are Sodoma's 1505 panels juxtaposing Lucretia with Judith; cf. *Textband*, p. 164, illustration in *Tafelband*, 1. 157, n. 735.

22. Walton, pp. 183-184; Richard Krauthheimer, "The Tragic and Comic Scene in the Renaissance: The Baltimore and Urbino Panels," *Gazette des Beaux-Arts*, VI, XXIII (June 1948), 327-346. See also Parronchi, pp. 37-45.

Parronchi has identified as the backdrop for the first performance of *Mandragola,* placed by Parronchi in September 1518.[23] Whether the Urbino panel was, in fact, the scene for *Mandragola,* it is likely that the *apparato* for Machiavelli's play resembled it, for a description of the stage set of Bibbiena's *La Calandria,* one of Machiavelli's immediate dramatic models, has survived, often attributed to Baldessar Castiglione. The description is of a classicizing scene, with friezes and reliefs depicting Roman heroes, including the Horatii.[24] In the context of Machiavelli's own literary practice and political interests, it is hardly speculative to assert that a conspicuously classicizing backdrop for the bourgeois comedy of *Mandragola* would provide an ironic visual "perspective" on the action of the play just as the evocation of Roman Lucretia in the name of Nicia's wife Lucrezia provides *verbal* irony. An idealized antiquity represented both by allusion to Livy and the visual allusions of architecture frames the action of *Mandragola* and imposes a perspective from which the audience views and judges the events of the plot.

My exposition of Lucrezia's fall will be in three parts, with a prologue. After consideration of some general aspects of Machiavelli's use of Livy's text, the first part will consist of a description of the principal parallels between Livy's history and *Mandragola.* A calculation of the differences between the Roman and Florentine Lucretias yields an inventory of the differences for Machiavelli between the heroic civic virtue of the Romans and the corruption of the civic body in early cinquecento Florence. The second part of the study examines the function of ritual action in the two texts. In Livy's narrative, the episode of Lucretia and Brutus functions as an etiological fable: Lucretia's suicide makes her the sacrificial victim, the *pharmakos* whose destruction is instrumental in precipitating the expulsion of the tyrants and establishing the Roman republic. As such, Lucretia's tragedy is one of a series of episodes in the first decade that exemplify Aristotle's view in the *Politics* that offenses to women may serve as

23. Parronchi, pp. 54-56.

24. For the description, see Walton, p. 183; Bonino, pp. 445-448, reprints an even lengthier extract.

25. See the *Politics,* V. 10-15, 1311a34-1311b22. For examples from Machiavelli's text, cf. *Discorsi,* I.2, I.40, II.16, III.6, 26—whose rubric is: "Come per ragioni de femine se rovina uno stato."

catalysts precipitating revolutions in the state.[26] Machiavelli's interest in
Lucretia's story—as in the first decade of Livy in general—springs largely
from his concern for the problems of political innovation, whether during
the original foundation of a city or as a part of constitutional reform or
violent revolution. Thus *Mandragola,* too, as some readers have observed,
is itself an etiology of a new community, albeit one founded not on heroic
sacrifice but on the rational calculation of private advantage, on
acquisitiveness or *guadagno.* Third and finally—in the wake of studies
showing how the lore of the mandrake root penetrates the language and
action of the play—I turn to a discussion of the potent, ambiguous
medicine *mandragola* from the perspective of Lucretia herself as the *pharmakon* that purges Rome from the disease of tyranny.[26] The ambiguous
function of *mandragola* is the play's principal link to the sacrificial economy operating in Livy's account of Lucretia's suicide and its aftermath;
and it is only after an elucidation of the full semantic domain of *mandragola* in the play that we can begin to unravel the play's teasing final
ironies—foremost of which is the magnificent rejuvenescence of Lucrezia
herself. Because Lucrezia is the cynosure, the uniquely virtuous element in
the generally corrupt world of the play, both her submission and her final
transformation are central to our understanding of the play's meaning.

The specific parallels between Livy's text and Machiavelli's play are
framed by Machiavelli's use of several important Livian themes in *Mandragola.* First, Machiavelli's notorious remarks in the verse prologue,
referring to the corruption of the present age, repeat the fundamental
premise of Livy's vast history, which would, in the historian's words,

trace the progress of our moral decline . . . the sinking of the foundation of
morality as the old teaching was allowed to lapse, then the rapidly increasing
disintegration, then the final collapse of the whole edifice, and the dark dawning
of our modern day when we can neither endure our vices nor face the remedies
needed to cure them. The study of history is the best medicine for a sick mind; for
in history you have a record of the infinite variety of human experience plainly set

26. See Giovanni Aquilecchia, "Mandragola la favola si chiama," in *Collected Essays in
Italian Language and Literature Presented to Kathleen Speight,* (Manchester, 1971), pp. 74-
100; Ezio Raimondi, "Il veleno della *Mandragola,*" in *Politica e Commedia,* pp. 253-264;
Hugo Rahner, "Moly and Mandragora in Pagan and Christian Symbolism," in *Greek Myths
and Christian Mystery,* (London 1963), pp. 224-277.

out for all to see; and in that record you can find for yourself and your country both examples and warnings . . .[27]

Machiavelli, who identified profoundly with Livy's role as *laudator temporis acti*, adopts both in the *Discourses* and the prologue to *Mandragola* not only the idea of the monitory value of history but also the Livian metaphor of the state as a diseased body—a metaphor that will return in the medical-pharmaceutical register of *Mandragola*.[28] Second, Livy's treatment of the story of Brutus and Lucretia, condensing and focusing the prolix account of Dionysus of Halicarnassus, presents the events in strikingly *dramatic* terms.[29] Indeed, Livy explicitly compares the indigenous Roman tragedy of Lucretia to the Hellenic flavor of the parricidal Tarquins:

In ancient Greece more than one royal house was guilty of crime which became the stuff of tragedy; now Rome was to follow the same path, but not in vain, for that very guilt was to hasten the coming of liberty and the hatred of kings . . .[30]

One consequence of Livy's conspicuously dramatic treatment is that his episode follows the tragic unities: the rape and suicide of Lucretia, and Brutus's speech over her body, are narrated as if occurring without interruption; they all occur in Collatia, where Lucretia, the wife of Collatinus, resides; and the sequence of events presents a closely articulated plot, a rigorous sequence of cause and effect that culminates with the flight of Tarquin.[31] The fact that the sequence of events continues

27. *AUC praefatio* 6-9, trans. Aubrey de Selincourt, *The Early History of Rome* (London, 1960), p. 34.

28. Cf. *Discorsi*, I, *proemio*; "Nè ancora la medicina è altro che esperienza fatta dagli antiqui medici, sopra la quale fondano e medici presenti e loro iudizii. Nondimanco, nello ordinare le republiche . . . non si trova principe nè republica che agli esempi delli antiqui ricorra; II, *proemio*: "Laudano sempre gli uomini, ma non sempre ragionevolmente, gli antichi tempi, e i presenti accusano"; III, i: "Egli è cosa verissima come tutte le cose del mondo hanno il termine della vita loro . . . E perchi'io parlo de' corpi misti, come sono le republiche e le sette, dico che quelle alterazioni sono a salute che le riducano inverso i principii loro."

29. Dionysus of Halicarnassus, *Roman Antiquities*, trans. E. Cary, Loeb Classics (Cambridge and London, 1952), II, 473-577.

30. Livy, *Early History*, p. 42.

31. For the dramatic thrust of Livy's account, see the remarks of R. L. Ogilvy, *A Commentary on Livy, Books I-V*, (Oxford, 1964), pp. 218-219.

through the night is made explicit in Ovid's version of the Lucretia-Brutus story in the *Fasti,* which follows Livy closely.[32] Whichever the textual stimulus for Machiavelli, in *Mandragola* the play's observation of the unity of time is ostentatiously proclaimed by the corrupt priest Timoteo at the beginning of the fifth act.[33] In the context of Livy's theatrical treatment of the Lucretia story, Machiavelli's religious observance of the unity of time is both vestige and elaboration of the dramatic tendencies in the historical text.

Finally, the Livian account of Sextus's violence against Lucretia is framed in terms of his father Tarquinius Superbus's siege of Rutulian Ardea; it is because the siege is stalled that Sextus and the other officers, including Collatinus, fall to boasting of their wives' virtue, that "muliebris certamen" that leads directly to Sextus's fatal infatuation with Lucretia.[34] The original context of the siege continues *as metaphor* through Sextus's attack and defeat of Lucretia's virtue, justifying Livy's reference to her loss of chastity with the formulaic term for the reduction of a city or fortress: "expugnatum decus."[35] Livy's metaphor is hardly lost on Machiavelli the student of military strategy and the psychologist of human competition, and thus the action of *Mandragola* is more than once conceived in the terms of a siege operation: the protagonists Callimaco and Nicia bear the names of generals, one imaginary, one real; and the terminology of assault and resistance appears in Callimaco's calculation of Lucrezia's virtuous opposition to his desire ("mi fa la guerra la natura di lei

32. P. Ovidius Naso, *Die Fasten,* ed. Franz Böhmer (Heidelberg, 1957), vol. I, *Fasti* II. 685-856. Ovid's emphasis on the nocturnal hour is noted by A. G. Lee, "Ovid's Lucretia," in *Greece and Rome* (1953), pp. 115-117.

33. For discussion, see E. J. Webber, "The Dramatic Unities in the *Mandragola,*" *Italica,* XXXIII, no. 1 (March 1956), 20-21, and C. S. Singleton, "Machiavelli and the Spirit of Comedy," *MLN,* LVII (November 1942), 585-592.

34. *AUC,* I.57.3-6.

35. Compare "expugnato decus" of Lucretia's chastity with Livy's expression for the expulsion of the Tarquins, I.59.2: "Ut praeceptum erat iurant; totique ab luctu versi in iram, Brutum tam inde *ad expugnandum regnum* vocantem sequuntur ducem." Livy also establishes a relation between the initial attempt of Tarquin's forces to seize Ardea by storm—"temptata res est, si primo impetu *capi* Ardea posset" (I.57.3)—and Sextus's own capture by the desire to rape Lucretia; "Ibi Sex. Tarquinium mala libido Lucretiae per vim stuprandae *capit*" (I.57.20).

che è onestissima . . ." I.i., p. 62).[36] In the play's penultimate operation, the metaphor of siege is made comically explicit as Callimaco, disguised as the surrogate *garzonaccio,* is caught in the grip of a two-horned phalanx rallied to the cry of "San Cucù"—Saint Cuckoo. The disguised Callimaco, inserted into Lucrezia's bedroom, might be viewed as a sapper, a mine designed to "blow up" Lucrezia, the object of the play-as-siege.[37]

Machiavelli's borrowings from Livy the moralist, Livy the dramaturge, and Livy the poet and mythographer—drawing parallels between the chastity of a Roman matron and the integrity of the city—would give *Mandragola* a Livian cast even in the absence of more specific parallels with Livy's history. But specific parallels there are. Those that I will discuss immediately following are, with one major exception, known, though their implications for the interpretation of Machiavelli's text have remained largely unexplored. They are drawn from crucial junctures in Livy's episode and play correspondingly important roles in Machiavelli's comedy.

I

The first major parallel serves to link Sextus Tarquinius's mimetic desire for Roman Lucretia with Callimaco's for Lucrezia. The terminology of René Girard is strikingly appropriate to the triangle of Collatinus, Sextus, and Lucretia as Livy presents it.[38] Sextus conceives his desire for Lucretia *because* of her husband's ostentatious demonstration of her superior beauty and virtue. Because he desires to be the victor in the competi-

36. Callimaco's terms here for Lucrezia's chaste *natura* echo Machiavelli's twenty-fifth chapter of the *Principe*: "Io iudico bene questo, che sia meglio essere impetuoso che respettivo, perché la Fortuna è donna, et è necessario volendola tenere sotto, batterla e urtarla . . ."

37. The metaphor of Lucretia's virtue as a citadel is worked exhaustively in Shakespeare's *Rape of Lucrece,* vv. 221, 441, 465, 485-487, 723, 1172-1173.

38. For the mechanisms of mimetic desire and its role in ordering rivalry, cf. René Girard, *Violence and the Sacred,* trans. Patrick Gregory (Baltimore and London, 1975), esp. pp. 145, 169, 174-175. Girard gives a succinct definition on p. 145: "Rivalry does not arise because of the fortuitous convergence of two desires on a single object; rather, the subject desires the object because the rival desires it. In desiring an object the rival alerts the subject to the desirability of the object."

tion to decide whose is the most exemplary wife, Collatinus excites a rivalry that is only satisfied with Sextus's triumph over Collatinus's dearest possession, his wife:

Collatinus, pleased with his success, invited his friends to sup with him. It was at that fatal supper that Lucretia's beauty, and proven chastity, kindled in Sextus Tarquinius the flame of lust, and determined him to debauch her.

Thus Sextus desires Lucretia *because* she is chaste, *because* she belongs to another. And not merely any other. For Collatinus and Sextus are relatives; their rivalry echoes the archetypal fraternal rivalry stretching back in Roman history to the twins Romulus and Remus.[39] The web of consanguineous rivalry extends even to Brutus, himself related to both Collatinus and Sextus, though Brutus's response to Lucretia, though passionate, is more filial in its sexuality.

In *Mandragola*, Callimaco's desire for Lucrezia is instigated by the praises of another as well. And even more indirectly: Callimaco falls in love with a verbal report of Lucrezia's beauty given by Cammillo Calfucci, a relative of Nicia, Lucrezia's husband. That Callimaco has not yet seen Lucrezia when he falls in love with her is a result of literary history, which interposes between the model of Livy's history and *Mandragola* the rich medieval and Boccaccian examples of desire instigated by verbal report.[40] But these distinctions should not cloud the significance for Machiavelli's play of the fact that the desire of the seducer is stimulated in a context that is, immediately, that of masculine rivalry. As Callimaco notes in his opening soliloquy, the news of Lucrezia's beauty comes to him at the

39. The genealogical relationships of the Tarquins to Collatinus and Brutus are explained in detail in *Roman Antiquities*, vol. II, IV.64.1–4 and IV.68, 1-2 (pp. 473, 481). Boccaccio, in his *Commento alla divina commedia*, ed. D. Guerri (Bari, 1913) I, 54, recalls his lineage: "Bruto fu per legnaggio nobile uomo di Roma, perciochè egli fu d'una famiglia chiamata i Giuni, ed il suo nome fu Caio Giunio Bruto, e la madre di lui fu la sorella di Tarquino Superbo, re de' romani." Though Boccaccio's genealogy differs from Dionysus's (in fact makes much better sense), the point is maintained that Brutus is kin to the Tarquins.

40. The *vida* of the troubadour Jaufré Rudel, who falls in love with the countess of Tripoli by hearing reports of her beauty and grace, is the most famous example. (Cf. J. Boutière and A. H. Schutz, *Les biographies des troubadours* [Paris, 1964], pp. 16-17.) But Machiavelli's immediate examples are those of the *Decameron*, I,5; IV.4; VII.7.

instance of *Fortuna,* who thus disturbs an existence chiefly remarkable for
its freedom from rivalries:

. . .I lived quietly pleasing everyone and taking pains to offend no one, so that I
was accepted by the townspeople, by the gentlemen, by strangers, by the poor,
by the rich . . . But when Fortune decided that I was having too easy a time of
it, she ordered that one Cammillo Calfucci should arrive at Paris . . .
                                                                    (I.1.61)

The excitement of sexual desire for Lucrezia deprives Callimaco of this
tranquility and initiates him into the *certamen,* the competition of insatia-
ble masculine desire, immediately provoked by the vehemence of Calfucci's praise, just as Collatinus's praise of Lucretia has excited Sextus:[41]

. . . he named madonna Lucrezia, wife of messer Nicia Calfucci, whose beauty
and manners he praised so lavishly as to leave all astonished, and awakening in me
such a desire to behold her that without further deliberation, and setting aside
any consideration of war and peace in Italy, I set on coming here . . .
                                                                    (I.1.61)

There are close incidental parallels to Livy in the above passage: Cammillo's excitement ("quasi che irato") recalls Collatinus's ardor in
proclaiming his wife's virtue "certamine accenso";[42] Callimaco's indifference to the military situation between France and Italy echoes the
abandonment of the stalled siege of Ardea by the soldiers and their trans-
fer of interest to the "muliebris certamen." These minor parallels are
significant especially in terms of the long-range effects of new passion on
Callimaco. In a Machiavellian context, erotic passion, no less than political ambition, subjects its victim to the whims of Fortune—as Callimaco
acknowledges—and plunges him into an uncertain world of risk. Though
it is true that in the course of the play's action Callimaco, with considerable help from others, reaches his goal, there is more than one hint that

41. Machiavelli offers a pessimistic theory of competition in the *Discorsi,* I.37: "La
cagione è, perchè la natura ha creato gli uomini in modo che possono desiderare ogni cosa e
non possono conseguire ogni cosa: talchè essendo sempre maggiore il desiderio che la
potenza dello acquistare, ne risulta la mala contentezza de quello che si possiede, e la poca
sodisfazione d'esso."
    42. *AUC,* I.57.7.

points to Callimaco as the plaything of Fortune. Callimaco's tedious posturing, his Petrarchan protests of suicidal despair, mark him as a victim of erotic furor, of the *aegritudo amoris* recognized as a disease since the time of Hippocrates.[43] Moreover, if we look closely at the text, it is apparent that Ligurio's objection, early in the play, to pursuing the corruption of Lucrezia at the public baths because of the presence of other suitors permits Machiavelli a sly acknowledgment of Callimaco's personal mediocrity as well as a glance at the intrinsic instability of the enterprise on which Callimaco has embarked.[44] As we shall see, these disturbing possibilities implicit in Callimaco's project are realized at the play's conclusion. For the present, it may be recorded that the first principal parallel with Livy's episode, describing the moment of the origin of desire and thus the mainspring of the action, establishes the grounds for the ironic subversion of Callimaco's erotic triumph, even as it provides the occasion of tragedy in the Roman text. In the ferocious world of rivalry that Machiavelli envisions as the stage of all public and private ambitions, Callimaco's entry into the *certamen* for the favors of Lucrezia engages him in a gamble which he cannot win, for in the slippery world of *Fortuna*, triumph is the prologue of defeat. In Ovid's words: "Quid victor gaudes? haec te victoria perdet."

By way of a corollary to the first major parallel to Livy, Machiavelli has veined his text with unmistakable allusion to the Roman historian by using the name of Cammillo Calfucci. Camillus, who saves Rome from the Gauls, is the hero of Livy's first decade if there is one; Machiavelli

43. Radcliff-Umstead's strongly positive view of Callimaco (*The Birth of Modern Comedy in Renaissance Italy,* pp. 124-125) is, to this reader at least, exaggerated; Callimaco's behavior and his dependence on Ligurio are reminiscent of Roderigo's simpering dependence on Iago in *Othello.*

44. Act I, scene 3 (p. 66): ". . . e potrebbe venirvi uomo a chi madonna Lucrezia piacesse come a te, che fussi più ricco di te, che avesse più grazia di te; in modo che si porta pericolo di non durare questa fatica per altri, e che intervenga che la copia dei concorrenti la facciano più dura, o che dimesticandosi la si volga ad un altro e non a te." Callimaco's willingness to seize any expedient ("per pigliare qualche partito bestiale, crudo, nefando," I.3 p. 67) is probably also an allusion to the resolution of Sextus—not Livy's Sextus, but Ovid's in the *Fasti,* II.781 ff.: " 'exitus in dubio est, audebimus ultima!' dixit, / 'viderit! audentes sorsque deusque iuvat.' "

remembers him generously and often in the *Discourses*.[45] It is Camillus
who spends his exile from Rome precisely at Rutulian Ardea, the city
besieged by Sextus and Collatinus—providing a topographic link between
the story of Lucretia and the illustrious career of the savior of Rome.[46]
Thus Cammillo Calfucci, Fortune's *agent provocateur* in Machiavelli's play,
evokes a standard of political high seriousness against which the characters
of the play, and their narrower concerns, will finally be judged.

To my knowledge, the second of the principal parallels I will discuss
has not been noted in the literature on Machiavelli's *Mandragola*, though
an ancillary source in a *novella* of Boccaccio has long been recognized.[47]
The parallel is spread over two distinct episodes in the play. Preparing
Callimaco for his placement inside Lucrezia's bedroom, Ligurio suggests
that the lover persuade the wife to accept his suit by threatening to
damage her reputation if she refuses: "dicale el bene le vuoi; e come sanza
sua infamia la può essere tua amica, e con sua grande infamia tua nimica"
(IV.iii.p.96). Ligurio's threat is a glancing but unmistakable echo of
Livy's text, where it is Sextus's offer to destroy Lucretia's reputation that
breaks her resistance to his lust:

But all in vain; not even the fear of death could bend her will. "If death will not
move you," Sextus cried, "dishonor shall. I will kill you first, then cut the throat
of a slave and lay his naked body by your side. Will they not believe that you have
been caught in adultery with a servant—and paid the price?" Even the most
resolute chastity could not have stood against this dreadful threat. Lucretia
yielded. Sextus enjoyed her [*expugnato decore*], and rode away, proud of his suc
cess.[48]

45. For Camillus in the *Discorsi*: I.29, where he is juxtaposed to Consalvo Ferrante, the
great Spanish soldier; II.23, where he is praised as an example of the rejection of the
halfway measures in military and political decisions; II.2, cited in the text, where his exile
to Ardea is an example of Fortune's manipulation of human events; III.23, on the reasons
of Camillus's exile from Rome; III.30, where Camillus is remembered for his effective
measures in the protection of Rome, and juxtaposed to the imprudence of both Savanarola
and Soderini, who did not know how to manage the envy of their rivals.

46. *AUC*, V.44.

47. For the parallel with Boccaccio's story of Catella and Ricciardo Minutolo, *Decameron*, III.6, cf. Raimondi, pp. 180-181.

48. *AUC*, I.57.3-4.

Sextus shatters Lucretia's resistance by making of her greatest strength, her commitment to her reputation, a fatal weakness. It is the dilemma into which Sextus's threat forces her that necessitates her subsequent suicide, which, she maintains, can alone convincingly witness her innocence of any complicity with Sextus. Sextus's threat is thus the precise weapon that batters down the fortress of Lucretia's chastity and prepares the tragedy that ensues.

The echo of Sextus's proposal in Ligurio's coaching of Callimaco disappears from the report that Callimaco gives in the last act, after his success with Lucrezia. But Callimaco does relate Lucrezia's own testimony as to the accumulation of causes that forced her to yield to her lover. The passage is therefore functionally parallel to the moment where Roman Lucretia realizes that she must succumb to Sextus if she is to preserve her reputation:

Given that your cleverness, the stupidity of my husband, the simple-mindedness of my mother, and the unscrupulousness of my confessor have led me to do what I should never have done on my own, I judge [voglio iudicare] that all this results from a heavenly command that has so wished it . . .

(V.iv.109)

Lucrezia's enumeration and evaluation of causes here is important for several reasons: it reiterates a pattern often used in the play (indeed a pattern favored by Machiavelli in his analytical works), from the dramatis personae in the authorial canzone ("uno amante meschino / un dottor poco astuto, / un frate mal vissuto," etc., vv. 40-43, p. 57) to the rhetorical schemes adopted during the course of the play by Callimaco, Liurio, and Timoteo. Ligurio's version is the most succinct, as he argues regarding the possibility of corrupting the priest Timoteo:

CALLIMACO
Who will persuade the confessor?
LIGURIO
You, me, and money; our wickedness—and theirs.

(II.vi.77)

In effect, Lucrezia's list retrospectively reflects the plot of the play, which, under Ligurio's direction, has pitted the combined efforts of parasite, lover, husband, mother, and confessor against the resistance of Lucrezia's chastity. Significantly, however, the forces Lucrezia enumerates as acting upon her are not so much powers as defects—with the exception of *astuzia,* which is not Callimaco's in this case but Ligurio's. Where, in Livy's account, Lucretia is broken by the terror of infamy and Sextus's *victrix libido,* Florentine Lucrezia is constrained by *simplicità, tristizia,* and *sciochezza.* There is a calculated degradation in the nature of the forces that impinge on the chastity of Lucrezia, the cynosure; she succumbs not to violence but to cumulative, circumambient corruption.

Lucrezia's decision to accept Callimaco's offer entails her will alone, for her body has by then been conceded to the supposed *garzonaccio,* the surrogate who is to absorb the toxic properties of the *mandragola.* The distinction of mind and body is pertinent to the third of the principal parallels, noted recently by Ezio Raimondi.[49] In Livy's text, Lucretia's husband and father remind her that since she has not consented to Tarquin's violence willingly her mind remains free of guilt. This Lucretia concedes, without however exempting herself from punishment: "ego me etsi peccare absolvo . . . supplicio non libero" (I.57.9-10).[50] In *Mandragola* it is frate Timoteo who attempts to persuade Lucrezia that

> Now that the act is a sin is nonsense, because it is the will that sins and not the body. And the cause of sin lies in displeasing the husband, but you please him; in enjoying pleasure, but you are displeased.
>
> (IV.ii.89)

The distinction drawn here focuses its irony on the passage discussed in the previous major parallel. Callimaco's proposal of love requires not the physical submission of Lucrezia, but the full complicity of her will. On the face of it, this consent is fully granted to the lover. Lucrezia, continuing her account of why she surrenders to Callimaco's offer, appears to place herself entirely in Callimaco's hands:

49. See Raimondi, *Politica e Commedia,* pp. 202-203.

50. Boccaccio's version of the tragedy in his *De claris mulieribus* emphasizes Lucretia's motive in preserving her life so as to proclaim her innocence, "Fearing that if she died there would be no one to avenge her innocence, she unwillingly gave her body to the adulterer," trans. in Guido Guarino, *Concerning Famous Women* (New Brunswick, N.J., 1964), p. 102.

. . . I am not strong enough to refuse what heaven wishes me to accept. Therefore I take you as lord, master, guide: I wish that you be my father, my defender,
and my entire good: and what my husband has wanted for a single evening, I
wish him to possess forever. You will become his godfellow; you will come to
church, and from there you will come to breakfast with us . . .

                                                                    (IV.iv.109)

Whether we choose to interpret Lucrezia's surrender to Callimaco's offer as
the fabliau-inspired victory of a *mal mariée,* or as the index of the corruption of the Florentine civic body, there can be no doubt that Lucrezia here
submits to Callimaco and comes to will what he wills. But the imperious
tone of the future tenses at the conclusion of the passage above also
suggests that Lucrezia's will, though placed under Callimaco's rule, has
taken on a very lively willfulness of its own—a crucial point to which I
shall return at the conclusion of my argument.

The three Livian parallels with *Mandragola* outlined above are central to
the development of Machiavelli's plot: one concerns the moment of Callimaco's embarcation on the slippery paths of desire and *Fortuna*; one the
etiology of Lucrezia's fateful submission to her seducer; one the ironically
pregnant fullness of her sudden complicity with Callimaco's desires.
Taken together, these three junctures profile Machiavelli's transformation
of Livy's episode of ritual, cathartic violence into a sly and cynical fable of
bourgeois accommodation and civic corruption. The defection of
Florentine Lucrezia from the example of heroic resistance and self-sacrifice
established by Roman Lucretia is the more striking because it had been
the explicit *purpose* of the Roman heroine to set an example of severity and
self-discipline for the benefit of future generations of free Romans: "nec
ulla deinde impudica Lucretiae exemplo vivet" (I.57.10). The seduction
of Florentine Lucrezia therefore marks a failure of the "antica virtù" to
maintain itself in the Florence of *Mandragola.* With the fall of Lucrezia,
cynosure of the play's intrigue and last surviving spark of ancient virtue,
the corruption of the present age advertised in the play's prologue appears
fully demonstrated.[51]

---

51. Consider a passage like *Discorsi* II, *proemio,* referring to the current conditions of
Italy: "perchè in questi (tempi) non è cosa alcuna che gli ricomperi da ogni estrema
miseria, infamia e vituperio, dove non è osservanza di religione, non di leggi, non di
milizia, ma sono maculati d'ogni ragione bruttura . . ."

II

Yet the most significant parallels between the text of Livy and that of Machiavelli remain to be discussed. These concern the *results* of Lucretia's suicide at Rome and of Lucrezia's submission at Florence. The last act of Machiavelli's comedy is by common consent a tour de force of comic harmony; the ambitions, however questionable, of all the principal characters are stunningly reconciled. Nicia anticipates an heir; Callimaco possesses his Lucrezia, Timoteo may look forward to alms, "grascia" for good works, Sostrata will be cared for in her dotage, while Ligurio, the chief architect of the successful conspiracy, earns his *pappo,* his free meals at Nicia's expense. The felicitous cooperation of flagrant self-interest diagrams a proleptic Hobbesian utopia, and few critics have resisted applauding the compelling, amoral joy that Machiavelli's sleight-of-hand provides.[52] Moreover, as Raimondi has noted, the final scene of the play is rich in references to both carnival festivity and Christian ritual, to the fulfillment of cyclical patterns of rebirth that Northrop Frye has termed the fundamental argument of comedy.[53]

Some form of rejuvenation is attributed to most of the characters: Nicia is to be reborn through his "figlio maschio," his male offspring ("Tu mi ricrei tutto quanto. Fia egli maschio?" III.8.p.86) though he starts to swell and blossom with self-regard well beforehand. "io paro maggiore, più giovane, più scarzo . . ." (IV.viii.p.101). Callimaco, in turn, must repeatedly be pulled back from the brink of suicide by Ligurio's stratagems, termed *rimedi* ("tu mi risusciti," I.iii.p.68), though such expressions often go no further than the stock gestures of Latin comedy.[54] More significant language is found in the play's final scene, as Timoteo observes to Sostrata that, in becoming a grandmother, she has "sprouted a

52. Leo Strauss, *Thoughts on Machiavelli* (Glencoe, Ill., 1958), pp. 284-286.

53. Raimondi, *Politica e Commedia,* pp. 214-216, 264; Aquilecchia, p. 99, n. 43. Lucrezia's remark (III.10, p. 88) "io sudo per la passione" and the chalicelike "bicchiere d'argento" (IV.3, p. 96) in which the potion of *mandragola* is administered infuse the lady's sacrifice of her body (as well as the "ordeal" of the *garzonaccio*) with parodic allusion to the Passion.

54. See, for example, Machiavelli's translation of Terence's *Andria,* II.i (ed. Gaeta, p. 16): "Tu mi hai risuscitato . . ."

new shoot on the old stock" ("messo un tallo in sul vecchio,"
V.vi.p.112).[55] In context, the remark works as a sly reference to the
insertion of a vigorous young breeding male in the household of the sterile
Nicia, a graft that promises to rejuvenate the declining house of
Calfucci.[56]

But the one rejuvenescence that makes all the others possible is, of
course, that of Lucrezia, who is marvelously refreshed, indeed transformed, by her night with Callimaco. "Gli è proprio, stamane, come se tu
rinascessi," Nicia announces with delight, marveling at Lucrezia's vivac-
ity ("tu sei molto ardita") where previous to her night with the *garzonaccio*
she had seemed half dead, "mezza morta." Most telling of all, Nicia
invokes one of the notoriously phallic totems of carnival to describe his
re-energized wife: "La pare un gallo."[57] In terms of the carnival humor
that pervades the last act of the play, the immediate reasons for Lucrezia's
revival are clear. The same *materia medica* that teaches Callimaco, disguised as a Parisian doctor, to analyze Lucrezia's *segno* (urine sample) as
cruda for lack of proper covering ("mal coperta")—technically speaking,
for lack of the proper decoction of the menses by the heat of male seed—
would reveal that a night of normal, healthy intercourse has purged
Lucrezia of the noxious humors accumulated due to Nicia's neglect of his
marital duties.[58] Lucrezia, with Callimaco's aid, has literally undergone a
healthful purge—a *catharsis*.[59]

---

55. The expression "un bel tallo" refers to the phallus in the fifteenth century "canto
carnascialesco" known as the "canzona degli ortolani." See C. S. Singleton, ed., *Canti
carnascialeschi del rinascimento* (Bari, 1936), p. 5.

56. The idea of the rejuvenation of the house of Calfucci should be viewed against the
background of Dante's remark, through Cacciaguida, that the Calfucci had become extinct
by Dante's day (*Paradiso*, 16.106). An undercurrent of futility, as well as folly, veins
Nicia's ambitions.

57. For the rooster as a symbol of fertility associated with carnival, see Emmanuel le
Roy Ladurie, *Carnival in Romans*, trans. Mary Feeney (New York, 1980), p. 323. See also
Paolo Toschi, *Le origini del teatro italiano* (Turin, 1955), p. 139.

58. For the ultimate authority on the operation of the semen on the female blood in
the *matrix*, cf. Aristotle's *Generation of Animals*, I.xx (729a10); II.iv (739b20); IV.iv.
(772a20).

59. On female purgations analogous to pollution among men, see the remarks of
Trotula of Salerno, *The Diseases of Women*, trans. Elizabeth Mason-Hohl (Los Angeles,
1940), pp. 1-3. Machiavelli uses the idea of a purge in *Discorsi*, II.v, for the historical
upheavals that obliterate civilizations: ". . . conviene di necessità che il mondo si purghi
per uno de' tre mod. . ."

Despite the rich Saturnalian flavor of the final act, it is important to emphasize that the play's festive rejuvenescence, as well as the sexual themes that pervade the action, are linked to the political outcome of Lucrezia's rape and suicide in Livy's history.[60] Livy's episode has a ritual function in Roman history as the first great conjuncture of the Roman constitution, a climacteric in the maturation of the Roman citizenry.[61] Placed strategically at the end of the first book of the *ab urbe condita,* Lucretia's suicide precipitates a chain of events that leads to the expulsion of the kings and the establishment of a republic; indeed, Livy, and the writers that follow him—including Boccaccio and Petrarch—are explicit in noting that it is precisely because of Lucretia's tragedy that Rome is re-founded as a republic.[62] The crucial turn of events begins when Lucius Junius Tarquinius Brutus, disguised as a simpleton in order to survive the tyranny of Tarquinius Superbus, jumps forward as Lucretia falls and draws the knife from her body. Since the passage is central to my argument, I quote at some length:

Her father and husband were overwhelmed with grief. While they stood weeping helplessly, Brutus drew the bloody knife from Lucretia's body, and holding it before him cried: "By this girl's blood—none more chaste till a tyrant wronged her—and by the gods, I swear that with sword and fire, and whatever else can lend strength to my arm, I will pursue Lucius Tarquinius the Proud, his wicked wife, and all his children, and never again will I let them or any other man be King in Rome."[63]

60. The carnival aspect of the play must not be underestimated. In addition to those carnival elements underlined by Raimondi (p. 215) and Toschi (pp. 12, 306-307) the *Mandragola* is set—if Ridolfi's deductions are correct—in late January or February, which is carnival time. In Machiavelli's day plays like *Mandragola* were conventionally staged during carnival festivities, whether their subject had any explicit link with carnival or not (Machiavelli's *Clizia,* for example, is set during carnival: "Ed è pur carnesciale," II.3., ed. Gaeta, p. 129).

61. Livy's description explicitly identifies the event with the pubescence, so to speak, of Rome as a political entity: "Dissipatae res nondum adultae discordia forent, quas fovit tranquilla moderatio imperii eoque nutriendo perduxit ut bonam frugem libertatis maturis iam viribus ferre possent" (*AUC,* II.i.6).

62. See note 21 above and the text, pp. 000-000. In the *Africa* (ed. N. Festa, [Florence, 1926]), III.651-802, Petrarch relates the story of Lucretia's suicide as the occasion that sparked the expulsion of the kings ("causa novande," l.651); cf. also Cicero, *De finibus bonorum et malorum,* II.66: "Stuprata per vim Lucretia a regis filio testata cives se ipsa interemit. Hic dolor populi Romani, duce et autore Bruto, causa civitati libertatis fuit, ob eiusque mulieris memoriam primo anno et vir et pater eius consul est factus."

63. *AUC,* I.58.12-59.2.

The vehemence of Brutus's oath, and the miracle of his sudden, albeit artificial, transformation ignite the others, who follow their new leader in swearing an oath; led by Brutus, they raise a tumult that frightens Tarquin from Rome. These results have been predisposed by Lucretia herself, who before her suicide challenges the men of her household to avenge her if they are men enough, "si vos viri estis." Her challenge, and Brutus's response, have the effect of galvanizing the passive, grief-stricken men (cf. "luctu occupatis") into citizens worthy of political independence.[64] Lucretia provides Brutus not merely with the perfect opportunity for his sudden and dramatic self-manifestation as *liberator*;[65] she also provides the *culter*, the knife symbolic of the *virga* of power, flowing ("manatem cruore") with her generous blood, which Brutus seizes and passes to the others, joining them in a fraternal conspiracy of *liberi*.[66] Armed with her strength, they expunge the tyranny in retaliation for the expunction of her chastity. Lucretia's role is that of scapegoat, the *pharmakos* who assumes the virulence and opprobrium of the tyrant in her own person by literally incorporating his seed. Killing herself, she expiates her defilement and becomes (as in the later practice of *devotio*) an instrument for the renewal of Rome.[67] In addition, if she is herself the sacrificial victim, her blood— whose defilement by the "regia iniuria" is punctiliously mentioned by Brutus—is a *pharmakon*, a remedy both virulent with the tyrant's seed and virtuous because of Lucretia's sacrifice.[68] Touching it as it flows from the

64. As Ogilvy notes (p. 228), the fact that the Romans are described in Livy's text as "opifices ac lapicidas" (*AUC*, I.59.9) means that they were like slaves. That Spurius Lucretius, Lucretia's father, and Collatinus are overcome with grief implies that they have been unmanned; the effect is made more strongly in Ovid, *Fasti*, II.835-836: "ecce, super corpus communia damna gementes / obliti decoris virque paterque iacent."

65. For Machiavelli's concern with the importance of correct timing, "occasione," see *Il principe*, vi. See also *Discorsi*, II.29; for discussion, Gilbert, p. 159.

66. Cf. Ovid, *Fasti*, II.839: "stillanteque tenens generoso sanguine cultrum"; Petrarch, *Africa*, III.740-741: "Ille cruentum / Fervidus educens spumanti vulnere ferrum."

67. Ogilvy notes that the story of Lucretia is based on Greek stories including accounts of the expulsion of the Peisistratids. Recently, the function of the *pharmakos* in *Oedipus Rex* has been studied with brilliant results by J. P. Vernant, "Ambiguité e renversement; sur la structure enigmatique de *"Oedipe-Roi,"* in *Echanges et communications: Mélanges offertes à Claude Lévi-Strauss* (Mouton, 1970); see also Girard, *Violence*, pp. 108-109.

68. Both the nourishing and medicinal or lustral aspects of Lucretia's blood (and its pollution by the seducer) are strongly implicit in the accounts; Ovid's "generoso sanguine"

phallic *culter,* the conspirators, wailing with effeminate grief, regain the masculine *virtù* that tyranny had stripped from them.

That Lucretia's power is, at the moment of her death, that of the phallus is unmistakable if Livy's passage is scrutinized.[69] Subsequent versions of the story, modeled on Livy's render more nearly explicit the sense in which Lucretia, through her heroic act, becomes masculine. Thus Ovid, in the *Fasti,* refers to her as "matrona virilis animo," a phrase echoed by Valerius Maximus, who makes Lucretia the chief (*dux*) of Roman chastity and ventures that her soul, truly virile, was misplaced in a woman's body by an error of Fortune: "Dux Romanae pudicitiae Lucretia, cuius virilis animus maligno errore fortunae muliebre corpus sortitus est . . ."[70] Ovid, too (though not Livy), gives to Lucretia the gesture of modesty at the moment of death attributed to the murdered Caesar, who fell so as to prevent any possibility of exposing himself.[71] And Livy's own description of Lucretia's fall—"prolapsa in vulnus moribunda cecidit"— echoes the fall of male heroes on the epic battlefield.[72] More significant still is the fact that Lucretia's insistence on exacting the full penalty for her minimal complicity with Sextus provides an example of that unyielding respect for the law that Machiavelli—among others—admired among

---

(*Fasti,* II.839) and "fortem castumque cruorem" are expressive of the enhancement of Lucretia's virility precisely because of her rape by the virulent Sextus. The idea is taken to its extreme form in Shakespeare's *Lucrece,* where Lucretia's blood separates: "Some of the blood still pure and red remained / And some looked black, and that false Tarquin stained" (vv. 1742-1743). For a brilliant dissection of *pharmakon* as a radically ambiguous term in Plato's language, see J. Derrida, "La pharmacie de Platon," in *La dissémination* (Paris, 1972), pp. 69-197.

69. The spotlight on the *culter* as phallic is in evidence from the point where Sextus enters armed into Lucretia's room ("stricto gladio," I.58.2; "ferrum in manu est," I.58.2) and continues when Lucretia draws her knife from beneath her garments ("Cultrum, quem sub veste abditum habebat . . . " I.58.11). Again, it is in Shakespeare's *Lucrece* that the phallic imagery becomes pervasive; cf. vv. 359, 364, 505, 1843 (364: ". . . at the mercy of his mortal sting").

70. Valerius Maximus, *Dicta et facta memorabilia,* ed. C. Kempf (Leipzig, 1888), VI.1 (p. 271).

71. *Fasti,* II. 830-831. See also Ogilvy's note to I.59.1, p. 226.

72. For example, the death of Pallas in the *Aeneid* (itself imitating Homer) X.486-489.

the Romans of the republican period.[73] Lucretia's act establishes the rigor of the law as above any and all circumstantial mitigation. It is thus no accident that Brutus, who is in a sense both Lucretia's final lover and her true spiritual offspring, is remembered by Machiavelli for his willingness to sacrifice his own sons to the rigor of the law when they conspire to return kings to Rome.[74] Because she establishes the primacy of law, because she reinvests Roman manhood with their lost phallic virtue, Lucretia is a true founder of the city, *urbis conditrix,* justly ranked in that small class of lawgivers and city-founders Machiavelli admired above all other persons.[75] *Contra* Augustine, who chops logic in dismissing the virtue of Lucretia's act in the *City of God,* Lucretia's exemplary demonstration of inflexible adherence to a draconian law for the sake of the future republic is not a private act of escape from shame but a public ritual, a sacrifice.

Another, related dimension of Lucretia's suicide must be mentioned at this point. I suggested earlier that Sextus's threat to dishonor Lucretia's memory—and Lucretia's submission to that threat—necessitate her suicide. Her death both punishes her justifiable moment of weakness in yielding physically to Sextus at all and frees her memory from any taint of blame in so doing. As the early Christian fathers (and, much later, Boccaccio), recall the event, Lucretia's suicide is lustral, washing her soul clean of Tarquin's lust and of any doubts regarding her own complicity.[76] Because Lucrezia's resolution and courage are described by Roman writers as virile, her suicide appears as a victory not only over her shame, but over her female nature. Thus, Livy's account of Tarquin's entrance into Lucretia's chamber stresses her physical vulnerability before the rapist:

Lucretia opened her eyes in terror; death was imminent, no help at hand. Sextus

73. Passages include *Discorsi,* I.1; I.11; I.18; I.23, III.22.

74. *Discorsi,* III.3.

75. "Discourse on reforming the government of Florence," in *The Prince and Other Works,* trans. Allan Gilbert (New York, 1941), p. 91: "In addition to this, no man is so much raised on high by any of his acts as are those who have reformed republics and kingdoms with new laws and institutions."

76. Jerome, *Adversus Jovinianum* I.46 (PL 23.287). See also Boccaccio, *Concerning Famous Women,* p. 103: "she cleansed her shame harshly."

urged his love, begged her to submit, pleaded, threatened, used every weapon that might conquer a woman's heart [*versare in omnes partes muliebrem animum*].[77]

The fear of loss of reputation vanquishes her resistance, and Tarquin's lust, significantly a feminine noun, emerges the victor (*victrix*):

Quo terrore cum vicisset obstinatum pudicitiam velut victrix libido . . .

The subsequent heroic, virile behavior of Lucretia marks the transformation that has taken place since the rape—indeed, because of the rape, for Lucretia's body transforms the virulent seed of the Tarquins into the force that restores the Romans—and the sense in which Lucretia's suicide, a typically masculine gesture in Roman culture, signifies her triumph over the feminine debility that necessitated her physical submission to Sextus.

The episode of Lucretia's suicide and its effect on Lucius Brutus and Rome is often alluded to in Machiavelli's *Discourses*.[78] It is discussed most extensively at the beginning of the third book, where Brutus's opportunism in seizing the moment offered by Lucretia's suicide is singled out for special praise:

. . . when on the occasion of the death of Lucretia, in the midst of the father, husband, and other relatives, he was the first to pluck the dagger from her breast and to make all present swear henceforth to suffer no king to reign in Rome.

(III.2)

In the following chapter, Brutus's severity in condemning his own sons for conspiring against the republic is also praised. The discussion of Brutus's merits takes place in the context of the thesis that opens the third

---

77. Ovid's version links Lucretia's physical vulnerability to Sextus with psychological vulnerability stemming from fear of dishonor: "quid faciat? pugnet? vincentur femina pugnans" (*Fasti*, II.801); "succumbit famae victa puella metu" (II.810). In *Discorsi*, I.19 Machiavelli points to the need for the successive kings of Rome to return periodically to the Romulean virtue of the city's foundation in order to prevent the onset of "effeminacy": "era bene poi necessario che gli altri re ripigliassero la virtù di Romolo, altrimenti quella città sarebbe diventata effeminata."

78. See I.3; I.9; I.16; I.17; I.25; I.28; I.58. The examples of the expulsion of Tarquin and the life of Camillus are in fact among the most frequently cited in the *Discorsi*.

book of the *Discourses*. The principle is elaborated in the medical terminology that Machiavelli uses following Livy's diagnoses in the histories:[79]

> . . . and the means of renewing them is to bring them back to their original
> principles. For, as all religious republics and monarchies must have within them-
> selves some goodness, by means of which they obtain their first growth and
> reputation, and as in the process of time this goodness becomes corrupted, it will
> of necessity destroy the body unless something intervenes to bring it back to its
> normal condition. Thus, the doctors of medicine say, in speaking of the human
> body, that "every day some ill humors gather which must be cured."
>
> (III. 1)

In the context of the pathology of the civic body as Machiavelli presents it
in the third book of the *Discourses*, the analysis of Lucretia's suicide as a
remedy, a *pharmakon* that buys the health of the state and returns Rome to
the pristine, virile origins of Romulus and Numa appears consistent with
both the political and metaphoric dimensions of Machiavelli's thought.[80]
But even after putting the suicide of Lucretia in the context of the political pharmacopoeia of the *Discourses*, and noting the continuity of medical
terminology uniting the *Discourses* and *Mandragola*, we may well ask how
the episode of Lucretia as an etiology of the republic can be translated into
the narrower, bourgeois world of Machiavelli's comedy.

First, the function in Machiavelli's political typology of Lucretia's
suicide as the opportunity for Brutus to return Rome to its principles
informs Machiavelli's insertion of political details in *Mandragola*. As
noted before, the date of action is placed in 1504, ten years after the
invasion by Charles VIII that initiated the ruin of Italy but also provoked
the restoration of republican rule to Florence. Thus, by the end of the date
of the play's action, Florence had been a republic for a decade, exactly one

---

79. References to the sickness and health of the body politic are abundant in
Machiavelli's text; cf. *Discorsi*, I.4: "e sono in ogni republica due umori diversi"; I.7; I.17:
"e che quella corruzione che era in loro si fosse cominciata ad istendere per le membra,
come le membra fossero state corrote era impossibile mai più riformarla"; II.1; II.5; II.30;
III.49.

80. For the process of corruption in the civic body, see J.A.G. Pocock, *Machiavellian
Moment* pp. 203-211. On the intrinsic difficulties of restoring a corrupted city, see *Discorsi*, I.17-18. See also Raimondi, p. 153.

of the intervals Machiavelli, in the *Discourses*, recommends might separate attempts to return the state to its principles after inevitable corruption:

It would be desirable therefore that not more than ten years should elapse between such executions, for in the long course of time men begin to change their customs, and to transgress the laws; and unless some case occurs that recalls the punishment to their memory and revives the fear in their hearts, the delinquents will soon become so numerous that they cannot be punished without danger.

(III. 1)

Lest the common interval of ten years appear too general to establish the parallel between *Mandragola* and the *Discourses*, it may also be noted that the relation between the invasions of the French armies and the invasion of the Gauls in early Roman history (like Lucretia's suicide, the event shocked the Romans into undertaking constitutional reforms) is made explicitly by Machiavelli, again in the *Discourses*. In Machiavelli's own terms, then, historical Florence, ruled by the complacent Pier Soderini and the *Otto di balia* is, or rather might have been, ripe for a constitutional crisis that would benefit the health of the republic.[81] That no such crisis is precipitated—that, in fact, the parallel of Roman and Florentine history invoked by Lucrezia's name is defective—is precisely the point: the intrigue of Callimaco and Lucrezia occurs not in a heroic political context uniting ancient Rome and modern Florence, but rather in the indigenously Florentine world of the Boccaccian bourgeois *novella*, the world of the ingenious trick, the *beffa*.[82] As Machiavelli argues in the *Discourses*, if the corruption of the citizenry proceeds too far the opportunity to "riprendere lo stato" and return it to its principles is irretriev-

---

81. *Discorsi*, III.43 and I.56. In Machiavelli's view Florence was faced with a historical obstacle to maintaining its freedoms because of its former servitude to Rome; see *Discorsi*, I.49 and II.1, for the harm to citizenship caused by servitude.

82. Machiavelli's debts to the *novelle* of Boccaccio are well established; for some inventories see Russo, *La commedia*, pp. 26-39, and Raimondi, pp. 180-181. For Machiavelli, Boccaccio's masterpiece suggests a world of bourgeois mercantilism which the "antica virtù" of the Romans—who played off private interest against public need—cannot penetrate. The political tragedy of Renaissance Florence, incapable of regaining the virtue of a true republic, is played out in the struggle between the Livian *fabula* of Lucretia and the Boccaccian register of the *beffa*.

ably lost.[83] The very transformation of literary genre from Livy's narrative tragedy to Lucretia to Machiavelli's *beffa*-inspired comedy is eloquent testimony of Machiavelli's typology of historical cycles at work: in *Mandragola,* an economy of seduction and accommodation replaces the catharsis of heroic violence in ancient Rome; the *virtù* that stood in Lucretia's suicide falls with Lucrezia's submission to the suffocating alliance of *astuzia, sciochezza, semplicità,* and *tristizia.*[84]

Second, just as Lucretia's suicide and its effects stage the foundation of a new community bound by her virile blood, Ligurio's plot in the comedy binds Timoteo, Nicia, Callimaco, Sostrata—and finally Lucrezia herself—in a new community based not on the austere rigor of the law but, rather, on the programmatic corruption of the civic role of each member. Early in the play we see Ligurio the parasite, Timoteo the corruptible priest, and Callimaco, the comically ruinous lover, conspicuously pledging their questionable faith to one another.[85] The allegiance is not merely the routine complicity of Latin comedy. In a unique moment of professed emotion, Ligurio, the social parasite, acknowledges an intimate fraternal kinship with his client, Callimaco: "il tuo sangue si affà col mio" (I.ii.p.67). The utterance has sinister portent if we compare the words of Ligurio's other chief conspirator, Timoteo, reflecting on his own seduction by the parasite: "This devil of Ligurio presented himself to me, and made me dip (*intignere*) my finger into a fault, where I've since place my arm and my whole body" (IV.vi.99). No reader of the Latin Bible can fail to hear the priest's allusion here to the possession of Judas by the demon and to Christ's pronouncement that one who dipped his bread in the dish with him would betray him: "Qui intingit mecum manum in paropside" (Matt. 26:23). Ligurio's elegant plot to seduce Lucrezia, which depends on the corruption of each conspirator for its success, is the model of a community where the characteristic act is betrayal.

The socially microcosmic nature of the community of conspirators has often been remarked; Sumberg in particular has noted the constitutive

83. Cf. *Discorsi,* I.17-18, and Pocock, pp. 203-211.

84. For Machiavelli's view of the usefulness of state violence in restraining the corruption of the populace, cf. *Discorsi,* II.2. On the function of decimations of the army, cf. *Discorsi,* III.49; see also Raimondi, p. 156.

85. I.3 (p.67): "non dubitar della fede mia" (Ligurio); III.6 (p. 85): "parmi avere contratta tele dimestichezza che non è cosa che io non facessi" (Timoteo).

role of the pseudo-betrothal—the *parentado,* as Timoteo jokes—that will unite Callimaco and Lucrezia in holy adultery.[86] The play's final procession to the church of the Servi, the sacred space embracing the typical collectivity of Christian Europe, on a day that, given the reference to Lucrezia's *puerpere* or purification, may well be the Feast of the Purification of the Virgin (Feb. 2), strongly reinforces the notion that the six characters, destined to collaborate in the formation of a most unusual household, are also the nucleus of a new community: *Mandragola,* like Livy's story of Lucretia, is an etiological fable.[87]

The new community, by Machiavelli's standards in the *Discourses,* is utterly corrupt. The behavior of the principal characters systematically displays an inventory of violations of civil and canon law and traditional piety. Nicia, the *paterfamilias* (!), accepts the certainty that a fellow citizen will die on his behalf, though he has qualms about the possibility of getting caught;[88] he stands just at the point where the threat of punishment provided by the laws no longer represses criminal behavior.[89] As far as Timoteo is concerned, even in Machiavelli's supposedly skeptical terms the pliable priest undermines the legitimate social authority of the

86. The idea of the play as descriptive of the establishment of a community is suggested as well by allusions to the epoch of the biblical patriarchs: Timoteo's reference to the daughters of Lot (III. 11, p. 89) and to the sterility of Rachel (who therefore requested mandrakes, cf. Gen: 30, 1-16) supplement Machiavelli's references to the antiquities of Rome. Compare for example Callimaco's mention of Nicia's desire for children (I.1, p. 63: "hanno un desiderio che muoiono") with Rachel's plea in Gen 30:1: "Da mihi liberos, alioquin moriar."

87. V.2. The "washing" of Lucrezia and her reconsecration are usually the consequences of an actual parturition, not of a night of love. Nicia's anticipation of the ceremony continues the theme of Lucrezia's (and his) delivery from the toxic *mandragola.*

88. Cf. Nicia's extreme fear of the "Otto di balìa" (II.6 p. 77-78). In Machiavelli's terms Nicia's corruption resides not so much in his callousness as in his willingness to let another engage in a dangerous enterprise in his stead and on his behalf; cf. Pocock, p. 204, where it is pointed out that for Machiavelli the model of public irresponsibility is the hiring of mercenaries.

89. *Discorsi,* I. 11-14. "Perchè dove manca *il timore di Dio,* conviene o che quel regno rovini o che sia sostenuto dal timore d'uno principe che sopperisca a' difetti della religione" (I.11). It is precisely such a "mancanza di divozione" that Timoteo (whose name recalls "timore di Dio) laments in the fifth act (p. 105). As Pocock notes (p. 192) "a substructure of religion is a prerequisite of civic virtue."

church—affirmed unambiguously in the first book of the *Discourses*—by violating the privileges of the confessional: "E si maravigliano poi se la divozione manca." Both Sostrata and Nicia cheerfully prostitute a virtuous wife in order to guarantee the legal and economic security that follows from having male heirs.

The principle in the name of which the characters engage in fundamentally antisocial acts is stridently inscribed in the *cognome* of Callimaco himself: *Guadagni*. Machiavelli, who draws from Dante's *Commedia* the family name of Nicia and Cammillo Calfucci (cf. *Paradiso* 16.106) has also remembered the poet's excoriation of the Florentine *nouveau riche* in the *Inferno*:

> La gente nova e i subiti guadagni
> orgoglio e dismisura han generate
> Fiorenza, in te . . .[90]

As Machiavelli writes in the *Discourses,* the pursuit of private gain at the expense of public good is one of the maladies that can afflict and destroy a republic.[91] So noxious is wealth to civic virtue, he argues, that it were better that the citizenry of a republic were kept poor so as to corrupt neither others nor themselves:

The cause of this is manifest, for it is not individual prosperity, but the general good, that makes cities great . . .

(II.2)

We have argued elsewhere that it is of the greatest advantage in a republic to have laws that keep her citizens poor.

(III.25)

By contrast, the characters of *Mandragola*—Nicia, Callimaco, even Sostrata—are explicitly prosperous. It is Nicia's great private wealth, and his desire to maintain it as such, that spurs him to desire the personal inconvenience of children:

90. Note Ligurio's instruction of Callimaco at IV.2 (p.96): "tu te la guadagni."

91. For Machiavelli's analysis of the effects of *acquistare* and *guadagno* on the political virtue of citizens, cf. *Discorsi*, I.5; II.i; II.30. For discussion, cf. Gilbert, pp. 175-176, 189.

. . . for having been married six years and not having had any children, the
desire that both he and she have of having some—since they're very rich—is
practically killing them.

(I.1.63)

Finally, as I have already suggested above, Machiavelli's metaphor for
the health and corruption of the political bodies is a traditional one: that
of the human body.[92] In this respect—whatever other models he may have
consulted—one principal source is Livy's history, where the preface draws
on the metaphor and whose first pentad includes the most important
Roman instance of the metaphor, the speech of Menenius Agrippa familiar to all students of Shakespeare's *Coriolanus*.[93] In different ways,
Machiavelli's echoes Livy's poem and its metaphor of the body in the
prefatory chapters to all three books of the *Discourses*.[94] The importance of
the metaphor of the body for *Mandragola*, whose title describes a remedy
for sterility, can hardly be overstated. In addition to what is explicitly
medical in the play—Callimaco's disguise as a Parisian physician and the
gynecological and pharmaceutical lore that he spouts—the medical lex-
icon that operates in the play is directly linked to the relationship between
Roman Lucretia as *pharmakos/pharmakon* for the Roman state and the
rejuvenation of the characters in the comedy, especially Madonna Lucrezia
herself. In Livy, the passage of the bloody knife, the *virga* of power, to
Brutus and the other conspirators initiates the resurgence of Rome; in
Mandragola, Lucrezia's restoration is attributed to the superior sexual
potency ("iacitura") of Callimaco. At the same time, however, the collapse of ancient virtue begins with the fateful transmission of Callimaco's
phallus to Lucrezia. To illuminate this important nexus linking Livy and
Machiavelli's comedy, the meaning of the play's title—and thus the lore
of the *mandragola*—must first be briefly considered.

92. For the conception of the state as a human body in antiquity and the Renaissance,
see Leonard Barkan, *Nature's Work of Art* (New Haven, Conn., 1974), esp. pp. 97, 100,
115, 119, 151, 158-159.

93. *AUC*, II.32-33.

94. Texts in note 28, above.

III

The importance of traditional lore on the *mandragola* for the plot of Machiavelli's play has been illuminated by several recent studies.[95] Intrinsically, however, *mandragola* serves as the comprehensive rubric for sexual meaning in the play. As Callimaco describes it, *mandragola* can be made into a *pozione* that promotes not only fertility, but impregnation itself: "non è cosa più certa a ingravidare la donna che darli bere una pozione fatta di *mandragola*" (II.vi.p.75). Callimaco is presumably leaving out an important step when he suggests that the potion will cause pregnancy without futher interventions of the male. But the omission is significant because it suggests a metaphorical equation between the natural cause of Lucrezia's pregnancy—Callimaco's seed—and the fabulous *mandragola.* Consequently the numerous terms in the play that refer to the remedy—*pozione, rimedio,* Nicia's colloquial *suzzacchera, hypocràs*—may also be taken to refer to the seminal efficacy of the male.[96] It is thus no accident that, given the rhizomatic analogy between the mandrake root and the male *radice,* the play abounds in double entendres for the phallus, woven deftly into the play's richly idiomatic texture of language such that the comedy becomes a sustained carnival song, a canto carnascialesco with all of its ingeniously veiled obscenity.[97] Expressions like Nicia's "zugo a piuolo" (III.vii.p.86), and references to the "tallo in sul vecchio" for which Sostrata hopes, to the *spadaccino* or bodkin worn by Nicia at the capture of the potent *garzonaccio,* to the bladder and bauble (*vesciche, badalucco*), to the white-headed leek (in sodomizing position, "porro di dietro") are all circumlocutions for the sex of the male. Nicia, anticipating the events to take place in his own bedroom, expresses confidence that

95. See note 26, above, for citations.

96. The analogy between the mandrake root and the phallus is suggested when Timoteo observes the removal of Callimaco from Lucrezia's room: "e' cavano fuora el prigione," where *cavare* (extract, dig out) recalls one of the common terms for digging up the mandrake root; cf. Raimondi, p. 257, who cites a commentary to Dioscorides (1518): "iactantque tanto periculo *effodi* humana forma."

97. Machiavelli wrote several obscene carnival-songs, including "di uomini che vendone le pine" (Gaeta, p. 337), where the pine cone is an image for the penis: "e che direte voi che dal pin cola / un licor ch'ugne poi tute quei nocchi . . ." For similar examples, see also Singleton, *Canti, passim.*

"Pasquina enterrà in Arezzo"—that is, that the phallus will enter the "dark place" (a rezzo) successfully.[98]

The most important reference to the male sex from the perspective of the links between Livy and Machiavelli's comedy is brilliantly indirect. It comes during the hilarious scene of Nicia's examination of the *garzonaccio*—Callimaco in disguise—to determine if there any signs (*bolle*, sores) of syphillis or other venereal disease. Nicia's role of health inspector is transparently a ruse: what he really wants to do is touch and see, "toccare e vedere," Callimaco's body and its splendid endowment. As he puts it, he wants to get to the bottom of the matter, "toccare a fondo." He goes so far as to make sure that the mystery to be consummated between Lucrezia and the *garzonaccio* is already well underway before he leaves the room: "e innanzi volli toccare con mano come la cosa andava" (V.ii.p.107). Now, Nicia's expression "toccare e vedere" reflects a formula of Latin comedy, adopted in its turn by the *novella*, usually appearing in the mouth of a clever servant promising to show his master the facts of a given matter.[99] But Machiavelli's little scene in the fourth act also has more proximate literary antecedents in several tales of Boccaccio and in the *Calandria* of Bernardo Dovizi, where touching the facts of the matter has the same meaning: the phallus is the truth, the *fondo* of things.[100] For

98. "Tallo sul vecchio" as a circumlocution for the penis appears also in Singleton, *Canti*, p. 5. The phallic suggestiveness of the *spadaccino* or *stocco* is illuminated by Machiavelli's use of a similar double entendre in his *Clizia*, where Nicomacho—in bed with the servant Siro disguised as Clizia—is repeatedly poked by what Nicomacho takes to be a dagger ("mi sento stoccheggiare un fianco e darmi qua sotto el codrione cinque o sei colpi de' maladetti!" (V.3, p. 160). "Pasquina enterrà in Arezzo" (Pasquina will enter in Arezzo [the town] [in the dark place]) is for Nicia a fairly transparent circumlocution of the event that he anticipates in his bedchamber; cf. Boccaccio, *Decameron*, VI, *introduzione*, where Licisca refers to "Ser Mazza" (Sir club, staff) entering *Montenero* ("black mountain"). In addition to terms specific of the penis, Nicia is also fond of colloquial references to the backside, "Cacastecchi," "Cacasangue," "Scingasi!" ("stickshitter," "bloodshitter," "let him drop his pants," etc.).

99. For some examples, cf. *Decameron* III.6.19; IV.4.9; VII.7.34—significantly, the last two tales include the love-by-report device adopted in *Mandragola*.

100. See *Decameron*, II.3.30; III.10.17-18; Bibbiena's *Calandria* is one of Machiavelli's richer veins of suggestion for the language of his own play (I count some 28 parallels), especially phallic imagery, which is central in the *Calandria* because of the hero's disguise as a woman. The play's resolution thus requires some positive identifications: "Tutto l'ho

our play, Nicia's handling of his rival is not only the grotesque nadir of his cuckoldry and a strong suggestion of why he has failed to produce children, but also a parody of the ritual transmission of phallic virtue depicted in Livy's episode of Lucretia and Brutus: in other terms, it is a *translatio stultitiae* rather than, as in Livy's history, a *translatio legis* and *imperii*. I will return to this point in a moment.

Mandragola is not to be decoded as seminal virtue only; it is also to be interpreted as a figure for the scheme of sexual differentiation itself, for sexedness as the master *segno* at stake in the play. Alongside the ingenious references to the phallus there are marked references to the female sex: Nicia's exclamation ("potta di San Puccio") and the profoundly obscene reference by Timoteo to the *sgocciolatura*, the "draining" of the surrogate from Lucrezia's bedroom (V.i.p.105), are examples. Nicia's joke about how much the *garzonaccio* has enjoyed the *unto* (grease, chrism, oil) provides an ambiguous term whose meaning ranges from sexual lubricants to the *mandragola* itself. There is good reason for the sexual ambivalence of terms associated with *mandragola*. In the traditional lore regarding the plant, the mandrake is always described as both anthropomorphic and sexed, having the shape of a human body and displaying the marks of sexual differentiation.[101] It is thus the symbol of the scheme spelled out explicitly by Callimaco disguised as physician when he explains, in simple

---

maneggiato e tocco . . ."; "Fulvia l'ha tocco tutto, e trovatolo femina . . ." (Bernardo Dovizi da Bibbiena, *Calandria*, in *Il Teatro italiano*, ed. Bonino, pp. 67, 72; see also pp. 68, 73).

101. For contemporary medical information regarding the mandrake, cf. Raimondi, pp. 257-258, where Beroaldo's commentary to Apuleius's *Asinus aureus* is cited: "duo sunt genera mandragorae, mas et femina." The Renaissance authorities are largely dependent on the medieval encyclopedias like those of Isidore and Bartholomaeus Anglicus (who gives generous excerpts from Dioscorides); Isidore's account is relatively complete and succinct: "Hanc poetae *anthropomorphon* appellant, quod habeat radicem forma hominis simulantem. . .huius species duae: femina, follis lactucae similibus mala generans in similitudinem prunorum. Masculus vero, foliis betae similibus . . ." (*Etymol.*, XVII.9.30, PL 82.627). Reference to the power of mandrakes to cure sterility is also a feature of carnival songs, e.g., Singleton, *Canti*, p. 17 ("per chi vuole ingravidare, che mandragola si chiama").

but conspicuous medical Latin, the possible reasons for the couple's failure to procreate.[102]

Nam causae sterilitatis sunt: aut in semine aut in matrice, aut in strumentis seminariis, aut in virga, aut in causa extrinseca.[103]

It is as a model of sexual differentiation that the traditional account of the *mandragola* is both remedy and poison is most telling for the meaning of the play. As Callimaco-physician describes the drug, it will impregnate Lucrezia but also kill the first male that lies with her: its effect on the female is vital and benign; on the male, mortal.[104] As Aquilecchia has demonstrated, the folklore motif of the poisoned lady, who annihilates her consorts, has been grafted by Machiavelli to the conventional lore of the mandrake found in the encyclopedias and medical texts of the Latin West. But the additional inclusion by Machiavelli of reference to the ordeal of Tobit's bride, Sarah, who must be detoxified for several days before Tobit can expect to survive a night with her,[105] points the way to the naturalistic referent behind the fabulous lore in the presumed toxicity of the female sex itself—marked most sensationally by the medical myth that the *menses* have virulent properties.[106] Thus *mandragola,* in its widest sense,

102. For "scientific" explanation of how the mandrake can aid fertility, we have the account of Bartholomaeus Anglicus, *De rerum proprietatibus* (1601; repr. Frankfurt, 1964) XVII.104: "quod mandragora sumpta modo debito matrice disponit ad conceptionem quando primitus calor nimis et siccus conceptionibus materiam impedivit. Mulieres calidas et humidas disponit ad conceptionem, cum sit frigida et sicca." Medically, then, the mandrake aids conception only in the special case of a woman who is excessively humid and hot (in traditional medicine women are normally humid and cold); otherwise, like most substances that are cold and dry, the mandrake is toxic and inimical to life.

103. Callimaco's scholastic form of reasoning here parodies Machiavelli's own technique of dividing one question in the first chapter of *Il principe.* For the consequences of Machiavelli's reliance on these patterns of thought, cf. Pocock, pp. 158-159.

104. For the motif of the poisoned lady ("concubitus velenatus"), cf. Aquilecchia. pp. 88-89, and Raimondi, p. 257-258.

105. For the reference to Tobit, see Raimondi, p. 257. The text (in the Vulgate) is Tobit 6:1-22.

106. See Isidore, *Etymologiae,* XI.141, translated in "Isidore of Seville: The Medical Writings," trans. with intro. and comm. by W. D. Sharpe, in *Transactions of the American Philosophical Society,* N.S., LIV, part 2 (1964), pp. 46-49: "On contact with this gore,

embraces the full gamut of oppositions active in the play: both the opposition of male and female sexual power and the ambivalent power of the drug, the *pharmakon*, the "remedy" that is both toxic and tonic, potion and poison, *virtus* and *virus*. Nicia's outburst when Callimaco-physician informs him as to the hitch in using the potent medicine describes the *mandragola* exactly, for he calls it a "*suzzacchera*," the name of a medicinal drink composed of vinegar and sugar, both sweet and sour. From this perspective, *mandragola*, the play's title, is the term that funnels into Machiavelli's text the coexistence of medicinal and toxic properties, of masculine and feminine aspects, in the defiled but virtuous blood of Roman Lucretia.

But there is one more decisive feature of *mandragola*. Also termed *rimedi* everywhere in the play are Ligurio's ingenious expedients for overcoming the obstacles to the execution of the plot, which has as its object the fertilization of Lucrezia.[107] Since Ligurio's need for constant resourcefulness enacts the Machiavellian commonplace that only a superior *virtù* can repeatedly overcome the obstacles of *Fortuna*, his *rimedi* also take their place under the rubric of *mandragola*, which thus sexualizes every device of the plot. It is perhaps this sexualization of Ligurio's *rimedi* that accounts for the alliance of Callimaco and Ligurio, for only Ligurio's skill makes Callimaco's sexual energy efficacious.[108] Both Ligurio and Callimaco are finally provided with keys to the "camera terrena" of Nicia's house, for both brains and brawn are needed to complete the execution of the brilliant *beffa*. If, in the *Prince*, Machiavelli compares the successful man of action to a centaur, because he can enlist both intelligence and feral violence for his designs, in *Mandragola* no single character embodies that ideal.

crops do not germinate, wine goes sour, grasses die, trees lose their fruit, iron is corrupted by rust, copper is blackened. Should dogs eat of it, they go mad."

107. For Ligurio's many *rimedi*, cf. pp. 67, 71 (3 times), 75, 76, 77 (3 times), 79, 83, 91, 94, 95. The three uses on p. 77 (II.6) show Ligurio inventing new *rimedi* to overcome fresh obstacles, fulfilling the Machiavellian notion that new and innovative solutions are constantly required for the challenges of Fortune.

108. The sexual dimension of male *virtù* is rendered most brutally explicit in Machiavelli's notorious reference, in the 25th chapter of the *Prince*, to Fortune as a woman who must be treated roughly by the man who would master her.

The richness of Machiavelli's title, which should be rendered without the article ("la favola *Mandragola* si chiama") so as to preserve its comprehensiveness, should be evident: *mandragola* covers nearly everything in the play and, reflexively, the function of the play itself as an ambiguous *rimedio* administered to its audience. It is both full of the bitterness of the satirist who confesses in the prologue that he, too, knows how to speak ill of others—"sa dir male anch'egli"—and potentially a *rimedio* offering relief to its author and illumination to its audience, if not the definitive healthy purge that would restore the vigor of the Florentine civic body.

The function of *mandragola* in embracing both the sexual dyad and the ambivalent efficacy of the *pharmakon* is important for understanding the meaning of the transformation of Lucrezia at the conclusion of the play. As noted above, Lucrezia's reported words when presented with Callimaco's proposal display a strikingly healthy faculty of willing.[109] By submitting to Callimaco and the "miraculous" power of his sex, she has become a powerful, even commanding figure. Much is at stake here. Nicia's admiring comparison of his wife to the rooster, the phallic totem of carnival virility, testifies to Lucrezia's assumption, through submission, of a masterful power that parallels Roman Lucretia's assumption of heroic virtue through her suicide. In terms of the lore of *mandragola,* Callimaco's night with Lucrezia has drawn the imaginary toxicity from her body into himself; she, in return, has retained his seed and, in effect, his masculine potency. Translated back into the realistic psychology of the play, Lucrezia enters into the possession of a new and subtle mastery over those who appear to have triumphed over her virtue, just as Lucretia triumphs over her seducer through the effects of her sacrifice. Lucrezia is transformed from the single remaining spark of ancient virtue to the absolute mistress of the corrupt world of the play; as Ligurio puts it early in the play, Lucrezia is "atta a governare un regno," and it is that realm that she inherits at the play's end.

Cured of her resemblance to Roman Lucretia, Lucrezia comes to stand

---

109. V.6, p. 111: "Io l'ho molto caro, e vuolsi che sia nostro compare"; p. 112: "Dategliene dieci," Lucrezia's last words in the play, order her husband to give ten *grossi* to Timoteo, echo the circumstances at the conclusion of *Decameron* VII.7.36 ("datigli sette gigliati"): a suggestive parallel, as Peronella, too, has just finished cuckolding her husband in his presence.

for an ambiguous female power that thwarts the ideal political agendas of the male *virtù* that, in Machiavelli's typology, strives to conquer history and fortune.[110] Indeed, Lucrezia finally represents the female personifications Fortuna and Natura themselves, the traditional adversaries of the designs of masculine desire.[111] In this respect the contrast with Roman Lucretia is again telling. In Livy's episode, Lucretia is powerful because she becomes like a man, she triumphs over a timorous female nature, she becomes "matrona animi virilis." Through her, the Roman virtue triumphs over nature and natural corruption, restoring the state to its pristine strength. In *Mandragola*, Lucrezia's submission to Callimaco marks the final defection of ancient *virtù*; her alteration ("ell' e stamane up po' alterata," Nicia remarks) is itself a change of nature, as Callimaco had hoped at the play's outset, that makes her a representative of changeable nature herself, "semper varium et mutabile."[112] In her defection, the corruption of nature triumphs over obstinate virtue.

The triumph of nature in Lucrezia's ascendancy requires a re-evaluation of the apparent success of Nicia and Callimaco in the play. For the consummation of Ligurio's ingenious plot marks the defeat not only of ancient virtue but also of the illusion of Callimaco's (and Nicia's) triumph. It is clear, in retrospect, that Nicia and Callimaco have been driven by Nature and Fortune throughout the play: Nicia because he wishes to preserve his fortune by propagating himself—the work of *Natura*—and Callimaco because it was Dame Fortune herself who inflamed his desire with the verbal images of Lucrezia's beauty.[113] Indeed,

110. For this view of male *virtù* in Machiavelli's works, see Gilbert, pp. 192-198; and Pocock, pp. 156-182, esp. p. 167, for an acute analysis of *virtù* as finally self-destructive.

111. For Machiavelli's view of *virtù* besieged by fortune—which it can surmount—and by nature, which it cannot, see his letter 119 (ed. Gaeta, 1961, pp. 230-231); also *Il principe* xxv (ed. Cantimori, pp. 92-94); *Discorsi,* III.9; "capitolo di fortuna," vv. 108-114 (ed. Gaeta, *Il teatro* . . ., p. 315). For discussion, cf. Pocock, p. 180.

112. For the problem of mutability, cf. *Discorsi,* I.42. For an analysis of corruption as an irreversible change of nature, see Pocock, pp. 207-208.

113. That Nicia is victimized by his desire for offspring is clear from the play; but Callimaco, too, is shown driven by a *libido* beyond his control: he threatens repeatedly to adopt violent remedies or destroy himself; e.g., I.3 (p. 67); IV.4 (p. 97): "io mi gitterò in Arno o io mi appiccherò o io mi gitterò da quella finestra o io mi darò d'un coltello in sullo uscio suo." In Act IV.1 (p. 92) Callimaco gives a description of his condition ("le gambe

as the play progresses Callimaco and Nicia, whose relationship is established with exchanges of university Latin, become increasingly similar. Not only are they to be god-fellows, *compari,* because Lucrezia wills it, but their names, already linked by common recourse to military etyma, are doubly related: as echoes of Machiavelli's reliance on Boccaccio's character Calandrino (*Dec.* 8.3, 6; 9.3, 5) and on Bibbiena's related Calandro (from the *Calandria*) as models for Nicia; and as dispersed homophonies of Machiavelli's own full name.[114] Thus Calandro/Calandrino's prefix disappears from Nicia's first name and reappears in front of his last (*Cal*fucci) and in *Call*imaco's name, while *Nicc*olò *Machi*avelli yields the elements of Nicia and Callimaco. The point, I believe, is that Nicia becomes Callimaco's true father, which means that Callimaco is destined to become, in his turn, another Nicia. If Lucretia's suicide provides the perfect opportunity for the "stupefied" Brutus to become miraculously wise and purposeful, the *translatio stultitiae* conducted by Nicia in Lucrezia's bedroom marks the initiation of Callimaco into a household ruled and represented by the idiotic Nicia.[115]

As a figure of Nature and Fortune, Lucrezia is, at the conclusion of the play, the mistress of a world wholly in the grip of those two powers because of the loss of the ancient resolve to stand at any cost against the

---

triemono, le viscere si commuovono, il core mi si sbarba del petto   ") that, as Raimondi notes (p. 202) is taken from Lucretius's sharply satirical view of erotic passion in the *De rerum natura* III. 152-158.

114. Machiavelli's flair for playing with names is beyond doubt. The protagonist of the *Clizia,* Nicomacho, is a collapsed version of *Niccolò Machiavelli* (cf. Ridolfi, p. 247). For the meanings of the names Nicia (= victorious) and Callimaco (= beautiful in battle) cf. R. Sereno, "A Note on the Names of the Personages of Machiavelli's *Mandragola,*" *Italica,* XXVI (1949), 56. Machiavelli's own nickname, *Machia* (cf. Ridolfi, p. 210), represents an operation on *Machiavelli* similar to that of *Nicia* on *Niccolò.* Machiavelli was, of course, well aware from Thucydides and Plutarch that *Nikia* was the name of the Athenian general who led the disastrous Sicilian expedition during the Peloponnesian War; cf. *Discorsi,* I.53; III.16.

115. As Hugo Rahner points out, Dioscorides gives as one of the names of *mandragola* the term *morion,* because the drug made from the plant is narcotic. In the context of our play, however, it might be suggested that the effect of *mandragora* in the broadest sense is *stupidity.* Cf. Rahner, p. 224, citing *De materia medica,* IV, 75, 7.

entropy of history.[116] A remarkable episode placed at the very heart of the play suggests, in an oblique but highly suggestive way, the depth of Machiavelli's melancholy understanding of the failure of the Florentine republic. In the third act (scenes iv, v, vi of twelve) Ligurio tests Timoteo's willingness to cooperate with the plan against Lucrezia by first suggesting an even more scandalous scheme: Timoteo is to persuade the abbess of a nunnery to administer a *pozione* to the pregnant daughter of Cammillo Calfucci so that she will miscarry. Citing the advantages to all concerned, and garnishing his reasoning with hints of subsequent contributions to the Church, Ligurio overcomes the pliant scruples of Timoteo, who agrees to attempt the service. The episode is striking for being an inverse parallel to the principal action of the play. Both of Ligurio's schemes are *rimedi* that entail administering a *pozione*. In one case, however, the object is impregnation; in the other, abortion. Both schemes call out the formulaic Machiavellian skill in assessing the pros and cons of a plan. In one case that skill is applied by Ligurio:

Observe how much good results from the course of action: you maintain the honor of the monastery, the girl's reputation and that of her family . . . and on the other hand you offend nothing more than an insensible unborn piece of flesh, which can be lost in a thousand ways [*che in mille modi si può sperdere*]

(III.v.84)

in the other case, by the newly converted Timoteo, who persuades Madonna Lucrezia with the same kind of argument: "el fine si ha a riguardare in tutte le cose: el fine vostro si è riempire una sedia in paradiso, contentare il marito vostro."

Another, deeper similarity also links the two schemes: the economy of sacrifice. In the scheme that Nicia accepts, adopting the treatment of *mandragola* for Lucrezia, a provision is made for the sacrifice of the surrogate who is to absorb the toxic properties of the drug. The life of the *garzonaccio,* whose ugliness and social marginality mark him as a traditional scapegoat, a *pharmakos,* is to be the price of the rejuvenescence of

116. For the destructive forces of the historical process, cf. *Discorsi* II.5; Gilbert, p. 198; Pocock, pp. 216–218. As Pocock points out, the republican system of Rome was also intrinsically unstable, though a virtuous republic can concentrate its energies and succeed politically for a long time.

Lucrezia and the household of Calfucci. By contrast, in Ligurio's test scheme for Timoteo the sacrificial victim is the imaginary unborn infant of Calfucci's imaginary daughter. That an infant, the desired object of the major plot, is the sacrificial victim of the imaginary microplot is not merely an exposure of the moral flexibility of the principal conspirators. The point of the episode is to place at the play's center a symbol of that which, in the full Machiavellian sense, is sacrificed by all the characters in the play: the "antica virtù" itself, precisely that which, in the Roman tragedy of Lucretia, is born. Ligurio argues to Timoteo that the abortion of the fetus is trivial because it tends to be lost in so many ways, "in mille modi si può sperdere." His idiom is hauntingly reminiscent of a passage in the *Discourses* where Machiavelli points to the multiple ways in which a republic may be betrayed:

. . . no adequate remedies existing for similar disorders arising in republics, it follows that it is impossible to establish a perpetual republic, because in a thousand unforeseen ways its ruin may be accomplished [*per mille inopinate vie si causa la sua rovina*].

(III.17)

One of the funniest plays ever written, *Mandragola* holds at its heart an etiological fable of the defection of ancient virtue and the failure of a free republic. The tale of Lucretia, for Machiavelli the inception of a utopian ideal of civic virtue, gives the measure that permits *Mandragola* to be grasped as the etiology of dystopia.

The Art and Meaning of Gammer Gurton's Needle

J. W. ROBINSON

GAMMER GURTON, the Widow Twanky of the Christ's College school of drama (ca. 1553-ca. 1598), and her well-organized yet volatile play hold more in store for the attentive student than at first sight seems probable. Rooted deeply in the mundane life of Tudor England, and at the same time boldly cast as a weapon in the war among the dramatic critics, the play is both a clever exercise in early modern English rhetoric and a significant religious statement. The playwright, a Christian humanist with a fondness for the Gospel according to St. Luke and *The Canterbury Tales,* fuses his drama with the customs and exigencies of the stage to produce truly theatrical revelations, as well as joyous laughter, as the play is performed. Its meaning is both more specific and more general than has been thought; the Gammer's village is Girton (Cambs.) and simultaneously the world.

An early version of this article was read as a paper at the Sixteenth International Medieval Congress, Western Michigan University, May 1981. I would like to thank my auditors, and also Mr. Richard Axton (Christ's College, Cambridge) and especially Ella Robinson for their comments.

Soon after it was reprinted at the Restoration *Gammer Gurton's Needle*[1] was recognized—since it is divided into acts and scenes, has a list of speakers (including "Mutes"), obeys the unities of time, place, and action, takes place in a street in front of two houses, and ends with a "plaudytie"—as the first "regular" English comedy. At the same time Thomas Warton in his history of English poetry complained of the "lowness of incident" in the play; and, ignoring William Hazlitt's romantic lecture—"such was the wit, such was the mirth of our ancestors:—homely, but hearty; coarse perhaps, but kindly"—Victorian critics managed to judge the play severely: Collier regretted that the author "did not apply his dramatic talents to a better subject," and Professor Ward found the plot to be "of the most childish nature."[2] A nagging sense of its triviality, together with a current tendency to emphasize the strength of the popular and native English dramatic traditions, have perhaps led to some recent neglect of the play.[3] The standard view is that it is an "attempt to present a picture of contemporary rustic life in the form of a regular comedy," and as such its deftness of plot and "realistic" depiction of life in a Tudor village—"the miry winter weather, the impassable roads, the sluttishly kept houses, the state of society in which a needle is a coveted possession, and therewithal the rude comfort which does not lack a slip of bacon, a draught of ale, and a game of trump by the fire"—have

1. I quote from the edition by H.F.B. Brett-Smith, *Gammer Gvrton's Nedle*, Percy Reprints, no. 2 (Oxford, 1920). Unless I note otherwise, I quote all other plays from the Malone Society Reprints. Biblical quotations are from *The Geneva Bible a Facsimile of the 1560 Edition* (Madison, Wis., 1969), and quotations from *The Canterbury Tales* are from *The Works of Geoffrey Chaucer*, ed. F. N. Robinson, 2d ed. (Boston, 1957).

2. [James Wright], *Historia Histrionica* (London, 1699), p. 28; Thomas Warton, *The History of English Poetry* (London, 1775-1781), III, 208; William Hazlitt, *Lectures on the Dramatic Literature of the Age of Elizabeth*, 2d ed. (London, 1821), p. 213; John Payne Collier, *The History of English Dramatic Poetry to the Time of Shakespeare* (London, 1831), II, 463; A. W. Ward, *A History of English Dramatic Literature to the Death of Queen Anne* (London, 1875), I, 143.

3. It is entirely ignored, for example, in Robert Weimann, *Shakespeare and the Popular Tradition in the Theatre* (Baltimore, Md., 1978) and almost ignored in Leo Salingar, *Shakespeare and the Traditions of Comedy* (Cambridge, Eng., 1974). There is no good edition of the play, although it has been anthologized as frequently as (if not more frequently than) any other early Tudor play, beginning with Dodsley (1744) and Hawkins (1773).

been admired,[4] but "everything here is for entertainment" only. When first performed, the play provided holiday fare for "scholarly persons," who, "living in academic celibacy, have often a singular taste for the manners of low life, and find in the crude humour and gross speech of the rustic a diversion from the niceties of classical culture." It is "a college-man's indulgent laugh at unlearned country folk," and "pure fun." "Its moral, whatever it may be, has successfully escaped detection."[5]

Although the art of *Gammer Gurton's Needle* has been praised, it has not, I think, been fully understood; similarly, the play is richer in meaning than is normally thought. In the following essay, I first point out that three academic Anglo-Roman plays of the mid-sixteenth century—*Ralph Roister Doister* (performed ?1552 and published ?1553 and again in ?ca. 1566), *Jack Juggler* (written ?1553 and published in ?1562), and *Gammer Gurton's Needle* itself—deliberately invite interpretation, and that in the case of *Gammer Gurton's Needle* the tradition of drama and dramatic criticism at Cambridge also suggests that it is unlikely that the play is as frivolous as it is commonly assumed to be. I invoke in the course of the essay the plain evidence of other plays which should be associated with *Gammer Gurton's Needle*—including *Misogonus* (written ca. 1560-1577), Fulwell's *Like Will to Like* (printed in 1568), Merbury's *The Marriage Between Wit and Wisdom* (printed in ?1579), and Porter's *The Two Angry Women of Abington* (written ca. 1585-1598).[6] I next try to show that in Englishing the *servus* and parasite as a "Bedlam" the dramatist has

4. Henry Bradley in Charles M. Gayley, ed., *Representative English Comedies* (New York, 1903), p. 203; F. E. Schelling, *Elizabethan Playwrights* (1925; repr. New York, 1965), p. 34, Brett-Smith, p. viii. The deftness of the plot is elaborated on in R. W. Ingram, "*Gammer Gurton's Needle*: Comedy Not Quite of the Lowest Order?" *SEL*, VII (1967), 257–268; and W. B. Toole, "The Aesthetics of Scatology in *Gammer Gurton's Needle*," *ELN*, X (1974), 252–258.

5. F. P. Wilson, *The English Drama 1485–1585* (Oxford, 1969), p. 110; Brett-Smith, p. vii; D. M. Bevington, *From* Mankind *to* Marlowe (Cambridge, Mass., 1962), p. 33; Alan S. Downer, *The British Drama* (New York, 1950), p. 53.

6. Three of these plays are also perhaps connected with the same college as *Gammer Gurton's Needle,* and so might be said to form a small Christ's College school of drama. Francis Merbury entered Christ's College in 1571 (T.N.S. Lennam, "Francis Merbury, 1555–1611," *SP*, LXV [1968], 207–222). The MS of *Misogonus* (R. W. Bond, ed., *Early Plays from the Italian* [Oxford, 1911], pp. 159–258) is signed by Laurence Johnson, who

awakened echoes of both proverbial and biblical folly, or of natural and divine simplicity; and that an examination of Diccon's exact position in the village reveals that—unlike the Vice, with whom he is normally associated—he has a sufficient motive for his actions, and also that they serve to uncover or illuminate the true nature of the village. Further, a number of other slight biblical allusions, together with an insistence on the part of the dramatist on the characteristic nature of village names and activities, help reduce the village to its true significance—an intepretation confirmed by an array of compelling proverbial allusions, which I explore in the next section. The proverbs and parables, which sometimes overlap, contradict, or coincide with each other, are acted out rather than spoken (and hence escape immediate notice), and this dramaturgical method can be found in a number of other Tudor plays, including *Jack Juggler*.

The proverbs and parables constitute an important part of the "witte and inuention" noticed in the play in 1588.[7] They also lend meaning to the play, suggesting that the academic dramatist views the antics of his Bruegelian peasants with the same humanistic circumspection with which Erasmus, for example, viewed the little world of man, epitomized, in this case, in a small village just to the north of Cambridge; and giving some depth to the joke in the 1590s about the "Tragedy" of *"Mother Gurtons needle."*[8] In the concluding section I briefly return to *Ralph Roister Doister* and *Jack Juggler* and show that in them also (as in *The Comedy of Errors*)

---

matriculated at Christ's College in 1570 (G. L. Kittredge, "The 'Misogonus' and Laurence Johnson," *JEGP*, III [1900], 335–341, and D. Bevington, "*Misogonus* and Laurentius Bariωna," *ELN*, II [1964], 9–10). Henry Porter the dramatist may well be the Henry Porter who matriculated at Christ's College in 1584 (E.H.C. Oliphant, "Who Was Henry Porter?," *PMLA*, XLIII [1928], 572–575). Fulwell had no connection with Cambridge, as far as is known (Irving Ribner, "Ulpian Fulwell and his Family," *N & Q*, CXCV [1950], 444-448). On the connections between these plays and *Gammer Gurton's Needle*, the earliest acted and published, see notes 42, 46, 67, and pp. 68-70 below. Later Christ's College dramatists are Richard Bernard, translator of Terence (1598); William Hawkins, author of *Apollo Shroving* (1627), a play for schoolboys; Francis Quarles, author of *The Virgin Widow (1649);* and John Milton.

7. *Oh Read Over D. John Bridges* (1588), p. 10; passage reprinted in E. K. Chambers, *The Elizabethan Stage* (Oxford, 1923), IV, 229.

8. *Histrio-Mastix* (1610; facsimile repr. *Old English Drama*. Students' Facsimile Edition, 1912), sig. C3.

Roman comedy, more thoroughly than has been recognized, has been rendered as moral and religious as the rest of the English drama; and that the methods of their dramatists are shared by the author of *Gammer Gurton's Needle,* who works in ways more intellectual and oblique than those favored by the authors of the more numerous allegorical moral interludes. My general conclusion is that the dramatic art of *Gammer Gurton's Needle* is rich, complex, and Chaucerian, in a modest way, and its meaning profound.

Plays at Cambridge,
and Anglo-Roman Comedy

A Ryght Pithy, Pleasaunt and merie Comedie: Intytuled Gammer gurtons Nedle: Played on Stage, not longe ago in Christes Colledge in Cambridge is an Anglo-Roman Cambridge play, published in 1575 by Thomas Colwell. Colwell's title pages are not necessarily to be believed; however, he published other works by Cambridge dramatists (Thomas Ingelands's *Disobedient Child,* ?1569, and John Phillips' *Patient Grissel,* ?1569), and also the translations of Seneca's *Medea* (1566) and *Agamemnon* (1566) prepared by John Studley, "Student in Trinitie College in Cambridge," and there is no reason to doubt his assertion on the title page that *Gammer Gurton's Needle* was "Played on Stage . . . in Christes Colledge in Cambridge." The further phrase "not longe ago" is vague (probably deliberately so), and the composition and performance of the play have not been exactly dated with any certainty, although the former at least occurred before 1563, when Colwell registered the play with the Stationers' Company.[9] In all probability the play was written, and performed at Christ's College, very early in Elizabeth's reign, although a case can be made for an earlier date, 1553.[10]

9. W. W. Greg, *A Bibliography of the English Printed Drama to the Restoration* (London, 1939-1959), I, no. 67. Colwell may well have also published an edition (no longer extant) of the play shortly after he registered it.

10. The case for 1553 rests largely on the assumption that the author of the play was William Stevenson; and that for a later date on the belief that the author was John Bridges. The arguments are discussed in Frederick S. Boas, *University Drama in the Tudor Age* (Oxford, 1914), pp. 80–88. In either case, the pre-Reformation tone of the play, com-

By 1560 Cambridge had seen productions of plays by Terence and
Plautus (beginning in 1510) and even, on occasion, Aristophanes; biblical
tragedies; Seneca's tragedies; political and religious allegories (including a
notorious performance of Kirchmayer's fanatical *Pammachius* at Christ's
College in 1545); morality plays in Latin; and prodigal-son plays and
school plays, including Fullonius's *Acolastus* and dialogues by Ravisius
Textor.[11] Given this repertoire, and even if Colwell's advertisement of
Gammer Gurton's Needle as "Ryght Pithy" (i.e., "strong", "significant") is
set aside as merely formulaic,[12] is is desirable to consider the play as
something more than empty entertainment.

In his *De honestis ludis* (1551 and 1557) Martin Bucer, the Regius
Professor of Divinity at Cambridge and earlier a friend of Erasmus,
although opposed to "impious and disgusting interchanges of buffoonery"
on the stage, believes it possible to compose tragedies and comedies which
show the "wisdom of living to God," *viuendi Deo sapientiam.*[13] The plays of
Terence and Plautus were frequently thought (for example, by Erasmus—
who stayed at Cambridge from 1511 to 1514, immediately after the
publication of the *Praise of Folly*) to be full of "moral goodness" and to
have been written "for the purpose of showing up men's vices."[14] Similarly, the "buffoonery" of peasant life can be made to reveal meaning, as
the work of Mr. S.'s contemporary, Bruegel, shows, and as does Chaucer's
farcical tale of measure for measure in the village of Trumpington.[15] Like
Trumpington, Girton (the place-name from which the surname

---

bined with the reference to an arrest in the "kings name" (V. ii. 236), must be a "literary
artifice," as Boas suggests. The "Kings peace" in *The Two Angry Women of Abington* (l.
2512) confirms this suggestion.

11. G. C. Moore Smith, in *College Plays Performed in the University of Cambridge* (Cambridge, Eng., 1923), pp. 50-72, provides a chronological list of performances.

12. Colwell's *King Darius* (1565) and *Albion Knight* (ca. 1565) are both "pithy and
pleasant": Greg, I, nos. 38, 40.

13. Chambers, IV, 188-190 (in Latin); Glynne Wickham, *Early English Stages* 1300-
1660 (London, 1963), II, i, 329-331 (in English).

14. *The Correspondence of Erasmus,* trans. R.A.B. Mynors and D.F.S. Thomson, *Collected
Works of Erasmus,* vol. 1 (Toronto, 1974), p. 59; Chambers, IV, 185 (in Latin).

15. Like *Gammer Gurton's Needle, The Reeve's Tale* concludes with proverbs; on the
biblical allusions in it, see P. A. Olson, *"The Reeve's Tale*: Chaucer's *Measure for Measure,"*
SP, LIX (1962), 1–17.

"Gurton"—unique in English drama—comes[16]) is a village just outside Cambridge, and the members of Christ's College are about to witness something taking place in their own backyard—a fair assumption, I think, especially since the action in *The Two Angry Women of Abington* takes place just outside Oxford.

The Anglo-Roman comedies make a special point in their prologues of the wisdom and morality hidden in them. The prologue to *Ralph Roister Doister* includes this passage:

> The wyse Poets long time heretofore,
> Under merrie Comedies secretes did declare,
> Wherein was contained very vertuous lore,
> With mysteries and forewarnings very rare.
> Such to write neither Plautus nor Terence dyd spare.
>
> (ll. 16–20)

Similarly, the prologue-speaker in *Jack Juggler* says that even though they deal with "trifles," "mattiers of non importaunce," only, the Roman comedies "conteine mutch wisdome & teache prudent pollecie" (ll. 54–55, 69) or, as Sir Thomas Elyot writes in *The Governor* (1531), "sens good and wise mater." [17] This seems to draw attention to something of greater or deeper significance than the *sententiae* for which Terence had long been famous, and raises the question of the meaning of these plays. What are these "mysteries . . . rare"? In *Gammer Gurton's Needle* Diccon, when he realizes the opportunity placed in his path, says, "Here is a matter worthy glosynge / Of Gammer Gurtons nedle losynge" (II, ii, 7–8). He speaks ambiguously and coyly to his academic audience, using the same pun as Chaucer's Summoner causes his friar to utter in the Summoner's Tale (l. 1793), and meaning not only that in this situation some misdirection is possible, but also that they may, if they will, see some meaning in the play, interpret it.

---

16. P. H. Reaney, *A Dictionary of British Surnames,* 2d ed. (London, 1976), p. 146. There are no other Gurtons or Girtons in Thomas L. Berger and William C. Bradford, Jr., *An Index of Characters in English Printed Drama to the Restoration* (Englewood, Colo., 1975).

17. Chambers, IV, 187.

Servus, Parasite, Vice, Fool, and "Bedlam"

The very first line of the play opens the door to the world of the English peasantry; Gammer Gurton is no gentle and nimble needlewoman: "As Gammer Gurton, with manye a wyde styche / Sat pesynge & patching of Hodg her mans briche." The last line is equally as firmly from Roman comedy: "For Gammer Gurtons nedle sake, let vs haue a plaudytie." In Englishing Terence and Plautus the dramatists found English equivalents for the characters and added a sense of plot to traditional English drama, finding in Terence, as Roger Ascham wrote in *The Schoolmaster* (1570), "all his stuffe so neetlie packed vp, and wittely compassed in euerie place";[18] and also a sense of haste and urgency, [19] of some importance in *Gammer Gurton's Needle,* since the success of Hodge's wooing, he feels, depends on his having a presentable pair of breeches by the morning. The author has, in fact, as has been explained, followed precisely the formula of the Terentian plot as analyzed and recommended in 1550 by the academic Willichius.[20] He has also, like the authors of *Ralph Roister Doister* and *Jack Juggler,* learned from Roman comedy how to propel his plot by means of the inventiveness of the ubiquitous *servus* and parasite, and these characters, not postclassical types, required domesticating. As has been often recognized, the native English Vice, who first appears in English drama in John Heywood's plays in the 1530s and appears frequently in plays throughout the remainder of the century, especially in the 1560s and 1570s, was available for this purpose. In Professor Wilson's words, Mathew Merygreeke, who "entangles Roister Doister in absurd situations reminds us as much of the mischievous Vice of the morality plays as of the classical parasite"; and Diccon, who "sets all at sixes and sevens" in *Gammer Gurton's Needle,* is "Vice-like."[21] Mercury in Plautus's *Amphitruo* has become Jack Juggler, and is named as "the vice" on the title

18. *Ibid.,* IV, 192.

19. L. Potter, "The Plays and the Playwrights," in Norman Sanders et al., *The Revels History of Drama in English 1500–1576* (London, 1980), pp. 216–217.

20. T. W. Baldwin, *Shakspere's Five-Act Structure* (Urbana, Ill., 1947), pp. 228–251, 409–410.

21. Wilson, pp. 109–111. So also Bernard Spivak, *Shakespeare and the Allegory of Evil* (New York, 1958), pp. 323–327; E. P. Vandiver, "The Elizabethan Dramatic Parasite," *SP,* XXXII (1935), 411–437; F. H. Mares, "The Treatment of Classical Material in Some

page of the play of that name. More generally, the dramatists are drawing on a native English tradition of clowning and jesting, of which English dramatists were particularly fond, and which even those writing or adapting neo-Latin academic plays embraced.[22] In the first English prodigal son play, "The Prodigal Son" (probably—only a fragment is extant—a version of Textor's *Iuvenis, Pater et Uxor,* ca. 1530), for example, the *servus,* who has become Robin Runaway, speaks Skeltonical nonsense verse (11. 57–84); and in *Misogonus,* also a prodigal-son play, the wicked servant pretends to be a Fool, adopts the name Will Summer (Henry VIII's jester—I.i.199), does "skoggingly" feats (after John Scogan, Edward IV's jester—I.iii.28), and wears long ears and a Fool's coat (I.i.182; I.ii.63). In this way, while (like Diccon, Mathew and Jack) promising "good sport" (II.iv.299), he deceives the prodigal's father. The *servus* and the parasite are thus grafted onto the tradition of the Vice and the Fool. They in turn carry with them some sense of a topsy-turvy world, and even of that availability of truth through topsy-turvydom found in the birth of Heaven's king in a mean stable, and expressed, for example, in the Chester Shepherds' Play (a sixteenth-century work[23]), when the shepherds' boy wrestles and overthrows his masters, deposing, in the words of the Magnificat (which is recited in the previous play), the mighty from their seats; and expressed also, as has been recognized, in the licensed folly of Shakespeare's wise fools. As Misogonus's father's neighbor says, "Children & fooles they say can not ly" (I.i.185).[24]

English Plays of the Sixteenth Century," *AUMLA,* XV (1961), 74; Ola E. Winslow, *Low Comedy as a Structual Element in English Drama,* (Ph.d. dissertation, University of Chicago, 1926), pp. 83–84.

22. The fool's parts in Grimald's *Archipropheta* (performed at Oxford, 1546–1547) and in the Anglo-Latin version of Birck's *Sapientia Solomonis* (perhaps performed at Cambridge, 1559–1560) are much more prominent then in the dramatic sources of these two plays. In Udall's lost biblical tragedy *Ezechias* (performed at Cambridge, 1564) there was drollery and humor ("mirum vero quantum hic facetiarum, quantum leporis in re tam seria ac sancta"); and when dramatizing Chaucer's *Knight's Tale* (performed at Oxford, 1566) Richard Edwardes could not avoid introducing a clown (Boas, pp. 96, 103).

23. L. M. Clopper, "The History and Development of the Chester Cycle," MP, LXXV (1978), 227, 243.

24. The tradition of the wise fool is traced in Barbara Swain, *Fools and Folly during the Middle Ages and the Renaissance* (New York, 1932), pp. 27–52.

The author of *Gammer Gurton's Needle* is, I think, indebted to this spirit. His decision to make Diccon (uniquely) a "Bedlam" influences the whole play. The names given to the characters in academic drama are normally meant to be significant, as are the names in Terence and Plautus, the allegorical names in the morality plays and moral interludes, and also the type names (including all the names in *Gammer Gurton's Needle*) that appear in English drama in the sixteenth century. As John Palsgrave, translating *Acolastus* (1540), explains, the names are those "the auctour hath taken to serue to his purpose." [25] The *servus* or parasite becomes Robin Runaway, Jack Juggler, and Mathew Merygreeke, "a merry greeke, a pleasant companion, and in faith a good fellow" (*OED*, "Greek," *sb.*, sense 5). "Diccon" is an affectionate diminutive of "Dick," a common name, meaning any "fellow," [26] and this character is further thoroughly domesticated, made a recognized (if odd) member of society, by being conceived and presented as a Bedlam. The author takes pains to stress this point. Diccon is listed first among the "names of the Speakers in this Comedie" as "Diccon the Bedlem," and is referred to by that epithet in the prologue and throughout the play, which was itself originally registered as "Dyccon of Bedlam, &c." [27] The focus is on the Bedlam, and his appellation is meant to be significant.

Bedlams were persons discharged from the hospital for lunatics of St. Mary of Bethlehem in Bishopsgate. This institution was granted to the Mayor and citizens of London at the Dissolution and incorporated as a royal foundation; in 1560 Queen Elizabeth issued a proclamation authorizing the collection of funds for it; and in 1575 (when *Gammer Gurton's Needle* was published) it was partly rebuilt. [28] The word "Bedlam" is frequently used throughout the sixteenth century to mean "lunatic" or "complete fool," and "like a mad Bedlam" became a proverbial comparison. Wandering the countryside and begging for their food, Bedlams

25. P. L. Carver, ed., EETS, O. S. 202 (London, 1937), p. 14.

26. E. G. Withycombe, *The Oxford Dictionary of English Christian Names,* 3d ed. (Oxford, 1977), pp. 253–254.

27. Greg, I, no. 67.

28. C. L. Kingsford, ed., *A Survey of London by John Stow* (Oxford, 1908), I, 164-165, 319; "Bethlehem Hospital," in William Kent, ed., *An Encyclopaedia of London* (London, 1970); P. L. Hughes and J. F. Larkin, eds., *Tudor Royal Proclamations* (New Haven, Conn., 1969), II, 161–162.

were a well-known part of the problem of vagabondage, of "straunge beggeres," with which local authorities were at this time constantly concerned. The worthy poor were licensed to beg, and in Cambridgeshire the local authorities periodically put badges on them;[29] Diccon, like other Bedlam beggars, probably wears a tin badge engraved with a cross. He is always, in the play, "the bedlem," and he is "of bedlem," or from it. The notoriously tattered and half-naked appearance of Bedlam beggars is probably reflected in the refrain of the drinking song adopted as one of the entr'acte entertainments (between I and II) in *Gammer Gurton's Needle*— "Backe and syde go bare, go bare, / booth foote and hande go colde: / but Bellye god sende thee good ale ynoughe, / whether it be newe or olde"— and in Diccon's reference to the "colde wether" and his "naked armes" (II.i.4); and like other Bedlams, or "Abrahem" men, he is particularly fond of bacon.[30]

At the same time, in the words of a common sixteenth-century proverb (used by Sir Thomas Chaloner in his translation, published in 1549, of Erasmus's *Praise of Folly*), "oftentimes a foole maie speake to purpose." [31] Similarly, "a fool may sometimes give a wise man counsel," and "a fool's bolt may sometimes hit the mark," as the proverbs say, reflecting the tradition of the wise fool.[32] Further, the "wisdome of this worlde is foolishnes with God," "who hathe chosen the foolish things of the worlde to confounde the wise" (1 Corinthians 1:27 and 3:19), and the wisdom of the foolish can be attributed to Bedlams. Erasmus (whose *Praise of Folly* concludes with this theme) comments on 1 Corinthians in his *Enchiridion*, and Coverdale translates (1545) this passage as, "the world" judges those

29. L. F. Salzman, ed., *The Victoria History of the County of Cambridge and the Isle of Ely* (London, 1948), II, 92; J. D. Mackie, *The Earlier Tudors 1485-1558* (Oxford, 1952), pp. 453–455.

30. John Awdeley, *The Fraternitye of Vacabondes* (1575; repr. in Edward Viles and F. J. Furnivall, eds., *The Rogues and Vagabonds of Shakespeare's Youth*, New Shakspere Society, series VI, no. 7 [London, 1880]), p. 3: he "walketh bare armed, and bare legged . . . and caryeth . . . a styke with baken on it . . . and nameth himselfe poore Tom (first published 1561?); Thomas Dekker, *The Belman of London* (1608, *STC* 6480), sig. D2: he gets what he demands, "which is commonly Bacon."

31. C. H. Miller, ed., EETS 257 (London, 1965), p. 128.

32. M. P. Tilley, *A Dictionary of the Proverbs in England in the Sixteenth and Seventeenth Centuries* (Ann Arbor, Mich., 1950), F449, F469, F516 (cited hereafter as Tilley).

who follow Christ "to be fools, to be deceived, to doat, and to be mad bedlames." [33] So in John Foxe's *Christus Triumphans* (performed at Cambridge, 1562–1563) Ecclesia, the true church, now weak, ragged, and pitiful, is said by Antichrist to be fit only for Bedlam, *ad Bethlemitas insanam abducite* (V.i.65);[34] and Jenkin Careaway in *Jack Juggler* thinks Jack, who has truthfully shown Jenkin the folly of his ways, a "mad knaue in bedelem" (l.1125). The suitability of Edgar's disguising himself as mad Tom o'Bedlam lies in his ability in his "madness" to bring the painful truth to the Earl of Gloucester and to Lear.

Diccon in the Village of Girton Confounding the Wise

It is a mistake to see Diccon as a villain, especially a motiveless one. He is wise, in both the biblical and proverbial senses; he is also somewhat wanton, but ultimately much less seriously culpable than the villagers he has come among. Like some other rogues and fools, he stands "somewhere between the concept of folly as wisdom and folly as sin." [35] As a Bedlam, this English version of the parasite roams the countryside, begging for his food and drink, or, as a last resort, filching it (I.i.1-6). He is recognized, in a kindly manner, by the people of Gammer Gurton's village, as a frequent visitor. He is "no straunger" (II.ii.22), but is not one of them; he speaks standard English, while they speak the exaggerated dialect adopted by Tudor playwrights for rustic characters. On his arrival in the village, as the play opens, he finds Gammer Gurton's household in an uproar, "howlynge and scowlyng" and "whewling and pewling" (I.i.11–12), and concludes—interestingly for a Bedlam—that they "be not well in theyr wyts" (I.i.18). In the first act, a clumsy, superstitious, and futile search for the needle takes place; in the second, Diccon, having discovered the nature of the problem, begins to render the search even more futile by spreading false information, and the search goes more and more astray until the surprise denouement. When all the noisy and boisterous folly is

33. Myles Coverdale, *Writings and Translations,* ed. G. Pearson (Cambridge, Eng., 1844), p. 500.

34. John Foxe, *Two Latin Comedies,* ed. and trans. J. H. Smith (Ithaca, N.Y., 1973), p. 334.

35. P. R. Baumgartner, "From Medieval Fool to Renaissance Rogue," *A.M.,* IV (1963), 62.

over, and Diccon is found to have been misleading the villagers, the
Bailey, or Magistrate, requires him to swear, on Hodge's leather breeches,
that he will try to help Gammer Gurton find her needle. Diccon obliges,
but instead of merely placing his hand on Hodge's breeches, as on a copy
of the Bible, gives Hodge *"a good blow on the buttocke"* (V.ii.293), as the
stage direction indicates. In so doing he dislodges the needle, which has
never really been lost, since it has reposed all the while in Hodge's
breeches, where Gammer Gurton left it when she was interrupted in her
mending by the need to chase the cat away from the milk pan (I.iii.-
31-37).

I think it is significant that the one person in the play who, by common
agreement and official license, is the foolish one, is the one to find the
needle. The combined wisdom of Church, in the person of the Curate, Dr.
Rat—"estemed full wyse" by the villagers (Prologue, l. 13; III.iii.59)—
and State, in the person of the Magistrate, fails to do so; and, to emphasize the point, the needle turns up, as in one of Chesterton's Father Brown
stories, in the most obvious place. The world should feel extremely foolish
for failing to look there to begin with. The suggestion that "the play ends
with the needle aptly found by accident almost as an aftermath of no
importance" [36] is hardly acceptable. The play ends with a startling climax; and if, as is commonly assumed, the revelation of the needle is an
accident, it is a symbolic or extremely appropriate accident, demonstrating the truth of both the proverb and the biblical sentence.

Diccon ought to have found charity in the village; by 1556 poor relief
in Cambridgeshire was compulsory. [37] Since the villagers are preoccupied
with their own misery, he is reduced to helping himself to a slip of bacon.
The Fool in *Misogonus* also introduces himself as blissful only "with bakon
in my hande . . . & my bole full of drinke/ha ha ha" (I.ii.8–9), and
Tipple, the alewife in Colwell's other farce, *Tom Tyler and His Wife*
(?1565), [38] enters "with a pot in her hand, and a piece of Bacon" (ll.
147–149). Apart from the traditional fondness of Bedlams for bacon, and
of Fools (and of Roman parasites) for food and drink, bacon needs ale.

36. Ingram, p. 262; Glynne Wickham, *Early English Stages 1300–1660* (London,
1981), III, 121 (the end comes "quite fortuitously").
37. Salzman, II, 92.
38. Tom Tyler was not certainly published by Colwell: Greg, II, no. 820.

Diccon, however, has so far obtained his bacon only, and sets to thinking how he can turn the bacon into "a shoinghorne [an appetizer] to draw on two pots of ale" (I.i.24)—a thought not easily missed, not only because the expression is common[39] (and often associated with bacon and other savories), but also because this line forms the conclusion to the first scene. Here is the motive for his subsequent actions. To fail, as is usual, to notice that he even has a motive—to go so far as to suggest that he is a "village Iago"[40]—is to bring a charge against him verging on the frivolous. He turns the loss of the needle into an opportunity for himself. His plan, which develops as opportunity presents itself, has good possibilities throughout—from Dame Chat, for example, he almost immediately secures "a cup of the best ale" (II.ii.80) in return for warning her that Gammer Gurton has accused her of stealing and cooking her best rooster. Diccon enjoys the sport of his quest, and is far more notable for his perceptiveness than for his villainy.

Although he is guilty of barratry (inventing and sowing "false reports, whereby discord ariseth or may arise between neighbours"), a vexing matter for Elizabethan magistrates, it is not precisely the case that it is Diccon who "sets all at sixes and sevens" in the play. This is to ignore, among other things, the first act. The village is extremely disorderly, and the Bedlam has wandered into the world of Mankind's tavern. He sees the futility of what is going on in the village, sees into the darkness of the hearts and the disharmony of the lives of the uncharitable villagers. The tavern or alehouse, a real and constant source of disorderliness in early Elizabethan England, is a natural image for the neglect of Godly ways, and by the mid-sixteenth century is well established in English drama for this purpose.[41] The prodigal son plays (such as *Misogonus*) provided an additional *raison d'être* for them, since they could serve to demonstrate the bad company, the "harlots" and "riotous liuing" (Luke 15:13, 30), into

39. *OED*, "Shoeing-horn," sense 2, and Thomas Nashe, *Workes,* ed. R. B. McKerrow (London, 1910), I, 207; IV, 130–131, provide many examples.

40. C. F. Tucker Brooke, *The Tudor Drama* (1911; repr. Hamden, 1964), p. 163; and A. M. Kinghorn, *Mediaeval Drama* (London, 1968), p. 144 ("Diccon is a comic Iago").

41. F. G. Emmison, *Elizabethan Life: Disorder* (Chelmsford, 1970), pp. 12, 26, 139, 202-217; Wickham, III, 94-99.

which the prodigal had fallen.[42] As in *Misogonus* (II.iv), the atmosphere of
the tavern has in *Gammer Gurton's Needle* spilled over into the home. Like
Sir John, Dr. Rat despises his flock and tries to spend all his time
drinking, frequently lifting the pot so often with alewives that he can
hardly walk, as Diccon truthfully reports (V.ii.216), and haunting
Mother Bee's tavern, or Hob Fylcher's (III.iii.74-75; III.iv.26). Sir John
plays cards at the alehouse, carries a pack of cards instead of a prayer book,
and consents to play dice with Misogonus and his whore. Neither one
appears to have "one dropp of pristes bludd in him" (II.iv.52). The author
of *Misogonus* has chosen a common name for his priest ("every foolish priest
most commonly is called Sir John," says *A C. Mery Talys*, 1526);[43] the
author of *Gammer Gurton's Needle* produces not only a pun on "Curate,"
but renders his man of God as vicious and rodentlike (capable of creeping
into holes—IV.ii.136) as possible; and at the same time "Dr. Rat" (the
name is peculiar to this play) also becomes "Sir John" as Diccon is about
to demonstrate how very foolish he is (IV.ii.142). Dame Chat has a card
game going in her house, and lures her maid Doll (who with such a name
is probably all too easily persuaded)[44] into taking a hand (II.ii.22–30);
Gammer Gurton also plays cards (I.i.12). The villagers thus offend the
law; a "game of trump by the fire" is not so innocent, being contrary, like
dicing, to 33 Henry VIII c. 9 (1541).[45] They also break the peace by
brawling as vigorously as Bruegel's peasants ever did, not only indulging
in a spirited flyting but also vowing to kill one another (III.iii.54, 58).
This is certainly the place for Idleness, and it is the character of that name
who very appropriately comes into the scene of domestic turmoil at
Mother Bee's (ll. 1133–1255) in *The Marriage Between Wit and Wisdom*
borrowed from *Gammer Gurton's Needle*.[46]

42. L. Bradner, "The Latin Drama of the Renaissance (1340-1640)," *Studies in the Renaissance*, IV (1957), 45. Potter, p. 229, describes the general similarities between *Misogonus* and *Gammer Gurton's Needle*; I note the recurrence of the colloquialism "whochittall" (III.i.52) and "washical" (V.ii.116)—*OED*, "What-d'ye-call-'em."

43. P. M. Zall, ed., *A Hundred Merry Tales* (Lincoln, Neb., 1963), p. 65. "Sir" was commonly used for any nongraduate priest.

44. *OED*, "Doll," *sb*[1]., sense 1; Withycombe, p. 88.

45. Emmison, p. 218.

46. Scenes 6 and 7: Idleness acts and speaks like Diccon, Doll (also a character in *Gammer Gurton's Needle*) like Tib, Lob (whose breeches need mending) like Hodge, and

Diccon knows that the villagers' approach to their problems is devilish. Most of the action of the play takes place in darkness, either in the evening or in the dark corners of the two poorly lit houses, when, in true Roman fashion, the action is described as it takes place by someone standing by the door. These houses—Gammer Gurton's and Dame Chat's, one on each side of the "stage," I imagine—are, or seem to be, very stable three-dimensional structures. They have doorposts and strong doors; Dr. Rat climbs through a hole in the wall of Dame Chat's house, and Hodge chases the cat "vp the stayers" (I.v.24) inside Gammer Gurton's, and can be heard as he clambers around in the dark. Cambridge certainly built "houses" (presumably pre-Serlian) for its comedies, employing carpenters for that purpose, as college account books show.[47] Inside these houses, and in a sense in the entire village, light is very hard to come by, and the source of it hard to find:

> Goe hye thee soone, and grope behynd the old brasse pan,
> Whych thing when thou hast done
> Ther shalt thou fynd an old shooe, wher in if thou looke well
> Thou shalt fynd lyeng an inche of a whyte tallow candell,
>
> (I.iv.39–42)

says Gammer Gurton to Cocke, her boy, probably imitating the woman in Luke 15:8–10 who, "if she loose one piece, doeth . . . light a candel, & swepe the house, and seke diligently til she finde it."[48] For someone

---

Mother Bee (who is mentioned as an alewife in *Gammer Gurton's Needle*, III, iii, 74) like Gammer Gurton. Idleness restores the "lost" (he stole it) porridge pot. Hodge and the cat are mentioned.

47. Smith, p. 28, and also "The Academic Drama at Cambridge" in the Malone Society Collections, II, 2 (1923), pp. 206-209. Christ's College in 1551-1552, for example, paid the "carpenter for removing ye tables in ye haull & setting y^{em} vp agein wth ye houses & other things," and in 1559-1560, when one of the plays was possibly *Gammer Gurton's Needle* ("Mr. Steuensonnes play"), paid "carpenters wirkinge at ii playes." H. A. Watt, "The Staging of *Gammer Gurton's Needle*," in *Elizabethan Studies and Other Essays in Honor of George E. Reynolds*, ed. E. J. West, (Boulder, Colo., 1945), pp. 85-92, argues for the simplest possible staging, and ignores Smith's evidence, as does Richard Southern, *The Staging of Plays before Shakespeare* (London, 1973), pp. 399-423, whose only conclusion is that the staging was "novel."

48. Professor A. Velz, University of Texas, first pointed this allusion out to me. S. J. Kozikowski, "Stevenson's Gammer Gurton's Needle," *Expl.*, XXXVIII, no. 3 (1980), 17-18, also sees the parallel and says that "the needle's unexpected recovery . . . symbol-

with his name (*OED*, "Cock," *sb.*[1], senses 6 and 7) Cocke is perhaps sufficiently spry, but insufficiently accomplished. At any rate, there is no fire at which to light his small piece of candle, once he has managed to find it in the old shoe; and Hodge, who takes the task of lighting the candle over from Cocke, "lieth tomblynge and tossing amids the floure / Rakyng there some fyre to find amonge the asshes dead," finally mistaking the cat's eyes for sparks, while Tib, the maid, winnows the dust and straw, finding only the chaff unpleasing to the Lord as "He wil make cleane his flooer" (Luke 3:17 and I.iv.44-I.v.57).

This is the first English play whose action (as in the case of *A Midsummer's Night's Dream* and *The Two Angry Women of Abington*) consists of the mad mistakes of a night. There is, however, far more devil in this play than in the later "nocturnals." The constant groping in holes and heaps of rubbish, and the constant references to turds (Hodge breaks open a piece of cat's turd, and Tib, a piece of hen's turd in their desperate search for the needle) show the presence of the devil, which Diccon, unlike the villagers, detects. "The deuill I smell hym wyll be here anone," he says to Hodge (II.i.110), and the impending arrival of this black monster with claws causes Hodge to "berayc the hall" (II.i.106); the most devilish part of the human body is the arse-hole, and the lowest and therefore the worst place in Hell is the devil's own arse-hole, as the proverb says, and as Chaucer's Summoner knew.[49] The villagers are living in devilish darkness. Their moral obtuseness is only the more apparent if, as has recently been

---

izes the unsearchable mystery of God's redemption of man." He also refers to Acts 9:5 ("it is hard for thee to kicke against prickes"). A. C. Cawley ("The Mak Episode and *Gammer Gurton's Needle*," *English Society Papers*, 1 {1978}, pp. 2-4) finds an interesting number of parallels between *Gammer Gurton's Needle* and the Wakefield *Second Shepherds' Play*, pointing out that the theme of both is a search for something lost. Another significant interpretation of *Gammer Gurton's Needle* is by Joel B. Altman, *The Tudor Play of Mind* (Berkeley, Calif., 1978), pp. 152-157, where the play is said to be about the folly of *consilia* and the normalcy of mystery, and to be a parody of Tudor litigation.

49. Bartlett Jere Whiting, *Proverbs, Sentences, and Proverbial Phrases from English Writings Mainly before 1500* (Cambridge, Mass., 1968), D207 (cited hereafter as Whiting); the Summoner says (ll. 1693-1694) that the friars in hell are kept under the Devil's tail, and swarm "out of the develes ers" "as bees out swarmen from an hyve." Hodge uses this expression, saying that Tom Tankard's cow frisked her tail "as though ther had ben in her ars a swarme of Bees" (I.ii.33).

suggested,[50] their habit of swearing on each other's breeches is to be
regarded as their handy substitute for swearing on the "Breeches Bible,"
or the Geneva Bible (1560), the English common Bible. Hodge, who
bears a name common among agricultural laborers,[51] has not surprisingly
"no booke" (II.i.69), and is notable for his superstitiousness; his surliness
toward Gammer Gurton, whose servant he is, is less expected. Dr. Rat,
far from enlightening his flock and representing the Lord who "wil come
on thee as a thefe, and thou shalt not knowe what houre I wil come vpon
thee" (Luke 12:39–40; Revelations 3:3), comes upon them literally like a
thief, as the Magistrate observes (V.i.8); Dame Chat, unlike the goodman
of the house in the parable, has suffered her "house to be digged
through," (Luke 12:39; IV.ii.95–96)[52] and unlike him she is confronted
(she thinks) by a real thief, whose head she promptly breaks with the door
bar (V.ii.35) and who as promptly vows to seek revenge (IV.ii.156–157).

Diccon is not responsible for the situation in the village. He comes
across it, and all he really does is "make a playe" of it, hardly adding a
"worde." He'll "enlarge" it a bit, he says (II.ii.10–14). Of Dame Chat
and Gammer Gurton, he knows "what lieth in both their harts" (II.iii.4),
as he tells the audience. When blamed for the indignities suffered by Dr.
Rat when he crept through the hole into Dame Chat's kitchen he replies,
sensibly enough, that the Curate ought to have known better, and that he
"showeth himselfe herein ye see, so very a coxe," or so true a fool
(V.ii.230). His accusations are believed eagerly and with alacrity, and
viciously elaborated on by others. The villagers normally quarrel (I.ii.24),
and are perfectly capable in fact of stealing each other's poultry, and it is
from Hodge that Diccon gets the idea for his accusations in the first place
(I.ii.38). Tib, no doubt (like her sister Tibet Talk-Apace, maid to Dame
Christian), is naturally talkative, given to gadding about outside the

50. S. J. Kozikowski, "Comedy Ecclesiastical and Otherwise in *Gammer Gurton's Nee-dle*," *Greyfriar: Siena Studies in Literature*, XVIII (1977), 12-13.

51. Withycombe, p. 255.

52. Tyndale (1534) has "broken vp," the Bishops Bible (1568) "broken through," and the Vulgate "perfodi" or "perfodiri." Dame Chat says that "a hole broke down, euen wᵗ in thes ii. dayes"—a plausible situation, the wattle and daubed clay filling the gaps between the stubs of sixteenth-century timber-framed houses being liable to crumble; burglars not infrequently chose to "break a hole" in a wall rather than force a lock or window (Emmison, pp. 270-271).

house, and liable to misunderstand what she sees (*Ralph Roister Doister,*
ll.720–765), but no sooner has Diccon suggested to Dame Chat that Tib
has hinted to Gammer Gurton that Dame Chat has stolen her rooster,
than Gammer Gurton is immediately guilty: "Haue I, stronge hoore?,"
exclaims Dame Chat, on the attack already, anxious to "haue the yong
hore by the head, & the old trot by ye throte" (II.ii.43-45). Similarly,
both Gammer Gurton and Dr. Rat have insufficient reason in them to
question Diccon's story about Dame Chat's stooping down and picking
something up outside Gammer Gurton's door (II.iv.24 and IV.ii.132),
and even the Magistrate is gullible (V.ii.54-55). Information known only
at secondhand, from Diccon, is readily turned into firsthand knowledge;
Hodge swears that he himself heard the Devil "plainly" say to Diccon that
Dame Chat had the needle (III.ii.25–26), and Dame Chat that Tib
"plainly" said to Gammer Gurton that she had eaten her rooster
(V.ii.150). Diccon can accurately predict what nonsense the villagers will
get up to next even without his help; Gammer Gurton knows nothing of
his gnomic message from the Devil about "chat," "rat," and "cat"
(II.iii.19–28) when she decides to send for Dr. Rat (III.iii.59–66), and
neither does poor Gib, the cat (who bears a common—and a Skeltonic—
name for a cat, who is the first cat in English drama, and who, says
Hazlitt, "may be fairly reckoned one of the *dramatis personae*"),[53] when she
suddenly starts to choke (III.iv.2), a diversionary tactic in Gammer Gurton's opinion, so convinced is she that Dame Chat is guilty.

Diccon, then, does not so much lead the villagers astray as allow them
to lead themselves astray, a process begun long before he came on the
scene. They jump at the chance to get themselves even further confused
than they already are. Chasing around aimlessly in a village hell, the
villagers neglect their charitable obligations to the wandering Bedlam. To
his chagrin he quickly notices this, and with his superior perception
realizes the foolishness of their behavior, if not the very source of their
mistake. The madman provides them with an opportunity to demonstrate, in amplified detail, how truly small-minded and filthy they are.
He brings enlightenment to the village, showing the inhabitants not only

53. Hazlitt, p. 286. *OED,* "Gib," *sb.*[1], sense 1. Philip Sparrow was slain by "Gib our
cat" (Philip Henderson, ed., *The Complete Poems of John Skelton,* 4th ed. [London, 1964], p.
60).

where their precious needle really is, but also something of themselves. They respond by achieving a kind of social harmony. Diccon is hardly blameless, but even before the needle is discovered the Magistrate, aware of what his village needs, rather than punishing him, rewards him, although the rewards are ambiguous, reminiscent of a fool's paradise, and again suggesting the power of topsy-turvydom (V.ii.270–287). The needle is then found, and there is a general reconciliation and rejoicing. Dame Chat and Dr. Rat share in Gammer Gurton's supreme happiness, possibly with a touch of restraint: "By my troth Gossyp gurton," says the former, "I am euen as glad / As though I mine owne self as good a turne had" (V.ii.314–315). Diccon is included in Gammer Gurton's invitation: "let vs go in and drink" (V.ii.326). His ruse has finally succeeded.

The allusions to the parables of the lost sinner and of the coming of the Lord, the generally smelly and devilish darkness in which the action takes place, the hint of divine folly so much more enlightening than the worldly wisdom of the village, and the ordinariness of the names of the villagers—all serve to place the events that occur in the village *sub specie aeternitatis*. The careful woman of the "house" and the watchful good man of the "house" have become silly and warlike neighbors. This method of demonstrating human failings, and rendering them amusing, by referring them to their serious opposites or counterparts is similar to the method familiar in some of the English mystery plays (the Chester Shepherds' Play, for example), and also—more to the point, perhaps—in some of Chaucer's fabliaux. Divine history provides a framework for human activity, and reveals it for the buffoonery it really is. Diccon is more a revealer of truth than the devil's agent provocateur. He seeks not disorder for its own sake, or "with no other purpose than the gratification of his own super-subtle imagination,"[54] but comfort and truth, truth which he is at the end capable of stating and revealing.

Looking for a Needle in a Haystack: Paroemia

The "needle" itself possibly has some biblical and religious overtones. In *Piers Plowman* (published in 1550 and in 1561 by Owen Rogers,

54. Mares, p. 74; Brooke, p. 163.

sometimes a partner of Thomas Colwell[55]) divine love is said to be as light as a leaf and "portatiue & persant, as the point of an nedle." [56] Gammer Gurton's life appears to be empty of this charity. Nor does she heed the prick of conscience; unlike Paul, she finds it easy to "resist God when he pricketh & soliciteth our consciences" (Acts 9:5, marginal gloss). At the same time, the proverbial senses of "needle" as something both trivial and elusive are perhaps more obvious.

The pursuits of the villagers have a strong air of futility about them. A needle is, in fact, worth very little, even in a Tudor village. Needles were commonly sold by peddlers (John Heywood's peddler has a supply in his pack) and grocers, and were very inexpensive.[57] "Not worth a needle" is a proverbial saying (Tilley P334; Whiting N69) common in the sixteenth century, and Gammer Gurton's melodramatic laments can only be considered to be out of all proportion to her loss. The light of her life is gone. She is lost forever. "Alas my neele we shall neuer meete, adue, adue for aye" (I.v.8), she cries. To her, in her fine frenzy, it may be a "goodly tossing sporyars neele" (II.iv.10), but even to Hodge, who has more at stake in the matter than she has, it is a mere "washical" (V.ii.116) or "what-do-you-call-it," and in truth it seems to have been a simple needle, made of iron, or perhaps silver, since Hodge describes it as a "lytle thing with an hole in the end, as bright as any syller" (II.i.43).[58] The hardness of Gammer Gurton's heart has more relevance than any alleged scarcity of needles; after all, she has only to borrow one from Dame Chat, or Mother Bee, who may well (like Elinour Rumming) have a good assortment of them on the shelf, left in pledge by villagers for cups of ale received on credit.[59] Furthermore, needles are notoriously hard to find, whether really lost or not. One is usually advised not to bother to search. Again the proverb is a common one: Thomas More writes (1532) that to look for

55. *STC* 6774, for example.

56. *The Vision of Pierce Plowman* (London, 1561, *STC* 19908), sig. Biii (I.157 of the "B" text).

57. Emmison, (41, above), p. 263: in 1590, 16 laces, 2 lb. pepper, 4 lb. ginger, 1 lb. cinnamon, 20,000 pins, and 1,000 needles were together valued at £4.

58. T. K. Derry and Trevor I. Williams, *A Short History of Technology* (London, 1970), p. 136.

59. Skelton, "The Tunning of Elinour Rumming" (*Complete Poems*, p. 120).

something practically impossible to find is "to go looke a nedle in a medow" (Tilley N97; Whiting N71).

These two very familiar proverbs are half-buried in the title given *Gammer Gurton's Needle* when it was published in 1575, and are exploited throughout the play, which also demonstrates at the startling climax the truth of the proverb that the "fool's bolt may hit the mark." Although the play contains many proverbial phrases and comparisons, the proverbs themselves are not so plainly apparent because they are acted out rather than spoken.[60] From the beginning of the play, when Gib gets in the milk pan, I.iii.34 (i.e., "cat after kind sweet milk will lap," or Gammer Gurton's household is always in an uproar), there are more proverbs expounded than the ear actually hears (Tilley C139, C167; Whiting C109). The first act continues to unfold proverbially. Hodge first expresses his anger at Gammer Gurton by uttering two proverbs: "Might ha kept it when ye had it, but fooles will be fooles styll" (I.iv.7), and, "By gogs soule I thenk you wold loes your ars, and it were loose" (I.iv.16); he then proceeds to do a proverbially very foolish thing himself—"Set me a candle, let me seeke and grope where euer it be," he says (I.iv.36), thus "burning a candle to find a pin," or spending more on the search than the thing lost is worth (Tilley C46). Cocke is then sent to fetch the candle, and has difficulty lighting it (I.iv.46); in his impatience (I.iv.44–49), Hodge seizes the stump of candle from Cocke and tries to light it himself, only to be smothered in ashes (I.v.11–12), thus demonstrating the proverb that "he who worst may must hold the candle," or, in the end incompetence will prevail (Tilley C40; Whiting C23).[61] "Any small spark shines in the dark," but when he sees "in a darke corner two sparkes" (I.v.14) Hodge is in fact seeing only the cat's eyes (Gib, of course, "has cat's eyes") and finding no potential illumination at all (Tilley C180, S713, S714; Whiting C105, S559). When he blows on them Gib "shut

---

60. Bartlett Jere Whiting, *Proverbs in the Earlier English Drama*, Harvard Studies in Comparative Literature, vol. 14 (Cambridge, Mass., 1938), pp. 217-218, lists as proverbs I.iv.7 and 16 (quoted below), and also V.ii.163, 175, and 331. He does not acknowledge the proverbial implications of the title. He lists thirty-two proverbial phrases (as distinct from actual proverbs). The language of the play has not been fully studied.

61. This proverb concludes both *Tom Tyler and His Wife* (l. 894) and *The First and Best Part of Scoggins Jests* (1626; repr. in W. C. Hazlitt, ed., *Shakespeare's Jest-Books* [London, 1864]).

her two eyes, & so the fyre was out" (I.v.17), just as "the cat winked when both her eyes were out," or as one makes an effort or pretends to, even when the situation is hopeless (Tilley C174; Whiting C92). Meanwhile, Cocke searches the ground and thinks he sees the needle, but "when my fyngers toucht it, I felt it was a straw" (I.v.49): inside and outside Gammer Gurton's thatched house, leaving no straw unturned, the villagers are looking for a needle in a bottle of hay, and, to make matters even more hopeless, doing so in the dark.

Proverbs continue to provide material for the dramatist, to constitute and enrich his story, throughout the play. In the second act, for example, Diccon's conversation with Hodge draws attention to the dialect form of "needle" used consistently in the play, "neele" ("Her Eele, Hodge?" II.i.41); the proverbially elusive and slippery nature of eels (Tilley E60; Whiting E44, E45) well suggests the frustrating difficulty Gammer Gurton's household finds itself in, and Diccon may also know that you might as well try to hold a wet eel by the tail as deal with a woman (Tilley E61, W640; Whiting E48). He surely knows, as Hodge takes his oath and "*kysseth Diccons breeche*" (II.i.76 s.d.), that he could not in his chagrin more plainly have said, "Kiss my arse!," or expressed his contempt for Hodge.[62] "The Devil always leaves a stink" (Tilley D224), and when Diccon cries, "The deuill I smell hym wyll be here anon" (II.i.110), Hodge flees. In the third act, Gammer Gurton and Dame Chat confirm, as they brawl and exchange invectives, the truth of a number of proverbs, chiefly, perhaps that "women will be lightly wroth" and "many women many words" (Tilley W686; Whiting W497, W547) Dr Rat breaks into Dame Chat's house in the fourth act, and the echoes of Caxton's *Historye of Reynart the Foxe* (1481)[63] reduce the scene to the level of the barnyard. From the beginning of this act, or perhaps earlier, the audience has surely "smelled a rat" (Tilley R31), and Dr. Rat may well think,

62. *OED, Supplement,* "kiss," *v.*, sense 6. i, from 1705—but the expression is common earlier, and occurs in the Miller's Tale, the Wakefield *Mactacio Abel, Mankind,* Skelton's "Why Come Ye Not to Court," and in *Gammer Gurton's Needle* itself: Diccon alleges that Dame Chat said it to him (II.iv.31), and Gammer Gurton says it back to Dame Chat (III.iii.24).

63. J. H. Hanford, "The Source of an Incident in *Gammer Gurton's Needle,*" *MLN,* XXV (1910), 81; Boas, *University Drama in the Tudor Age,* pp. 70-71. *Reynard the Fox* was also published in 1525 and 1550.

trapped inside Dame Chat's kitchen, that "too late does the rat repent in the cat's paws" (Tilley R32) as he cries "Wo worth the houre that I came heare" (IV.ii.150). In the fifth act, Diccon, about to place his hand in oath on Hodge's torn breeches, as instructed by the Magistrate, says to Hodge, "take good heede now, thou do not beshite me" (V.ii.292), a necessary precaution, since "claw a churl by the arse and he shits in one's hand," as the Summoner's Friar John only narrowly escapes proving ("a chevle hath doon a cherles dede," cries the lady, l. 2204); in short, this village may be incurable (Tilley C386; Whiting C264). Moments later, Gammer Gurton has recovered her needle; perhaps she was never wise enough to say, "Here I left a needle and here I will find it" (Tilley N93). Diccon reminds her to thank him for "springing of the game" (V.ii.320), which, as John Scogan knew, can be done with a "pricke . . . in the buttocke."[64]

The play is, then, both based on proverbs and infiltrated and swollen with them, although few are actually spoken—a situation which perhaps led to the introduction of Nicholas Proverbes himself as a character in *The Two Angry Women of Abington*. The somewhat illogical suggestion conveyed unwittingly by Gammer Gurton (I.iv.5–6) and Hodge (II.i.43–44) that the needle, and the eel, are phallic[65] may be said to serve to help fill out the picture of life in the village. *The Two Angry Women of Abington* makes the same joke, unequivocally, and also by acting out the proverb rather than by simply stating it. This play, unlike *Gammer Gurton's Needle,* is a hearty and sexual romantic comedy. The young suitor, Frank, and his mistress, Molly, are seeking each other at night in the darkness of the "cunny greene" or "Cunny borough" (this expression has "some meaning in't I warrant yee," ll. 1913, 1927), but are kept chasing around in circles by the stubborn opposition of their mothers, the two angry women. Phillip, Molly's amiable brother, is to meet the young lovers there:

64. *The First and Best Part of Scoggins Jests* (1626; repr. in W. C. Hazlitt, ed., *Shakespeare's Jest-Books* [London, 1864]) p. 82. This (*STC* 21850.7) is another edition of the work first published by Colwell, ca. 1570, of whose edition only fragments of one copy remain (STC 21850.3).

65. Eric Partridge, *A Dictionary of Slang and Unconventional English,* 7th ed. (New York, 1970), "needle," sense 2. In *The Marriage Between Wit and Wisdom* the porridge pot has a sexual meaning (ll. 1185-1190).

PHILLIP

Keepe the Kings peace.

FRANK

How? art thou become a Constable?
Why *Phillip* where hast thou bin all this while?

PHILLIP

Why where you were not, but I pray whers my sister?

FRANK

Why man I sawe her not, but I haue sought her as I should seeke.

PHILLIP

A Needle haue yee not?
Why you man are the needle that she seekes,
To worke withall . . .

                                                       (ll. 2512-2519)

The proverb itself had earlier been uttered, together with strings of others, by Nicholas Proverbes, who (it is his humor) "learnedly prouerbde it" (l. 883):

He that worse may must holde the Candle, but my Maister is not so wise as God might haue made him, hee is gone to seeke a Hayre in a Hennes nest, a Needle in a Bottle of Haye, which is as sildome seene as a blacke Swan: hee is gone to seek my young Mistresse, and I thinke she is better lost then found, for who so euer hath her, hath but a wette Eele by the taile . . .

                                                       (ll. 2284-2290)

Abingdon is outside Oxford, whither Phillip will send Molly and Frank to escape the fury of their mothers and to meet their reasonable fathers to "determine of their mariage"; and Mrs. Goursey and Mrs. Barnes (names redolent of farm and countryside), whose quarrel came to a head when they were playing dice, are as furious with each other, "hart sick with hate" (l. 1125) and "black mouthd rage" (l. 570), as Gammer Gurton and Dame Chat are, also over a mere suspicion (l. 2857), in their village just outside Cambridge. Mrs. Goursey is aided and abetted by her servants, Dick (who has "drunke all the Ale-houses in Abingdon drye," ll. 1031-1032) and Hodge. She sets off for Mrs. Barnes's "house" (l. 1350) to pick a quarrel, and arranges for Dick, under cover of darkness, to "hit her and thou canst, a plague vpon her" (l. 1385; III.iii.28-58), their maledictions almost equal to Dame Chat's and Gammer Gurton's. Most of the play takes place in darkness. It is the darkness of unreason, a night of ignorance

(l. 2497). The husbands, eager to let "reason moderate" the "rage" (l. 1688) of their leaden-witted (l. 256) wives, hope to effect a reconciliation by marrying Frank Goursey to Molly Barnes, and are successful, especially with the intervention of Sir Ralph Smith as dawn breaks at the end of the play. This is clearly in part the younger generation's romantic sequel to *Gammer Gurton's Needle,* the Oxford version, and confirms (I think), together with the evidence of *Like Will to Like* and *The Marriage Between Wit and Wisdom,* my assumption that the Gammer's village is Girton, that *Gammer Gurton's Needle* is full of proverbs, and that the play's darkness is metaphorical.

The humanists had an especial fondness for proverbs, so pithy and unsuperstitious, as well as for fools, jest books, and Chaucer's writings.[66] Erasmus's *Adagia* was early translated and enlarged (by Nicholas Udall, among others, 1542, 1564), and Heywood's *Dialogue . . . of all the Proverbs* appeared in 1546. Many Tudor plays have proverbs for titles, especially after 1560, and more than one Tudor play may be considered to be, in essence, a dramatization, or proof, of a proverb. *Like Will to Like,* which shows the influence of *Gammer Gurton's Needle,*[67] is a clear example; most of the action consists of the Vice's putting like with like, beginning with the Devil and the collier, in exemplification of the proverb which provides the title. The plot of *Tom Tyler and His Wife* is also based on a proverb. Colwell seems to have had a fondness for proverbial lore and jests—he published three jest books, including *The Jestes of Skogyn* (ca. 1570) and the *Merie Tales of the Mad Men of Gotam* (ca. 1565),[68] both

66. John Buxton, *Elizabethan Taste* (London, 1963), pp. 223-230, and on the fabliaux, p. 226; Caroline Spurgeon, *Five Hundred Years of Chaucer Criticism and Allusion 1357-1900* (1925; repr. New York, 1960), I, at date 1520 ("Rastell"), 1533 (Elyot), 1533 (Heywood), 1535 (More), 1552 (Ascham), etc.

67. Ulpian Fulwell, *Like Will to Like,* in J.A.B. Somerset, ed., *Four Tudor Interludes* (London, 1974): this text is from the edition by John Allde, 1568. The reappearance of both "Gib our Cat" (l. 612) and "Hob Filcher" (ll. 444, 738) appears to establish a relationship between this play and *Gammer Gurton's Needle.* John Allde probably also published Merbury's *The Marriage Between Wit and Wisdom* (Greg, II, no. Θ 9). Some particular, but not strong, resemblances between *Like Will to Like* and *Misogonus* are pointed out by Bond, *Early Plays from the Italian,* p. 167.

68. *Scoggins Jests* (1626); A. B., *Merie Tales of the Mad Men of Gotam,* ed. Stanley J. Kahrl (Evanston, Ill., 1965).

alluded to in *Misogonus* (I.iii.28 and III.ii.10). There are some general resemblances between these jest books and *Gammer Gurton's Needle*. Scogan, who operates largely in Oxfordshire, is given to obtaining his necessities by means of "witty shifts," much like Diccon. He is especially good at setting people at odds with each other. Dr. Rat himself might well have danced to Scogan's tune—as, indeed, he actually does in the antimasque in Jonson's *The Fortunate Isles* (1624), together with Elinour Rumming (summoned by Skelton) to cheer up a melancholy student.[69] Many of Scogan's jests and shifts conclude, as do those in *A C. Mery Talys*, with proverbs or proverbial admonitions. Some are remarkably applicable to Diccon's shifts—"Here," for example, "it is good to mark that a man beleeve not every word that another doth speake, for some doe lie, some doe jest, some doe mock, and some doe scorne, and many men doe saye the very truth" (p. 106)—and others may be said to be the working out of proverbs; as Scogan himself says, at the conclusion of the final jest, "now the Proverbe is fulfilled." The mad men of Gotam are generally as empty-headed as the Girton villagers, and their wives, gathered in the alehouse (in the nineteenth jest), are certainly as sly. After originally registering the play as "Dyccon of Bedlam, & c.," Colwell may have felt the proverbial force of "Gammer Gurton's Needle," and altered the title accordingly. He may also have welcomed the sound of the alliterating name, "Gammer Gurton," with its suggestion of English or skeltonic fun (his other jest book is *Merie Tales . . . Made by Master Skelton*, 1567), and also noticed it in the titles of the other Anglo-Roman plays, *Ralph Roister Doister* and *Jack Juggler*, and his own *Tom Tyler and His Wife*, to which this kind of title is peculiar in early English drama.

The acting out of proverbs, proverbial phrases, and idiomatic expressions should be added to Professor Wickham's list of the "devices" out of which Tudor dramatists constructed their plays, and to Professor Whiting's list of the uses to which Tudor dramatists put proverbs (he conceives of them as didactic or ornamental, or as "used to characterize an individual or a class").[70] Peter Bruegel's peasants dramatize proverbs, most notably in *Netherlandish Proverbs* (1559). As in the case of *Gammer Gurton's*

69. *Ben Jonson*, ed. C. H. Herford and P. and E. Simpson (Oxford, 1925-1952), VII, 721.

70. Wickham, III, 65-155; Whiting, *Proverbs in the Earlier English Drama*, p. x.

Needle, one scene in this picture may demonstrate more than one proverb, and sometimes the connection between scene and proverb is oblique. Generally speaking, many of Bruegel's paintings render "idiomatic expressions literally," as has been observed. In this way, the most innocuous activities of the peasants sustain at least a moral interpretation, if not a religious one; when *Skating Outside St. George's Gate* was engraved (1559), the legend *Lubricitas Vitae Humanae* was added to it.[71] The point is soon, but not immediately, rather obvious: so it is with *Gammer Gurton's Needle.*

The effect of the acting out of proverbs, as Shakespeare must have realized when choosing the titles of some of his comedies and romances, is to lend them a subtlety not normally theirs; to invite speculation (since so many proverbs with the same elements in them have different meanings); and to render them thematically important—to embody in them the meaning, or part of the meaning, of the play. The "witte and inuention" (the phrase applied to the play in 1588) of *Gammer Gurton's Needle* consist in good measure of the amplification by the dramatist of his material by means of parables and proverbs. In a characteristic Elizabethan phrase, "wit" and "invention" go together. With their aid, one embellishes a theme and maintains a flow of ideas (or, in this case, dramatic action), which may, for example, be deduced from proverbs. Proverbs (and parables) are, in fact, among the chief riches and refinements of expression, as Erasmus and Thomas Wilson (a Cambridge M.A.), in *The Arte of Rhetorique* (1553, 1560), wrote.[72] As a matter of course a writer (especially, presumably, an academic writer) might take his subject through the various "topics of invention," looking for possibilities; and *paroemia*[73] especially endeared itself to the author of *Gammer Gurton's Needle.*

His subject (possibly with a nod in the opposite direction toward the faintness of love or the evanescence of the prick of conscience) is insignificance and buffoonery. It is hard to avoid the conclusion that his play is, in part, written in oblique response to dramatic criticism, for Terence and Plautus deal, in the words of the sixteenth-century critics,

71. M. Seidel and R. H. Marijnissen, *Brvegel* (New York, 1971), pp. 24, 38-43; Ludwig Münz, *Bruegel the Drawings* (London, 1961), p. 227 (no. 140).

72. William G. Crane, *Wit and Reason in the Renaissance* (New York, 1937), pp. 9, 21, 27, 71, 86, 102, and passim.

73. Miriam Joseph, *Shakespeare's Use of the Arts of Language* (1947; repr. New York, 1966), pp. 308, 310.

and as the prologue to *Jack Juggler* says, with insignificant "trifles." The lascivious "toyes" (Edwardes, *Damon and Pithias*, 1571, prologue), and the atmosphere of "sotle bawdes, and wilie harlots" [74] referred to by Roger Ascham (Fellow of St. John's College, Cambridge, 1534–1554) he has deliberately avoided altogether. His play does, however, deal with a complete and utter trifle, and just as some saw that Terence and Plautus, despite their insignificant subjects, yield good sense, so the English dramátist has (in a spirit, I think, of accomplishing good-humouredly something of a tour de force) "wonne morallyte" from the trifling affairs of his undignified Cambridgeshire village, "as the Bee suckes the honny from weedes," as George Whetstone, in the prefatory epistle to *Promos and Cassandra* (1578),[75] says grave Roman senators did from the plays of Terence and Plautus. From his lumbering human and nimble divine folly, expressed in tavern and village by parable and proverb and organized in a most academic five-act way, and from "the disgusting interchanges of buffoonery" found so reprehensible by the Regius Professor of Divinity, emerge "sens good and wise matter," and a demonstration of the wisdom of living to God. Henry Porter was impatient with this. His play is also "about a thing of nothing" (l. 1313), but a popular sweet nothing, not a domestic trifle; and he has turned the academic "plaudite" into a female epilogue.

Roman Comedy and English Piety

Roman comedy provided some Tudor dramatists with an opportunity not only for English high jinks and folly, but also for morality, piety, and even holiness. *Terens in englysh* (*STC* 23894, a version of *Andria,* published ca. 1520 and meant to be acted) shows this, if only in a mechanical way. At the end of the play, Davus's *vos valete et plaudite* becomes in English:

> I can no more now but the one. ii. And thre
> Saue you and kepe you both grete And small
> Reynyng aboue the Region etheriall,

74. Chambers, IV, 192, 193.
75. Chambers, IV, 201.

and the further epilogue provided with the English version also concludes with a blessing. The English dramatic tradition is religious and moral, and the normal blessing which fittingly ends most English plays is here simply attached to the end of the Roman comedy.

A more developed fusion is found in *Ralph Roister Doister,* which in comparison with Plautus's *Miles Gloriosus* and Terence's *Eunuchus* is suffused with morality and romance, as well as with folly; and also in *Jack Juggler.* Mathew Merygreeke and Jack Juggler both operate in much the same way as Diccon; like him, however "Vice-like" they may be, they are best understood not so much as causing confusions and entanglements but as permitting them to arise, expressing or extending what is already present. Like Diccon, Mathew opens the play as a wanderer, wondering where he will get his "meate and drink" next (l. 14). He is not the cause of Ralph's folly; rather, he provides Ralph with opportunities to show the folly already in him. At his first appearance Ralph asks, "Why did God make me suche a goodly person?" (l. 73), and such a man hardly needs any encouragement. It is he, not Mathew, who mispunctuates the crucial love letter, as has been pointed out.[76] Mathew tends to cap Ralph's absurdities with suggestions even more absurd: if Ralph is in love, Mathew will fetch the musicians; if determined to die, Mathew will begin conducting the funeral; if lacking armor for his attack on Dame Christian's house, Mathew will suggest he wear a kitchen pan on his head. Ralph jumps at these ideas, because they express his own empty-headed character so well. Unlike his counterparts, Gnatho in *Eunuchus,* and Artotrogus in *Miles Gloriosus,* Mathew tries long and hard but in vain to show Ralph that he is being foolish, and finally succeeds in making him realize that Dame Christian will not have him. Not only has good "sporte" (l. 55) been had in the process, but Mathew has also been able to reveal Dame Christian's "honestie" (l. 1568). Harmony and truth prevail in the end.

Similarly, in *Jack Juggler* (also a play for school boys to act), Jack's trickery (*OED,* "Juggler," senses 1-3) only results in Jenkin Careaway's revelation of his own "leude" and "negligent" (l. 931) ways. By showing them in himself (ll. 601–629), Jack reveals the same faults in him. Jenkin Careaway (as befits one with such a name) dawdles on his errands and

76. A. W. Plumstead, "Who Pointed Roister's Letter?" *N & Q,* CCVIII (1963), 329-331.

plays in the street too often. He "loses himself" (ll. 684, 843, 861)—
OED, "Lose," *v.*[1], sense 10; confronted with Jack claiming to be him (as
Mercury disguises himself as Sosia in *Amphitruo*) he realizes he has literally
lost himself (it is in this sense that Romeo, in love with Rosaline, says "I
have lost myself, I am not here"—*Romeo and Juliet,* I.i.195), and is led to
review the chain of schoolboyish immoralities that have resulted in this
predicament, blurting out the truth about his misdeeds to his master, and
thus finding himself again (ll. 1020–1044). Jenkin's final words to the
audience are clear: he says he has played truant so often that he can indeed
"wonder if he be I" (l. 1116) and prays that they will not "lose" themselves "homward as I have done" (l. 1142). So also a "good name is better
than riches" (Tilley N22; Whiting N12), and Jenkin, who has lost all his
money playing dice, blames himself, as he thinks about his encounter
with Jack, or "himself," for losing his name (that is, his reputation) by
plain negligence (l. 700), which is precisely what he has done. The person
who stole his good name from him was himself. From the beginning Jack
knew he could deceive Jenkin since the latter was in a mood to be
confused, being already "starke staryng mad" at his own mistakes (ll.
182–185); and at the end, when he has served his purpose, Jack abandons
the deceit and changes out of his disguise, aware, however, that he might
need it again "for a like cause" (ll. 884–885). Jack has his "sporte" (l.
873), Jenkin's guilt is revealed, and Mr. and Mrs. Boungrace are completely reconciled. The common expression (possibly with a glance at
Luke 15:24—"he was lost, but he is founde. And they began to be
merie") is provided with a moral sense and acted out both literally and
figuratively within the framework of the classical device.[77] Again, Shake-

---

77. This interpretation might replace or supplement those which see the play as an
attack on the doctrine of transubstantiation (Gayley, p. lxxix) and Jesuits (Wickham, III,
76-78); or as a demonstration of the psychological alienation that results from dislocations
in the social order (R. Marienstras, "Jack Juggler: Aspects de la conscience individuelle
dans une farce du 16ᵉ siècle," *Etudes Anglaises,* XVI [1963], 321-332); or as a "theological,
epistemological, or ontological metaphor" (Jackson I. Cope, *The Theatre and the Dream*
[Baltimore, Md., 1973], pp. 107-111). Like *Gammer Gurton's Needle, Jack Juggler* concerns
the search for something lost, takes place at night, requires a house with (apparently) a
practicable door, and has an angry woman (Dame Coy, "an angrie pece of fleshe and sone
displeasyd," l. 217) and a maid who gads about (Alice Trip-and-Go) in its cast of characters.

speare combines, as is recognized,[78] actions from *Menaechmi* and *Amphitruo* with themes from Acts 19 and Ephesians 4-6 to produce *The Comedy of Errors* (also an academic play), where wives, husbands, and servants must maintain a proper Pauline harmony in their relationships, and where the "lustes of errour" and "confusions" of Ephesus must be righted, the temple of Diana being replaced with the Priory.

There is, then, little reason a priori to fight shy of finding meaning in *Gammer Gurton's Needle,* of finding a farce not only artfully formed into a comedy, but given dramatic shape and meaning by the interlocking proverbs and parables—including the notion of the perceptive fool revealing in his simplicity, and the theatrical image of the house as a rattrap and a habitation—acted out in it, and purposively constructed out of a trifle. The peasant world and the village road are made to hold more meaning than the urban streets and alleys of Roman comedy. The Englishness of the content and the classicism of the form—both noticed early by the critics—produce, once married, more than something merely amusing. The enlightened members of Christ's College perhaps realized that they had witnessed an example of the foolish things of this world confounding the wise. Diccon certainly "confounded," or "confused," them all, tied them up in knots, and put them to shame (*OED,* "Confound," *v.,* senses 3-5). Proverbs, naturally associated with all people, appropriately balloon into the life of the village of man as seen by the humanist's eye. The college men undoubtedly laughed, but not (I think) at the countryfolk, and not without a larger perspective, no more than did Erasmus, who in *The Praise of Folly* (in Chaloner's version) writes: "Briefely, if one (as Menippus did) lokyng out of the moone, behelde from thence the innumerable tumultes, and businesses of mortall men, he shoulde thynke verily he saw a meny *of flies, or gnattes, braulyng, fightyng, begilyng, robbyng, plaiyng, liuyng wantonly, borne, bredde vp, decaiyng, and diyng*: So that it is scant beleuable, what commocions, and what **Tragedies**, are sterred vp, by so littell, and so short liued a vermyn as this man is." [79] Social class in this play is metaphorical. The victims of the Christ's College lampoonist are the mean and uncharitable of whatever worldly rank, and those di-

78. *The Comedy of Errors,* ed. R. A. Foakes, The Arden Edition of the Works of William Shakespeare (London, 1962, 1968), pp. xxiv-xxix, 113-115.

79. Erasmus, *Praise of Folly,* p. 70. The italics and bold-faced type are in the original.

verted by what is really nothing from more reasonable and Godly ways, like the energetic peasants in Bruegel's *Peasant Dance* (?1569), who all have their backs turned to the church, and ignore the picture of the Virgin Mary on the nearby tree.[80] *"Mother Gurtons neadle"* is indeed, in a way, a "Tragedy." The conclusion of *Misogonus* provides the moral: "beside godliness & learninge all thinges in this worlde are but transitorye." The humor has been embodied within the thoroughly dramatic homily.

80. F. Grossman, *Pieter Bruegel* (London, 1973), p. 201.

Imitations of Spenser in
A Midsummer Night's Dream

JAMES P. BEDNARZ

I N THE LAST ACT of *A Midsummer Night's Dream,* after the members of
the Athenian court have dined and are eager to be entertained,
Theseus's master of revels—Philostrate—tenders a list of theatrical performances ripe for presentation and asks his lord to choose a favorite.
Theseus selects the "tedious brief scene of young Pyramus / And his love
Thisby; very tragical mirth," only after rejecting out of hand the previous
three titles on Philostrate s list.[1] Each of these rejected suggestions is
totally unsuited to the occasion of an impending marriage. The first item,
"The battle with the Centaurs, to be sung / By an Athenian eunuch to the
harp" (V.i.44–45), conjures up images of castration and the attempted
rape, at her wedding feast, of Hippodamia, the wife of Theseus's friend.
This anti-epithalamion, warbled by a castrato, is clearly inappropriate.
The second choice promises to be equally indecorous. This interlude,
entitled "The riot of the tipsy Bacchanals, / Tearing the Thracian singer
in their rage" (V.i.48–49), evokes the kind of drunken, orgiastic frenzy
that the celebrants of weddings usually try their hardest to prevent. The

---

1. *A Midsummer Night's Dream,* V.i.56–57, in *The Riverside Shakespeare,* ed. G. Blakemore Evans (Boston, 1974). All quotations from Shakespeare's plays are from this edition.
Line numbers will hereafter be placed in the text.

third and final spurned offering is as ludicrously inadequate as the rest. Theseus reads its title—"The thrice three Muses mourning for the death / Of learning, late deceas'd in beggary" (V.i.52–53)—and registers his sense of its incongruity with the present celebration by observing that the work is "some satire, keen and critical, / Not sorting with a nuptial ceremony" (V.i.54–55). He is understandably reluctant to burden a wedding with funereal verse—with the Muses' tearful dirge for that dead beggar—Learning.

This final rejected title, however, is different from the rest for one important reason. Warburton, in his edition of A Midsummer Night's Dream, printed in 1747, is the first critic to have pointed out what has now become the consensus opinion— that Shakespeare is here alluding to a minor poem by Edmund Spenser, called The Teares of the Muses, first published in the Complaints volume of 1591.[2] The third title is consequently unique because it refers to an actual work by one of Shakespeare's more illustrious contemporaries. Its topicality explodes with the force of the unexpected—in a list of supposedly fictitious fictions—for a group of auditors who would have immediately sensed its significance. Warburton and Warton after him in the Variorum edition of 1773 assumed that Shakespeare's allusion was a compliment to Spenser, but the whole tone of the passage seems to militate against this explanation. As A. G. van Kranendonk remarks in an article published in 1932, there is "an unmistakable ring of mockery or irony in the wording, and in this respect it is in perfect harmony with the other items on the programme."[3] Not only is the work placed in such wretched company, but its very title announces its poetic deficiencies. With a deft stroke, Shakespeare characterizes Spenser's style as one of "facile circumlocution" epitomized by the phrase, "thrice three," which usurps the place of a more straightforward "nine." [4] He reinforces this parody with two key words from The Teares of the Muses, "learning" and "mourn," which reify the identification. The most intriguing question that this pattern of imitation poses is also the most basic: why should Shakespeare parody Spenser in A Midsummer Night's Dream?" This question is, I believe, inseparable from

2. Harold Brooks, the editor of the Arden edition of A Midsummer Night's Dream (Bungay, Sussex, 1979), p. xxxi, asserts that "the old suggestion" of Shakespeare's acquaintance with Spenser's poem "has been too hastily dismissed," and accepts the identification.

3. "Spenserian Echoes in A Midsummer Night's Dream," ES, XIV (1932), 209.

4. Ibid., p. 211.

its more particular formulation: why should Shakespeare parody *The Teares of the Muses* in this, his most Spenserian play? The answers to these questions become apparent only after we have examined the specific social pressures which contributed to the creation of *A Midsummer Night's Dream* and which are, in turn, reflected in its meaning.

In "The Occasion of *A Midsummer Night's Dream*," E. K. Chambers argued that the play's "epithalamic ending" suggested its "performance at a wedding" and that "the compliment to the 'fair vestal throned by the west' points to a wedding at which Elizabeth was present." [5] Chambers's observation is corroborated by the fact that this reference to Elizabeth is one of only three such allusions to the queen that exist in the entire corpus of Shakespeare's writing—the other two being the mention of "Our radiant Queen" in *The Merry Wives of Windsor* and the explicit mention of her birth in *Henry VIII*. The first allusion was meticulously crafted for a special auditor. Because of two traces in *A Midsummer Night's Dream* of events occurring in *1594*: (1) the unusually cold and damp weather, and (2) the proposal to include a lion in a processional celebrating the baptism of Prince Henry of Scotland on 30 August, Chambers was able to establish the *terminus a quo* in that year. He therefore suggested that the most plausible occasion for the play's composition was the wedding of William Stanley, Earl of Derby, and Lady Elizabeth Vere, daughter of the Earl of Oxford, granddaughter of Lord Burghley, and goddaughter and maid of honor to the queen—an event that transpired on 26 January 1595. Reviewing his evidence, however, Chambers was not able to exclude a second possibility: the marriage of Thomas, the son of Lord Berkeley, and Elizabeth Carey on 19 February 1596 [6] In *William Shakespeare: A Study of Facts and Problems*, published fourteen years after his article on the "occasion" of *A Midsummer Night's Dream*, Chambers had still not resolved the dilemma of dating he posed and tentatively concluded that "Either wedding would fit such indications of date as the play yields. It belongs to the lyric group of 1594-6." [7] A more rigorous examination of the social context for Shakespeare's parody of Spenser, however, adds further evidence to the argument that the Stanley-Vere match on 26 January 1595

5. "The Occasion of *A Midsummer Night's Dream*" is included in *Shakespearean Gleanings* (Oxford, 1946), p. 61. Reprinted from *A Book of Essays in Homage to Shakespeare*, ed. Israel Gollancz (Oxford, 1916).

6. *Ibid.*, pp. 66–67.

7. *William Shakespeare: A Study of Facts and Problems* (Oxford, 1930), I, 369.

establishes the *terminus ad quem* of the play's composition. This would
indicate its creation between 24 October 1594, when *A True Reportarie,*
describing the lion incident at the Scottish court, was registered, and 26
January 1595, the date of the Stanley-Vere wedding.

The marriage of Elizabeth Vere to William Stanley was a remarkable
personal triumph for William Burghley, Elizabeth's trusted lord treasurer. Burghley had expended considerable effort in attempting to secure a
suitable mate for his granddaughter, and with the death of William
Stanley's father and older brother in 1594, this young bachelor had suddenly become one of the wealthiest aristocrats in England.[8] The ceremony
was consummated at Greenwich, where the court was then situated, and,
soon after, Elizabeth arrived at Burghley House on the Strand with the
newly married couple to enjoy two more days of reveling. It is likely that
the lord treasurer's controlling presence behind the marriage acted as a
catalyst for Shakespeare's parody of *The Teares of the Muses,* a work included
in Spenser's *Complaints* volume, which repeatedly attacks Burghley for his
barbaric indifference to culture and his unrestrained self-aggrandizement.
Clever ridicule of Spenser would find a welcome audience at this gather-
ing.

Spenser's dislike for Burghley probably went back to 1579, when his
opposition to the lord treasurer's plan to solidify a proposed marriage
between Elizabeth and the Duke of Alençon led to his self-exile. Ten years
later, he again found himself in conflict with Burghley, whom he now
suspected of blocking his bid for patronage from Queen Elizabeth. Spenser arrived in London with his manuscript of the first three books of *The
Faerie Queene* late in 1589. He evidently expected some form of preferment
from the queen—a gift of money, a monopoly, or a government
position—and when it was not immediately forthcoming, the poet lashed
out at the lord treasurer. By the end of 1590, still in London and without
remuneration, Spenser had written and revised material for his *Complaints,*
which William Ponsonby registered on 29 December. Part of Spenser's
reason for issuing this volume was to express public resentment against
Burghley in a style reminiscent of Skelton's attack on Wolsey. Indeed,
some passages in the collection were so scandalous that the authorities
suppressed its publication and "called in" copies of the work.[9] One poem

8. Conyers Read, *Lord Burghley and Queen Elizabeth* (New York, 1960), pp. 502–503.

9. See the commentaries in the section entitled "Calling-In" of Appendix IV, in *The
Works of Edmund Spenser, A Variorum Edition,* ed. Edwin Greenlaw, Charles Osgood,
Fredrick Padelford, Ray Heffner, et al. (Baltimore, 1947), VIII, 580–585. This edition
will be cited as *Variorum* in the notes.

in the anthology—*Mother Hubberds Tale*—proved to be so vitriolic that it was never again printed until the death of Burghley's son Robert Cecil in 1612. Gabriel Harvey, in a published letter to Christopher Bird, dated 2 September 1592, confided that "Mother Hubbard in heat of choller . . . over-shot her malcontented selfe." This comment led Thomas Nashe in *Strange Newes* of 1593 to censure Harvey for reminding the world of an incident that could "rekindle" against Spenser "the sparkes of displeasure that were quenched." "If any man were undeservedly toucht in it," Nashe adds, "thou hast revived his disgrace that was so toucht in it, by renaming it, when it was worn out of al mens mouths and minds." [10] Harvey himself had gained notoriety in 1580 for his satire of Burghley's son-in-law, the Earl of Oxford, the father of Elizabeth Vere, in *Speculum Tuscanismi*. [11] Throughout his poetic career, Spenser constantly aligned himself with factions that opposed Burghley, as he supported, in turn, Leicester, Ralegh, and finally Essex. In part, because of these allegiances, Burghley would always stand menacingly between Spenser and the queen.

Mother Hubberds Tale included the harshest denunciation of Burghley, as a treasonous fox who plots to steal his sleeping monarch's scepter and diadem. But the entire *Complaints* volume is laced with similarly negative comments. In the first poem of the collection, *The Ruines of Time*, Spenser writes that Burghley "now welds all things at his will," [12] neglecting and disdaining soldiers and scholars, to which the poet adds a lament and a curse:

> O griefe of griefes, O gall of all good heartes,
> To see that vertue should dispised bee
> Of him, that first was raisde for vertuous parts,
> And now broad spreading like an aged tree,
> Lets none shoot up, that nigh him planted bee:
> O let the man, of whom the Muse is scorned,
> Nor alive, nor dead be of the Muse adorned.

(ll. 449–455)

10. *Variorum,* VIII, 580–581.

11. Harvey's poem was included in his published correspondence with Spenser, entered in the Stationers' Register on 30 June 1580. It appears in *Variorum,* IX, 467.

12. *The Ruines of Time,* l. 447, in *Variorum,* vol. VIII. All quotations from Spenser's poetry are from the *Variorum* edition, published from 1932 to 1957. Line numbers will appear in the text.

The editors of the Spenser first folio of 1611 revised these lines in deference to Robert Cecil, for the same reason that they excluded *Mother Hubberds Tale* from *The Collected Works of England's Arch-Poet*. Wedged between *The Ruines of Time* and *Mother Hubberds Tale* in the *Complaints* volume, *The Teares of the Muses* reiterates the poet's invective against the "foes of learning" (1.64) who are now found on all levels of society, even at the top:

> Ne onely they that dwell in lowly dust,
> The sonnes of darkness and of ignoraunce;
> But they, whom thou great Jove by doome unjust
> Didst to the type of honour earst advaunce:
> They now puft up with sdeignfull insolence,
> Despise the brood of blessed Sapience.
>
> (ll. 67–72)

The Teares of the Muses—the second of the complaints—merely expresses in generic form the personal invective of the collection's opening selection. The humor of Shakespeare's allusion to this work as "The thrice three Muses mourning for the death / Of learning, late deceas'd in beggary" depends for its effect, as I have previously indicated, on its inappropriateness to both the fictional world of *A Midsummer Night's Dream* and the historical context of the Stanley-Vere wedding. *The Teares of the Muses* was simply unthinkable as after-dinner entertainment. It was exactly what Theseus calls it—a "satire keen and critical," *certainly* not suited to the "nuptial ceremony" celebrated on 26 January 1595. It was quite clearly a work to be parodied and disgarded by the celebrants of *that* noble wedding.

But if Shakespeare parodied Spenser in the service of Burghley, he also had another and more personal reason for mentioning Spenser's lament. *The Teares of the Muses* had two principal targets: a barbaric aristocracy that refused to support learning and the ignorant rabble that currently passed as artisans. In the latter category Spenser included dramatists working in the public theater. After Clio, the Muse of History chastises "mightie Peeres" for misprizing "true wisedome" (l. 80), and Melpomene deems all life "a Tragedy" (l. 157). Thalia complains that she is now "the servant of the manie" (l. 223), since the "sweet delights of learnings treasure" which formerly graced "The painted Theaters" (l. 177) are no longer in evidence. The room once occupied by "glee" is now filled by "unseemly Sorrow":

And him beside sits ugly Barbarisme
And brutish Ignorance, ycrept of late
Out of dredd darknes of the deep Abysme,
Where being bredd, he light and heaven does hate:
They in the mindes of men now tyrannize,
And the faire Scene with rudenes foule disguize.

(ll. 186–191)

Spenser's taste in dramatic performances embraced academic and coterie works and excluded, on principle, the popular. In the complaints, more even than in *The Faerie Queene,* he states that his poetry embodies a strategy of exclusion—it concerns itself only with a minority, the elect.[13] Thalia, the Muse of Comedy, has kind words only for John Lyly, whose dramatic career had been terminated by the ecclesiastical authorities. Having been asked by the bishops to enter the propaganda war against a pamphleteer—known only as Martin Marprelate—Lyly's efforts were finally curtailed, when it appeared that they were merely inciting further invective.[14] Spenser, however, viewed Lyly's eclipse as a sign of the times, as a symptom of learning's demise. For Spenser, the playwright's theatrical banishment was self-willed, since

that same gentle Spirit, from whose pen
Large streames of honnie and sweete Nectar flowe,
Scorning the boldness of such base-borne men,
Which dare their follies forth so rashlie throwe;
Doth rather choose to sit in idle Cell,
Than so himselfe to mockerie to sell.

(ll. 217–222)

Thalia's lament for John Lyly—here referred to as "Our pleasant Willy" (l. 208)—bemoans, by implication, a serious blow sustained by coterie drama in 1590. Lyly's suppression coincided with the abolition of the company he composed for—The Boys of St. Paul's—who disappear from Court records after 1590.[15] Spenser's sympathies clearly lay with those

13. For a thorough treatment of Spenser's poetic of exclusion, see Michael Murrin, *The Veil of Allegory* (Chicago, 1969).

14. Lyly's connection with the Martin Marprelate controversy is detailed by E. K. Chambers, *The Elizabethan Stage* (1923; repr. Oxford, 1967), IV, 229–233.

15. *The Elizabethan Stage,* II, 18.

"little eyases," rivals of the adult companies to which Shakespeare belonged. For Spenser, the censure of coterie drama was only a victory for the vulgarity of the public theater, where,

> Each idle wit at will presumes to make,
> And doth the Learneds taske upon him take.
>
> (ll. 215–216)

Shakespeare, lacking scholarly accreditation, would have been numbered by Spenser among those who threatened the status of "learning," as it was defined by the rigid laws of neoclassical decorum advocated, if not always practiced, by the coterie dramatists. The young playwright was keenly aware of the fact that the public theater was one of the targets for Spenser's displeasure. Shakespeare's reaction to Spenser's complaint is mediated by the social dynamics of *status competition* and *mimetic rivalry*.[16] Their opposing conceptions of drama illustrate allegiances to what Alfred Harbage called "the rival repertories" of the popular and coterie theatrical companies.[17] Through his parody of Spenser in *A Midsummer Night's Dream*, Shakespeare met the coterie on its own ground—when his play was produced in the palace at Greenwich. His strategy—which employs humor for its effect—had both an offensive and a defensive aspect. Shakespeare aggressively seizes upon his opponent's pet phrase—"thrice three"—and turns it against him, just as he would use the words "humor" and "element" to lampoon Jonson in *Henry V* and *Twelfth Night*, respectively. In the context of Shakespeare's mimetic joke, Spenser's poem contains a kind of "learning" that is as vacuous as the language it engen-

16. I have derived the concept of "mimetic rivalry" from René Girard, who defines it at length in *Violence and the Sacred*, trans. Patrick Gregory (Baltimore, 1977), and applies it to the play under discussion in his essay "Myth and Ritual in Shakespeare: *A Midsummer Night's Dream*," published in *Textual Strategies: Perspectives in Post-Structuralist Criticism*, ed. Josué Harari (Ithaca, N.Y., 1971). Unlike Girard, however, I do not believe that Shakespeare projects an endlessly antagonistic system of desire in *A Midsummer Night's Dream*; instead, he is able to imagine a resolution of "triangular desire." The conclusion of my study consequently registers an implicit critique of Girard's reading of the play.

17. This distinction is, of course, the foundation of Alfred Harbage's *Shakespeare and the Rival Traditions* (Bloomington, Ind., 1952), especially his chapter "The Rival Repertories," pp. 58–89.

ders. Far from revealing the sacred knowledge that Spenser promises in the *Complaints* volume, it delivers the mundane—"nine"—but in an extravagantly refined form. If learning provides the leap from "nine" to "thrice three," it contributes nothing to the search for true wisdom. It represents instead the vanity of mere wordplay, the literary pretension that is also deconstructed in *Love's Labor's Lost,* where the question arises of whether or not "thrice three" does in fact equal "nine." [18]

It is surely no accident that the poet whom Theseus mocks earlier in the play fraudulently promises secret knowledge in a caricature of allegorical poetics. "The poet's eye, in a fine frenzy rolling, / Doth glance from heaven to earth, from earth to heaven" (V.i.12–13), seeking "The forms of things unknown" (V.i.15), but his pen, nevertheless, names "nothing." Attempts to secure transcendent knowledge, to join heaven and earth through a system of correspondence, are here treated with derision, until a more lenient Hippolyta describes the "strange" and "admirable" constancy of this act of ideal imitation. When Theseus swears that he "never may believe / These antic fables, nor these fairy toys" (V.i.2–3), his words reach beyond the play's immediate plot to become part of an ongoing critique of Spenserian poetics. A sixteenth-century speaker of English was free to pronounce the word "antique" with a stress on either the initial or final syllable, so that it was possible to give the word a double meaning. Thus, when Theseus says that he doesn't believe "antic fables," his phrase coincides with Spenser's description of *The Faerie Queene* as an "antique history." Anticipating the fact that his poem will be attacked as a futile exercise of imagination, Spenser, in the Proem to the Book of Temperance, remarks to Queen Elizabeth:

> Right well I wote most mighty Soveraine,
> That all this famous antique history,
> Of some th' abundance of an idle braine
> Will judged be, and painted forgery,
> Rather than matter of just memory, . . .

> (II. Proem 1)

It seems likely that Shakespeare exploited the linguistic instability of Spenser's phrase to emphasize the "antic" quality of his enterprise. The

---

18. See the dialogue between Berowne and Costard in *Love's Labor's Lost,* V.ii.484–495.

conjunction of Shakespeare's terms "antic fables" and "fairy toys" further solidifies their connection with *The Faerie Queene*. The word "toys," a derogatory expression for things absurd or trifling, was often used by Elizabethans to indicate contempt for literary efforts. *Vannetyes and Toys,* for instance, is the ironic title of Arthur Gorges's manuscript collection of poems. Used together, the words "antique" and "fairy" define the twin mimetic registers of Spenser's epic. Viewed as narrative modes, the "antique" and the "fairy" strains of Spenser's poem create the possibility of allegory; they are his primary vehicles for the release of imagination as well as being the primary means by which he displaces his own presence—his own immediate historical moment—to discuss events which occur in nonexistent worlds. They also provide, of course, the mimetic disguise Spenser needed to engage the world he pretended to be avoiding. Arthurian legend and Celtic mythology, or, if you will, "antique history" and "fairy toys," are Spenser's fundamental narrative modes, and as such they provide suitable targets for the barbs of Shakespeare's wit.

Shakespeare's parodies of Spenser exhibit that quality of mind which C. L. Barber has designated as the spirit of "festive abuse." [19] This abusive freedom is here shielded by the mask of fiction, the holiday of imagination, which expresses itself in *A Midsummer Night's Dream* through Spenser's narrative matrix—in a work that fuses the domain of Fairyland with the precincts of the antique world—where Oberon, King of Fairies, and Theseus, Duke of Athens, coexist. Indeed, Shakespeare absorbs so much of his predecessor's material that his parodies appear to be calculated attempts to exorcize a powerful influence, to assert independence and thereby resist the stigma of imitation. Ridicule of Spenser is an attempt to deny him the paternity of *A Midsummer Night's Dream*. More than at any other time in his career, Shakespeare in this play takes the works of Spenser as models for his own creation. Oberon's reference to Queen Elizabeth, for instance, praises her in a manner that parallels Spenser's treatment of Elizabeth as both Gloriana and Belphoebe in *The Faerie Queene*. In a style conforming to that of Shakespeare's mimetic rival, Oberon narrates a mythological account of Cupid's failure to molest the virgin queen:

19. C. L. Barber has named one of his subchapters "Festive Abuse," in *Shakespeare's Festive Comedy* (Princeton, N.J., 1959), pp. 73–86.

> A certain aim he took
> At a fair vestal throned by [the] west,
> And loos'd his love-shaft smartly from his bow,
> As it should pierce a hundred thousand hearts;
> But I might see young Cupid's fiery shaft
> Quench'd in the chaste beams of the wat'ry moon,
> And the imperial vot'ress passed on,
> In maiden meditation, fancy-free.

(II.i.157–164)

Shakespeare's tribute to Elizabeth's virginity as a symbol of her power is a less severe formulation of Belphoebe's triumph over the God of Love, who unsuccessfully tries to induce desire through her eyes:

> In them the blinded god his lustfull fire
> To kindle oft assayd, but had no might;
> For with dredd Majestie, and awfull ire,
> She broke his wanton darts, and quenched base desire.

(II.iii.23–26)

Although Shakespeare's description of this "fair vestal throned by [the] west" probably evoked memories of the pageant held in Elizabeth's honor at Elvetham in 1591,[20] it also bears one important resemblance to Spenser's passage. Both treatments of Elizabeth's immunity to Cupid's arrows exalt in the denial of sexuality, the "quenching" of desire, in works that are, to a large extent, celebrations of matrimony. The praise of Elizabeth in both *The Faerie Queene* and *A Midsummer Night's Dream* creates a double frame of reference that points in the directions of both chastity (or married love) and virginity. The expansive character of both works is evident in the way that they absorb these antithetical attitudes toward natural process, in order to address directly the vanity of an aging queen. The possibility of incorporating this ethical division may have been suggested to Shakespeare by Spenser's poem, which manages to set forth the same dichotomy without destroying its artistic integrity. In Spenser's poem and Shakespeare's play, Elizabeth becomes a privileged member of the audience, who finds her own image reflected by these "fairy toys."

---

20. E. K. Chambers mentions the Elvetham pageant in *William Shakespeare: A Study of Facts and Problems*, I, 359.

A Midsummer Night's Dream shows Shakespeare's wide-ranging familiarity with Spenser's work—a topic that has received little attention from literary scholars. Harold Brooks has shown that Shakespeare was intimately acquainted with both the eclogues and glosses of *The Shepheardes Calender,* and probably knew the *Amoretti* and *Epithalamion* as well as *The Teares of the Muses.*[21] He particularly focused on the floral imagery of Spenser's pastorals, when he sought matter of invention to furbish his imaginative landscape. Thus Spenser's "fragrant flowers . . . dewed with tears" (ll. 109, 112) of the December eclogue become "fragrant flowers . . . And . . . dew . . . Like tears" (IV.i.51–54) in *A Midsummer Night's Dream,* where the same passage employs the rather rarely used word "floweret," which E. K. annotates in the *Calender,* because of its peculiarity.[22] Brooks cites numerous Spenserian echoes of this order, such as the duplication of "My head besprent with hoary frost" (December, l. 135) in the "hoary-headed frosts" (II.i.107) lamented by Titania, or November's "coloured chaplets" (l. 115), transformed into "an odorous chaplet of sweet summer buds" (II.i.110). E. K.'s gloss on the phrase "Frendly faeries" in the June eclogue, which notes that "there be no such thinges, nor yet the shadowes of the things," might have supplied Shakespeare with the associative link between actors and these supernatural creatures which appears in Puck's closing words, "If we shadows have offended . . ."[23] The apparently diminutive creatures of the June eclogue are the elder brothers of Masters Peaseblossom, Cobweb, Moth, and Mustardseed, just as Gloriana in Spenser's epic is genealogically related to the life-sized and often imposing figure of Titania, the *other* Fairy Queen.[24] Another fecund passage in the October eclogue seems to have supplied Shakespeare with an imaginative bridge connecting *The Shepheardes Calendar* with *The Teares of the Muses.* Pierce's invitation to Cuddie:

21. See Harold Brooks's introduction to the Arden edition of *A Midsummer Night's Dream,* pp. xxxiv-xxxix and pp. lviii-lxii.

22. E. K.'s gloss is on line 25 of the June eclogue, in *Variorum,* VII, 64.

23. Puck's excuse can also be an apology for the topical allegory, which might be thought to be far too bold.

24. The two strains of fairy mythology found in both Spenser and Shakespeare are discussed in Minor White Latham, *The Elizabethan Fairies: The Fairies of Folklore and the Fairies of Shakespeare* (New York, 1930), and Isabel Rathborne, *The Meaning of Spenser's Fairyland* (New York, 1925).

> let us cast with what delight to chace,
> And weary thys long lingring *Phoebus* race
>
> (ll. 2–3)

is paraphrased twice by Shakespeare in rapid succession. Theseus first asks:

> what masques, what dances shall we have,
> To wear away this long age of three hours.
>
> (V.i.33–34)

He then demands of Philostrate:

> How shall we beguile
> The lazy time, if not with some delight?
>
> (V.i.40–41)

The October eclogue's argument describes it as portraying "the perfecte paterne of a Poete, which finding no maintenaunce of his state and studies, complayneth of the contempte of Poetrie." E. K. observes that it "is made in imitation of Theocritus his xvi Idilion, wherein hee reproved the Tyranne Hiero of Syracuse for his nigardise towarde Poetes." Shakespeare's imitation of lines from the October ecloguc, dealing with the neglect of poets, probably sparked his mention of *The Teares of the Muses,* only eleven lines later.[25] The two poems are based on an identical theme.

The likelihood that *A Midsummer Night's Dream* was composed by 1595 is suggested by a possible imitation of lines from the *Epithalamion,* which was registered for publication on 19 November 1594 and could have been available to Shakespeare immediately before he put the final touches on his work for 26 January. When conjuring the terrors of the night at the end of the play, Puck mentions in sequence "the screech-owl," "graves" that "let forth their sprite," and concludes with "we fairies that do run . . . Following darkness like a dream" (V.i.376–386). This acts as a

---

25. E. K. Chambers, *William Shakespeare: A Study of Facts and Problems,* I, 360–361, discusses Dover Wilson's theory that part of the fifth act—V.i.1–84—shows marks of revision. This may account for the two echoes of the October eclogue.

prelude to the fairies' blessing on the bridal chamber. Among the list of horrors that Spenser deflects from his own marriage bed are "the shriech Oule" and "damned ghosts cald up with mighty spels," as well as "hob Goblins," "the Pouke," and "other evill sprights" (ll. 341–347). The main problem with this attribution is revealed in the fact that Spenser's passage in the *Epithalamion* is one of the poet's many imitations of himself. Shakespeare's list of evils also echoes Hobbinoll's words in the June eclogue:

> Here no night Ravens lodge more black then pitche,
> Nor elvish ghosts, nor gastly owles flee.
> But frendly Faeries, met with many Graces,
> And lightfote Nymphes can chase the lingring night.
>
> (ll. 23–26)

The "Faeries" which "chase the lingring night" are transformed into the playwright's "faeries that do run . . . Following darkness like a dream," mentioned by Puck. Again, Harold Brooks cites several other imitative details which corroborate the theory that Shakespeare knew both works. Prominent among these is Helena's wordplay on the term "fair" (which means both "beauty" and "the fair one"), when she says to Helena: "Call you me fair? That fair again unsay! / Demetrius loves your fair: O happy fair!" (I.i.181–182). Spenser's Sonnet LXXIX begins with words rephrased by Helena: "Men call you fayre," and then commences to elaborate on the term's multiple meanings for the rest of his lyric.[26] Since no conclusive imitations of any work by Spenser published after the combined edition of the *Amoretti* and the *Epithalamion* has been detected in *A Midsummer Night's Dream,* it is likely that this recently issued collection of poems was perused by Shakespeare sometime between the date of its registry in November of 1594 and the Stanley-Vere wedding in January of 1595. *The Teares of the Muses* was at this time a scandalous work that could safely be mentioned, once the controversy had cooled, almost four years later. The *Epithalamion,* on the other hand, was a poem, hot off the press, commemorating a marriage, the subject to which Shakespeare was then devoting his considerable efforts. Placed in so timely a fashion in

---

26. Harold Brooks mentions this pun in his introduction to the Arden edition of *A Midsummer Night's Dream,* p. xxxvi.

Shakespeare's hands, some of its motifs soon found their way into his play-in-progress.

The similarities that exist between *A Midsummer Night's Dream* and the poetry of Edmund Spenser can be attributed to the fact that the Elizabethan court and the system of patronage it engendered comprised a small social universe in which the playwright and the epic poet strove simultaneously for recognition and advancement. Elizabeth and Burghley sat at the top of a social pyramid, dangling Philotime's chain for a handful of talented writers, who evidently strove alongside of, as well as against, each other. Spenser seems finally to have been quite pleased with the two gifts he secured from Elizabeth, after his long wait for favor—she granted him a pension of £50 a year for life and title to the lease on his Kilcolman estate.[27] Shakespeare similarly benefited from the arrangement through his continual productions before the queen as well as through the patronage of the lord chamberlain, which guaranteed his right to present plays in the public theater.[28] One of the reasons why Shakespeare would have taken notice of *The Teares of the Muses* is that the poem was dedicated to Lady Strange, the wife of his former patron, Ferdinando Stanley, the Earl of Derby. It is generally assumed that Shakespeare was one of Strange's Men until the death of his patron on 16 April 1594, after which his company was temporarily in the service of Lady Strange, before becoming affiliated with Lord Hunsdon, the lord chamberlain, by the end of the same year. Spenser and Shakespeare had, consequently, besides Elizabeth, a second patron in common.[29]

27. See Alexander Judson, *The Life of Edmund Spenser* (Baltimore, 1945), pp. 155–156.

28. The details of the conflict caused by the court's sanction of the public theater are set forth in E. K. Chambers, *The Elizabethan Stage,* I, 269–301, in "The Struggle of the Court and City."

29. Hazelton Spenser, *The Art and Life of William Shakespeare* (New York, 1940), p. 111, notes that "The company Shakespeare belonged to by the end of 1594 was known as the Lord Chamberlain's Men. . . . They had begun that year under another patron, Ferdinando Stanley, Lord Strange." Shakespeare remained one of Strange's Men until the death of his patron on 16 April 1594. Harden Kelsie, "Nashe's Rebuke of Spenser," *N&Q,* CXCVIII (1953), 145–146, cites Nashe's censure of the poet for not having included a dedicatory sonnet to Lord Strange in the 1590 edition of *The Faerie Queene,* a further substantiation of their relation. Kelsie conjectures that Spenser could not afford to honor a possible claimant to the throne and consequently omitted a tribute to him.

Spenser claims to have been related to Lady Strange—whose maiden name, Alice Spencer, indicates the connection. She seems to have recognized this familial bond, since in his dedicatory letter to her prefacing *The Teares of the Muses,* Spenser thanks her for both "particular bounties, and also some private bands of affinitie, which it hath pleased your Ladyship to acknowledge." Alice was one of the three daughters of Sir John Spencer of Althorpe who helped finance their poorer relation's poetic career and who are immortalized in dedicatory sonnets to *The Faerie Queene,* dedicatory letters prefacing the complaints, and the coterie allegory of *Colin Clouts Come Home Againe.*[30] Alice Spencer was also the sister-in-law of William Stanley, whose marriage to Elizabeth Vere was the occasion for a production of *A Midsummer Night's Dream,* during which a poem dedicated to her was ridiculed. E. K. Chambers notes that there was a feud in 1595 between Lady Strange and her brother-in-law "over the succession of the Derby estates," and that she had written to Burghley that she wished Elizabeth Vere "a better husband."[31] The marriage pleased Burghley because it mated his granddaughter with one of the richest men in England, and on 2 January 1595 he wrote to his son, Robert Cecil, of his pleasure:

Though my hand is unable to fight and my right eye unable to take a level, yet they both do stoop to return my humble thanks for continuance of her favour at this time when I am more fitter for a hospital than to be party to a wedding.[32]

Elizabeth must have also been gladdened by the prospect of William Stanley's marriage to Elizabeth Vere, because it finally obviated the threat to her sovereignty posed by Lord Strange, who had a remote claim to the throne through his mother, Margaret Clifford, granddaughter of Henry VIII's younger sister.[33] Elizabeth's fear that Catholic instigators would rally to Strange's call was permanently put to rest with his death and the

---

30. See Judson's chapter on "The Spencers" in *The Life of Edmund Spenser,* pp. 1–7.
31. Quoted from E. K. Chambers, "On the Occasion of *A Midsummer Night's Dream,*" in *Shakespearan Gleanings,* p. 65.
32. Quoted from Conyers Read, *Lord Burghley and the Queen,* p. 502.
33. *Ibid.,* p. 502.

marriage of his younger brother to Elizabeth Vere. The humorous suggestion that *The Teares of the Muses* should furnish the evening's entertainment
might have been doubly inappropriate, since it coupled Edmund
Spenser—who had previously insulted Burghley—with Alice Spencer—
who was certainly still opposed to her brother-in-law's marriage at the
time of Shakespeare's allusion to *The Teares of the Muses*. It would be hard
to overemphasize the compactness of the aristocratic society in which both
Shakespeare and Spenser moved, tied by the purse strings of patronage.
Shakespeare's success in the public theater lessened his direct dependence
on his social superiors. Indeed, the public theaters were tolerated because
they relieved the aristocracy of the financial burden of supporting the
actors as their servants. Shakespeare's company, the Lord Chamberlain's
Men, later the King's Men, was as integral a part of the courtly milieu as
Edmund Spenser ever was. Spenser read selections from *The Faerie Queene*
to Elizabeth, and Shakespeare may have even acted a part in his royal
entertainment. They orbited in the same closed social sphere. After William Stanley and Elizabeth Vere were married at Greenwich, where *A
Midsummer Night's Dream* was probably performed, the couple moved on
to Burghley House in the Strand, where they were scheduled to be entertained by—of all things—an "Epithalamion" of the Nine Muses, who
were commonly called upon to bestow poetic grace at weddings. Arthur
Throckmorton, hearing of Davies's proposed masque, wrote to Robert
Cecil in January of 1595, asking to be permitted to come before the muses
entered, for the purpose of offering Elizabeth:

> a ring made for a wedding ring set round with diamonds,
> and with a ruby like a heart placed in a coronet,
> with the inscription *Elizabetha potest*.[34]

Spenser incorporated this evidently stunning jewel in the 1596 sequel to
The Faerie Queene. Belphoebe—Queen Elizabeth—is there enticed by:

---

34. This historical analogue was first brought to my attention by J. R. Brink, "The
Masque of the Nine Muses: Sir John Davies's Unpublished 'Epithalamion' and the
'Belphoebe-Ruby' Episode in *The Faerie Queene*," *RES*, XXIII (1972), 445–447.

> a Ruby of right perfect hew,
> Shap'd like a heart, yet bleeding of the wound,
> And with a litle golden chaine about it bound.
>
> (IV.viii.6)

The same aristocratic occasion, duly recorded in Stowe's *Annals,* consequently exhibited a twofold influence on the literature conditioned by its power: it encouraged mimesis through patronage, shaping *A Midsummer Night's Dream,* even as it became the very groundwork of mimetic construction, in the "Belphoebe-Ruby" episode of *The Faerie Queene.*

The literary connection between Edmund Spenser and William Shakespeare that brought them closest together was their mutual acquaintance with Richard Field, a printer who operated a shop in the Blackfriars. Three years Shakespeare's senior, Field was also from Stratford, and his father knew John Shakespeare, William's father. On 18 April 1593, he entered *Venus and Adonis* in the Register at Stationer's Hall and commenced to print a poem so popular that it had already gone through three editions by 1596—it would see *sixteen* before 1640. When Spenser returned from Ireland to England again in the winter of 1595-1596 to arrange for the reprinting of the first three books of *The Faerie Queene* and the first edition of the final three, he probably corrected proofs of his poem in Field's possession. William Ponsonby registered the new installment on 20 January 1596, but the title page of the two new quartos bears the *Anchora Spei* device of Richard Field, who was evidently contracted to supply the editions. When Spenser visited Field's shop he might have perused the third edition of *Venus and Adonis.* Shakespeare, on the other hand, might have glanced through the new installment of Spenser's epic, which was being printed next to his own erotic epyllion. For this reason Alexander Judson has called Field's shop, which was just a short walk from Ponsonby's, "a physical link between the two poets." [35]

The struggle for literary status that I have been illustrating arises out of the similar social arrangement of patronage which molded the imaginations of both Spenser and Shakespeare. Spenser ignited the competition in a general way by condemning a public theater that rudely forced Thalia to become "the sevant of the manie" in *The Teares of the Muses.* The

---

35. Judson, p. 179.

stage was, according to Spenser, the home of "Barbarisme" and "Ignorance," except for that dramatist who wasn't at present writing, John Lyly, whose poetic name—"pleasant Willy"—must have surely intrigued Shakespeare who played on his own name "Will" so skillfully in Sonnets 135 and 136. G. K. Hunter has observed that *A Midsummer Night's Dream* is "Lylian" in its "construction" largely because its occasion is "aristocratic rather than popular." [36] Having decided to bring the scope of his synthetic imagination within the realm of coterie conventions, Will Shakespeare plundered "pleasant Willy's" plays for both memorable phrasing and the schematic pattern of confusions that traces the lovers' interactions. Moving closer to Spenser's imaginative terrain in *A Midsummer Night's Dream* coincided with a movement toward the work of Spenser's favorite English playwright.

If Spenser's satire excited Shakespeare's feeling of mimetic rivalry, the dramatist can be credited with personalizing it in Old Comedy fashion. Spenser, of course, had already particularized his abuse of Burghley, and for this reason he can be said to have triggered even this aspect of Shakespeare's response. The "rude mechanicals" who present their drama for the Athenian court embody the very qualities that Spenser deplored on the stage, and Shakespeare may here be acknowledging his superiority over the skills of lesser dramatists. The court was here entertained by brilliant actors pretending to be blockheads, always implicitly emphasizing their bond with an aristocratic audience which demonstrates both tolerance and mockery. Hippolyta warns Theseus not to be rude to the actors, but the pathetic spectacle of their failure secretly cements a bond between the Lord Chamberlain's Men and the court. By parodying artistic naïveté, the actors announce their standards, deflecting the thrust of Puritan and Humanist attacks on the stage—including Spenser's. But their play, besides being a critique of bad acting, is also a comic rendering of Golding's translation of the *Metamorphoses*. The tragedy of Pyramis and Thisbe divides its self-referential focus between the poles of wretched drama *and* racy, but seriously flawed translation.

The full scope of Shakespeare's imitations of Spenser in *A Midsummer Night's Dream* is available to us only when we acknowledge that Shake-

36. G. K. Hunter, *John Lyly: The Humanist as Courtier* (Cambridge, Mass., 1962), p. 318.

speare was both deeply impressed by Spenser's achievement and critical of it. The effect of parody I have been emphasizing had both a defensive and an offensive component. It warded off Spenser's influence even as it saw through his mistakes; it fused with its source even as it rebelled against it. *A Midsummer Night's Dream* is the sincerest form of flattery, in spite of the strategy of containment it employs to repress its source. At the Stanley-Vere wedding, the simultaneous pressures of status competition and mimetic rivalry converged in parody, but they were transformed into literature only because the *mythoi* of both Spenser and Shakespeare converged for this unique moment in Elizabethan history. Parody paradoxically coincided with acceptance of a deeper sort, and it is the existence of these two strands—of ridicule and reverence—that fully expresses the contradictory attitudes that Shakespeare felt toward his predecessor. Nowhere is this clearer than in my final example of Spenser's literary presence in *A Midsummer Night's Dream.*

Nick Bottom, who recalls his perplexing dream of a Fairy Queen, is simultaneously a parody of and an analogue to Spenser's Prince Arthur, who remembers a similar vision. The role that is given to Arthur in Spenser's poem is transferred to Bottom in Shakespeare's drama. Their visionary accounts of the Fairy Queen are crucial moments in these works: both speakers are master characters, who take us through all parts of the fiction. Arthur enters each book of *The Faerie Queene,* and Bottom participates in all subplots of *A Midsummer Night's Dream.* Bottom is the only character who enters each of the play's four social divisions: he joins the Fairy world as Titania's consort; he becomes one of the lovers; he leads the "rude mechanicals"; and he entertains at the court of Athens. As John Palmer remarks, he "holds together the gossamer structure" of *A Midsummer Night's Dream.*[37] His activities impart a kind of modal composition to the play, similar to that interlacement of episodes central to Spenser's method of writing. Concerned about Bottom's temporary absence from the company of actors, Flute observes that "If he come not, then the play is marred" (IV.ii.4). His remark can be applied to the play as a whole as well as to the lamentable comedy of "Pyramis and Thisbe."

Shakespeare debased Arthur by transforming a high mimetic character into its opposite: the lowly, ludicrous Bottom. But, on closer examina-

---

37. John Palmer, *Comic Characters of Shakespeare* (London, 1944), p. 92.

tion, the two dreamers and their accounts of the Fairy Queen are remarkably akin. They both, in spite of all differences, project a paradoxical, double vision of experience. The major similarity shared by Shakespeare's and Spenser's dreams of the Fairy Queen is the fact that they both connect the empirical and the ideal—the dreamer and his fairy mistress—and attack this relation as being fraudulent. Bottom's famous rendering of his vision is a wondrous confrontation with the unknown that parallels what I will call "Arthur's dilemma." In the First Book of *The Faerie Queene,* when asked to reveal "what adventure, or what high intent, / Hath brought you hither into Fairy land," Arthur admits his quandry:

> Full hard it is (quoth he) to read aright
> The course of heavenly cause, or understand
> The secret meaning of th' eternall might,
> That rules mens wayes, and rules the thoughts
>   of living wights.

(I.ix.6–10)

Having referred to the arcane character of human destiny, which is shaped by an obscure teleological plan, Arthur then goes on to relate a dream, the vanishing of which has caused him tremendous sorrow. In a line of poetry that Spenser places in the exact center of Arthur's narrative, the prince states that he is not certain whether or not he can believe the experience he remembers, since he cannot determine "whether dreames delude, or true it were" (I.ix.14). This epistemological dilemma was, I believe, seized upon by Shakespeare who exploits its fullest implications in Bottom's familiar words: "I have had a dream past the wit of man to say what dream it was. Man is but an ass if he go about to expound this dream" (IV.i.203–206). Stirred by wonder, Bottom refuses to interpret his experience, arguing that it resists comprehension, in a speech that provokes us to consider the question of uncertainty broached by Arthur. In St. Paul's language of negatives, Arthur recalls his vision and stresses its extraordinary nature: "Was never hart so ravisht with delight, / Ne living man like words did ever heare" (I.ix.13). The same passage that Spenser suggests—1 Corinthians 2:9—is garbled by Bottom in a manner that conveys both its vatic possibility and the severe mental handicap of this speaker who concedes:

The eye of man hath not heard, the ear of man hath
not seen, man's hand is not able to taste,
his tongue to conceive, nor his heart to report what my dream was.

(IV.1.211–214)

Bottom's words are complex because they reflect both the mystic folly of St. Paul and the sheer folly of the buffoon: they hover at once both above reason and below it, through synesthetic confusions, which are paradigms of teleological uncertainty.

The similarities that exist between Prince Arthur's and Bottom's dreams are to a great extent due to their common literary genealogy. Their common source is the frivolous burlesque romance of the "doughty swayne" Sir Thopas, narrated by an "elvyssh" Geoffrey Chaucer, who numbers himself among the pilgrims of *The Canterbury Tales*. Sir Thopas, awakening from sleep's solace, recalls his vision of the "queene of Fayere" and promptly sets out to seek her company.[38] His soliloquy announces his quest for the "elf-queene" in a singsong verse that maximizes its comic intensity, when he relates:

> Me dremed al this night, pardee,
> An elf-queene shal my lemman be.

(ll. 1977–1978)

Thopas's "Me dremed" is re-created by Arthur, who says:

> Me seemed, by my side a royal Mayd
> Her daintie limbes full softly down did lay.

(I.ix.13–14)

Both were precedents for Bottom's truncated echoes:

> Methought I was—there is no man can tell what.
> Methought I was, and me thought I had—

(IV.i.7–8)

38. Chaucer describes himself in the "Prologue to Sir Thopas," l. 1893; the phrase "queene of Fayerye" appears in "Sir Thopas," l. 2004. All quotations from Chaucer's poetry are from *The Complete Works of Geoffrey Chaucer,* ed. F. N. Robinson (1933; repr. Boston, 1961). The final quotation is cited in the text.

Spenser expresses the epistemological uncertainty of Arthur's dilemma through the theological categories of "nature" and "grace," which, as A.S.P. Woodhouse has noted, both confirm and deny the doctrine of intrinsic human perfection.[39] Spenser's borrowing of Chaucer's ridiculous tale, which the medieval poet's unamused companions prohibit him from completing, allows him to undermine subtly, with a single stroke, the basic frame of his ambitious poem, in a gesture that Angus Fletcher has called one of Spenser's "bad puns." [40]

Spenser's conception of human dignity was both strengthened and weakened by his attachment to the social hierarchy of the Elizabethan court, and one feels that his epistemological dilemma was the result of the ambivalent treatment he received throughout his career—the confirmation and rejection of mimetic desire certainly contributed to his teleological quandary. Shakespeare matured under similar conditions, in a social configuration that prompted both rivalry and introspection, leading to an ironic evaluation of others and a probing examination of a self subjected to the pressures of hierarchy, trapped in the endless dialectic of humility and aspiration, doubt and confidence, success and failure. Shakespeare returns the dream of Sir Thopas to its original low mimetic register, deflating Spenser's elevation, but their dreams were subjected to similar pressures and inevitably ended in the same perplexity. Shakespeare was clearly aware of the two sources for Bottom's dream of the Fairy Queen, since he takes a considerable amount of material from "The Knight's Tale," the great heroic narrative of *The Canterbury Tales*, diametrically opposed to the ridiculous "Tale of Sir Thopas." Indeed, the amorous rivalry between Demetrius and Lysander is modeled on that of Palamon and Arcite, a theme to which Shakespeare would return at the end of his career with John Fletcher in composing *Two Noble Kinsmen*. The rivalry early in the play of Demetrius and Lysander for Hermia's hand retraces that which separates Palamon and Arcite, who both love Emelye. Both pairs of lovers are discovered fighting by Theseus in a clearing in the woods. But where in Chaucer's account the interloper Arcite is ultimately destroyed, in Shakespeare's more benevolent variation the latecomer is given his own

39. See A.S.P. Woodhouse's seminal essay "Nature and Grace in *The Faerie Queene*," *ELH*, XVI (1949), 194–228.
40. *The Prophetic Moment* (Chicago, 1971), p. 99.

mistress, Helena, thereby erasing the point of conflict that made it impossible for the lovers to coexist. Shakespeare may parody Spenser, but he also mythically imagines a society in which competition is transcended, where each poet and each lover may enjoy his own unique desire and focus on objects that are inherently different, no matter how similar Helena and Hermia may strike us, no matter how similar *The Faerie Queene* and *A Midsummer Night's Dream* actually are.

A Woman Killed with Kindness
as Subtext for Othello

PETER L. RUDNYTSKY

C HARLES LAMB epitomized Heywood as "a sort of *prose* Shakespeare," [1] and many subsequent critics have noted the affinity of *Othello* with the genre of domestic tragedy, of which *A Woman Killed with Kindness* is a prime example. Representative is G. Wilson Knight's statement, "*Othello* is eminently a domestic tragedy." [2] But although incidental similarities between the two dramas have frequently been pointed out, and commentators on Heywood's play in particular have found the comparison with *Othello* irresistible, [3] no one has systematically explored these re-

1. Charles Lamb, *Specimens of English Dramatic Poets* (1808), in *The Works of Charles and Mary Lamb,* ed. E. V. Lucas (London, 1904), IV, 95. In urging that the reprinting of works by earlier English dramatists begin with Heywood, Lamb elaborated the comparison with Shakespeare: "He possessed not the imagination of the latter; but in all those qualities which gained for Shakespeare the attribute of *gentle,* he was not inferior to him. . . . I love them both equally, but Shakespeare has most of my wonder" (p. 419).

2. G. Wilson Knight, *The Wheel of Fire: Interpretations of Shakespearian Tragedy* (1930; repr. London, 1972), p. 108.

3. Comparisons between *Othello* and *A Woman Killed with Kindness* are to be found in: Robert B. Heilman, *Magic in the Web: Action and Language in "Othello"* (Lexington, Ky., 1956), p. 284; Moody E. Prior, *The Language of Tragedy* (New York, 1947), pp. 94-99;

semblances or attempted to determine whether there is a relationship of direct influence between Heywood and Shakespeare.

In speaking of *A Woman Killed with Kindness* as a "subtext" for *Othello,* accordingly, I propose to investigate two interrelated problems—one of reading, the other of writing. Heywood's play functions as a subtext of its virtually contemporary Shakespearean counterpart, first, in that an examination of its themes, structure, and language necessarily sharpens our critical responsiveness to *Othello.* Such a comparative analysis is independent of, and takes precedence over, any effort to argue that one play may be a source for the other; but once one has accumulated a sufficient number of parallels, it is impossible to repress the suspicion that these may be due to more than coincidence. At the close of this paper, I shall speculate that *A Woman Killed with Kindness* may be a subtext for *Othello* also in the second, more literal sense that was known to Shakespeare at the time he wrote his play.

The intertextuality between *A Woman Killed with Kindness* and *Othello* is mediated by the close connections of both plays to Shakespeare's early comedy, *The Taming of the Shrew.* Heywood's title is a proverbial phrase, but its most celebrated previous occurrence comes in Petruchio's description of his wooing of Kate: "This is a way to kill a wife with kindness, / And thus I'll curb her mad and headstrong humor" (IV.i.208–209).[4] Once again, it is tempting, though not essential, to wonder whether this echo is due to deliberate borrowing on Heywood's part. What is clear is

---

Michel Grivelet, *Thomas Heywood et le drame domestique Elisabéthain* (Paris, 1957), pp. 305-307; Robert Ornstein, "Bourgeois Morality and Dramatic Convention in *A Woman Killed with Kindness,*" in *English Renaissance Drama: Essays in Honor of Madeleine Doran & Mark Eccles,* ed. Standish Henning, Robert Kimbrough, and Richard Knowles (Carbondale, Ill., 1976), pp. 140–141; Peter Ure, "Marriage and the Domestic Drama in Heywood and Ford," *ES,* XXXII (1951), 207–208; Roger Stilling, *Love and Death in Renaissance Tragedy* (Baton Rouge, La., 1976), pp. 173–175. Perhaps the most amusing example of such a discussion is David Cook, "*A Woman Killed with Kindness*: An Unshakespearian Tragedy," *ES,* XLV (1964), which, its title notwithstanding, ends with the conclusion, "Indeed several of the objections that can be made against *A Woman* apply more or less forcibly to *Othello*" (p. 372). I shall return to many of these studies in the course of the present essay.

4. All quotations from Shakespeare's plays are to *The Riverside Shakespeare,* ed. G. Blakemore Evans (Boston, 1974), with act, scene, and line numbers included parenthetically in the text.

that there is a remarkable correspondence between his domestic tragedy and Shakespeare's comedy. In the opening scene of *A Woman Killed with Kindness,* Sir Francis Acton refers to his sister Anne, Frankford's new bride, as "A perfect wife already, meek and patient" (i.37).[5] This description of Anne Frankford strongly resembles the portrayal in the final scene of Shakespeare's play of Kate, who instructs her fellow brides on the duties wives owe to husbands. It thus seems as though Heywood takes up where Shakespeare leaves off, in dramatizing the story of an apparently "perfect wife" who is corrupted after her marriage.

Othello, similarly, is a tragedy built upon a comic structure, where the marriage of the protagonists comes not at the end but the beginning, and the action of the play consists in the shattering of the illusions of both Othello and Desdemona.[6] In depicting the unfortunate consequences of what initially seem to be ideal marriages, *Othello* and *A Woman Killed with Kindness* anticipate George Eliot's realization in the Finale to *Middlemarch* that "Every limit is a beginning as well as an ending," and that marriage in particular, "which has been the bourne of so many narratives," is also "the beginning of the home epic," in which the happiness of "complete union" is permanently won or lost.[7] Just as the reliance upon marriage as the ultimate happy ending in the great tradition of the English novel from Fielding to Austen may be traced back to Shakespearean comedy, so the questioning of that idealized convention by nineteenth-century novelists such as Eliot has its roots in Shakespeare's own "dark" comedies and in the Renaissance genre of domestic tragedy.

Beyond the simple fact that *Othello* begins where *The Taming of the Shrew* ends, the arrangement of characters in the two plays reveals a striking

---

5. All quotations from *A Woman Killed with Kindness* are to the splendid Revels Plays edition of R. W. Van Fossen (Cambridge, Eng., 1961), with scene and line numbers included parenthetically in the text.

6. On the relation of *Othello* to Shakespeare's comedies, see Carol Thomas Neely, "Women and Men in *Othello*: 'What should a fool / Do with so good a woman?'" *ShakS,* X (1977), 133–158; and Susan Snyder, *The Comic Matrix of Shakespeare's Tragedies* (Princeton, N.J., 1979), pp. 70–90; and for the tradition of *commedia dell'arte,* see Barbara Heliodora C. de Mendonça, "*Othello*: A Tragedy Built on a Comic Structure," *ShS,* XXI (1968), 31–38.

7. George Eliot, *Middlemarch: A Study of Provincial Life* (1872) (New York, 1964), p. 805.

parallel. In both plays there are three female characters, who are distributed across a spectrum so that they personify the alternatives of what might be termed idealistic, realistic, and sexual love. These alternatives are represented in *The Taming of the Shrew* by the complacent Bianca, the recalcitrant Kate, and the lusty Widow, "That shall be woo'd and wedded in a day" (IV.ii.51). In *Othello*, the role of idealist belongs to Desdemona, that of realist to Emilia, and that of sensualist to the courtesan Bianca; each woman, moreover, is paired with a suitable male counterpart. The precedent of *The Taming of the Shrew*, where Shakespeare is at pains to show the superiority of the arduous courtship of Petruchio and Kate over the superficial extremes embodied in the other two couples, illuminates *Othello* and warns us against assuming that the absolute love of Othello and Desdemona is meant to be taken in any simple sense as adequate or normative.[8]

The common filiation of *A Woman Killed with Kindness* and *Othello* and *The Taming of the Shrew* is reinforced by the fact that, as domestic tragedies, both plays focus intensely upon the marriage bond and depict the torments of a husband who is—or believes he is—being cuckolded. In *A Woman Killed with Kindness*, Nicholas, a servant, informs his master Frankford that the latter's wife has betrayed him with his friend Wendoll, whom he has invited into his home. After initially rejecting the accusation, Frankford says in an aside:

> 'Tis probable; though blunt, yet he is honest.
> Though I durst pawn my life, and on their faith,
> Hazard the dear salvation of my soul,
> Yet in my trust I may be too secure.
> 'May this be true? O may it? Can it be?
>
> (viii.72–76)

---

8. The same pattern obtains also in *Much Ado About Nothing*, where the role of idealist is assigned to Hero, that of realist to Beatrice, and that of sensualist to the lady-in-waiting Margaret, who allows herself to be inveigled by Borachio into the conspiracy against Hero. As Snyder points out in her analysis of *Othello*, "Twice before, Shakespeare had used comedy to explore the inadequacies of romantic courtship, cursorily in *Taming of the Shrew* and more thoroughly in *Much Ado*" (*The Comic Matrix of Shakespeare's Tragedies*, p. 75). My observations concerning Shakespeare's deployment of female characters corroborate Snyder's view of the close links between *Othello* and these two comedies.

Unlike Iago, Nicholas is telling the truth about Anne Frankford, but the roles of the two subordinates, and the responses of the two masters, are otherwise identical. In its configuration of characters, this exchange in scene viii of *A Woman Killed with Kindness* unmistakably recalls the great "temptation scene" (III. iii) of *Othello*. Frankford's description of Nicholas as "honest" likewise serves, of course, as the watchword for Iago throughout Shakespeare's play.[9] In addition to this repetition of "honest," and to the larger analogy between the situations of the characters, there are several more specific echoes of Frankford's speech in *Othello*. Frankford's willingness to "pawn my life, and on their faith / Hazard the dear salvation of my soul" is matched by Othello's oath, "My life upon her faith!" (I.iii.294), and his imprecation to Iago in the "temptation scene":

> Give me the ocular proof,
> Or by the worth of mine eternal soul,
> Thou hadst been better have been born a dog
> Than answer my wak'd wrath!
>
> (III.iii.360–364)

Combined with the evidence I shall adduce concerning the dates of the two plays, the closeness of the various verbal reminiscences of Frankford's speech in *Othello* provides the most compelling argument that *A Woman Killed with Kindness* is a subtext in the rigorous sense of having been deliberately imitated by Shakespeare in the writing of *Othello*.

The parallel between the "temptation scene" in *Othello* and its equivalent in *A Woman Killed with Kindness* points up, in any case, the intertwining of the themes of honor and perception in both plays. Othello's obsessive quest to obtain the "ocular proof" of Desdemona's infidelity is evoked in the continuation of the same dialogue between Frankford and Nicholas. Nicholas answers his master's query concerning the proof for his charges with the words "Eyes, eyes," to which Frankford responds, "Thy eyes may be deceiv'd I tell thee" (viii.81–82). The pairing of the words "eyes" and "deceiv'd" occurs also in *Othello* in the bitter warning of Brabantio, "Look to her, Moor, if thou hast eyes to see; / She has deceiv'd

---

9. The connection between Frankford's speech and *Othello* is noted by Stilling, *Love and Death in Renaissance Tragedy*, p. 174, who assumes that Heywood is here imitating Shakespeare.

her father, and may thee" (I.iii.292–293)—the same warning which calls
forth Othello's vow, "My life upon her faith!" Patricia Meyer Spacks,
whose analysis of the themes of honor and perception admirably brings
out the complexities of *A Woman Killed with Kindness,* has remarked:

Frankford may be virtuous, but he is not perceptive, and failure of perception can
be as disastrous in its effects as failure of goodness. The tragedy which befalls
Master Frankford is in a sense his own fault. . . . Frankford's characterization
presents the problem of perception from a different angle [from that of his wife]:
he is the false perceiver rather than the false object of perception.[10]

Spacks's account of Frankford's downfall as due to a "failure of perception"
and largely "his own fault" may be applied without modification to
Othello. A further indication of the affinity between the tragedies of
Othello and Frankford, moreover, is that both protagonists evince in their
jealousy an absolutist temperament, a tendency to view the universe in
all-or-nothing terms. Upon having his suspicions aroused by Nicholas,
Frankford says in so many words, "Till I know all, I'll nothing seem to
know" (viii.111), a cast of mind analogous to that of Othello in the
"temptation scene": "I'll see before I doubt; when I doubt, prove; / And
on the proof . . . / Away at once with love or jealousy" (III.iii.190–192).

The structural symmetry between these two scenes depicting the im-
plantation of suspicion is carried forward by that between scene xiii of *A
Woman Killed with Kindness,* where Frankford actually catches Anne and
Wendoll *in flagrante,* and the "brothel scene" (IV.ii) of *Othello.* In both
plays, the real or imagined infidelity of the wife leads to a conflation of
marriage with the thought of prostitution in the mind of the husband;
and this common associative link is once again expressed by Heywood and
Shakespeare in remarkably similar language. At the conclusion of the
immediately preceding scene in *A Woman Killed with Kindness,* when the
minor servant Jenkins is told that he is to be made porter for the night, he
replies, "Thus by little and little I creep into office" (xii.22). This use of
"office" to signify the duties of a bawd or pander finds a counterpart in the
ravings of Othello:[11]

10. Patricia Meyer Spacks, "Honor and Perception in *A Woman Killed with Kindness,*"
MLQ, XX (1959), 326.
11. See *A Woman Killed with Kindness,* ed. Van Fossen, p. 70.

> I took you for that cunning whore of Venice
> That married with Othello.—You, mistress,
>> *Enter* Emilia
> That have the office opposite to Saint Peter,
> And keep the gate of hell! You, you! ay, you!
> We have done our course; there's money for your pains.
>
>   (IV.ii.89–93)

Earlier in the "brothel scene," Othello registers his tortured reaction to the thought of Desdemona's adultery:

> But there, where I have garner'd up my heart,
> Where either I must live or bear no life;
> The fountain from the which my current runs,
> Or else dries up: to be discarded thence!
> Or keep it as a cestern for foul toads
> To knot and gender in!
>
>   (IV.ii.57–62)

When Frankford, in his equivalent to the "brothel scene," returns home surreptitiously to entrap the guilty couple, he examines the key to his bedchamber:

> But this, that door that's bawd unto my shame,
> Fountain and spring of all my bleeding thoughts,
> Where the most hallowed order and true knot
> Of nuptial sanctity hath been profan'd.
>
>   (xiii.10–13)

Frankford's description of his "profan'd" bedchamber as the "Fountain and spring of all my bleeding thoughts" seems to resonate in Othello's veneration of Desdemona's chastity as "The fountain from the which my current runs." There is thus a simultaneous congruence between *Othello* and *A Woman Killed with Kindness* at the levels of diction, character, and scenic structure.

Later in the same scene, after Frankford has surprised Anne and Wendoll and the latter has fled, Anne begs her husband for forgiveness:

To call you husband—
O me most wretched, I have lost that name;
I am no more your wife.

(xiii.81–83)

She invokes the example of Christ to plead for a single boon from Frankford:

. . . even for his sake
That hath redeem'd our souls, mark not my face
Nor hack me with your sword, but let me go
Perfect and undeformed to my tomb.

(xii.97–100)

Both these passages have duplicates in *Othello*: the former, Anne's confes-
sion "I am no more your wife," parallels Othello's stammered insight after
he has killed Desdemona, "My wife! my wife! what wife? I have no wife"
(V.ii.97);[12] and the latter, Anne's request that she be sent "Perfect and
undeformed to my tomb," mirrors Othello's resolution to murder Desdemona bloodlessly:

Yet I'll not shed her blood,
Nor scar that whiter skin of hers than snow,
And smooth as monumental alablaster.

V.ii.3–5)

Underlying these specific resemblances is the fact that both Frankford and
Othello are obsessed with reconciling the conflicting claims of justice and
love in determining the fate of their erring (or supposedly erring) wives.[13]

In scene xiii, when Frankford first comes upon Anne and Wendoll
asleep in each other's arms, he checks his desire for vengeance:

But that I would not damn two precious souls
Bought with my Saviour's blood and send them laden

12. See Ure, "Marriage and the Domestic Drama in Heywood and Ford," pp. 207–208.
13. See Winifred M. T. Nowottny, "Justice and Love in *Othello*," *UTQ*, XXI (1952),
330–344.

> With all their scarlet sins upon their backs
> Unto a fearful Judgement, their two lives
> Had met upon my rapier.

(xiii.44–48)

This refusal to damn Anne and Wendoll by not giving them a chance to repent before killing them contrasts with, and is directly modeled upon, Hamlet's unwillingness to kill Claudius at his prayers lest he go directly to heaven (see *Hamlet*, III.iii.73-96).[14] Heywood's imitation of a scene from *Hamlet* in a play which is otherwise most closely tied to *Othello*, and whose title may be borrowed from *The Taming of the Shrew*, demonstrates his familiarity with Shakespeare and attests to the complexity of the intertextual relations between these two dramatists.

The analogies between *Othello* and *A Woman Killed with Kindness*, as I have tried to show, are embedded as much in the rhythm and scenic structure of the plays as they are in the language and imagery. Additional evidence that this is so is provided by the reliance on dramatic irony in both plays, whereby the end is anticipated in the beginning. In the opening scene of *A Woman Killed with Kindness*, as the wedding of Anne and Frankford is being celebrated, the banter produced by a call for music possesses serious overtones:

ACTON
Some music there! None lead the bride a dance?
MOUNTFORD
Yes, would she dance "The Shaking of the Sheets":
But that's a dance her husband means to lead her.
WENDOLL
That's not the dance that every man must dance,
According to the ballad.

(i.1–5)

These lines are ironic, not simply because of their bawdy allusion to the wedding night, but also because "The Shaking of the Sheets" refers to a dance ballad, the opening stanza of which is glanced at by Wendoll:

---

14. See *A Woman Killed with Kindness*, ed. Van Fossen, p. 73.

> Can you dance the shaking of the sheets
> a dance that every man must do?
> Can you trim it up with dainty sweets
> and every thing that longs thereto?
> Make ready then your winding sheet
> And see how you can bestir your feet,
> For death is the man that all must meet. [15]

The ambiguous meaning of "The Shaking of the Sheets" thus brings together sexuality and death and prefigures the death of Anne Frankford, which is the consequence of her dancing "The Shaking of the Sheets" with a man other than her husband.

The full impact of this joking comes with the recognition that *Othello*, too, might be regarded as an extended gloss upon the double meaning of "The Shaking of the Sheets." Desdemona's wedding sheets literally become her winding sheet. On the night of her murder by Othello, she asks Emilia to lay her wedding sheets on her bed, and adds, "If I do die before thee, prithee shroud me / In one of these same sheets" (IV.iii.24–25). But the almost mystical quality of Desdemona's request is counterbalanced by another mention of wedding sheets in *Othello*. As Iago and Cassio, before carousing on Cyprus, are discussing the Moor's recent marriage, Iago responds to Cassio's rapturous praise of Desdemona with the cynical benediction, "Well—happiness to their sheets" (II.iii.29). As domestic dramas centrally concerned with the sexual bond at the heart of marriage, both *Othello* and *A Woman Killed with Kindness* make conspicuous thematic use of wedding sheets; but the divergence between the tones of Iago and Desdemona indicates the wider range of attitudes toward love encompassed by Shakespeare's play.

In an effort to remove *Othello* from the category of domestic drama exemplified by *A Woman Killed with Kindness*, Moody Prior has contended that not only is Frankford's character "defined in terms which cannot embrace actions and feelings of great power, but his basic qualities remain in large part unthreatened by the action"; as a consequence, Prior concludes, "*Othello* is tragic; *A Woman Killed with Kindness* is sad and pathetic." [16] We have already seen, however, that the violation of his

---

15. Quoted in *A Woman Killed with Kindness*, ed. Van Fossen, p. 4.
16. Prior, *The Language of Tragedy*, p. 96.

"nuptial sanctity" poses a threat to Frankford that goes to the core of his being. But Prior's observation that Heywood's play lacks the true tragic power of *Othello* is borne out by the comparatively limited range of points of view to be found in *A Woman Killed with Kindness*. Put differently, Heywood's treatment of adultery, unlike that of Shakespeare, is frankly didactic. As Frankford retires to consider a suitable sentence for his wife's transgression, Anne addresses the female spectators in a soliloquy:

> O women, women, you that have yet kept
> Your holy matrimonial vow unstain'd,
> Make me your instance: when you tred awry,
> Your sins like mine will on your conscience lie.
>
> (xiii. 141–144)

There is in *Othello* no stable moral benchmark comparable to this speech by Anne Frankford. When, for instance, Desdemona naïvely asks Emilia whether "there be women do abuse their husbands / In such gross kind" (IV.iii.62–63), and Emilia answers by asserting "But I do think it is their husbands' faults / If wives do fall" (IV.iii.86–87), there is as much reason to sympathize with the realistic relativism of the latter as with the unworldly idealism of the former. No more than Desdemona does Emilia have the last word, however, for her own somewhat priggish respectability is challenged by the courtesan Bianca. To Emilia's branding of her as a "strumpet," Bianca retorts, "I am no strumpet, but of life as honest / As you that thus abuse me" (V.i.122–123); and in view of Emilia's defense of infidelity, Bianca's reply carries considerable justification.

Heywood's insistence on using his drama to inculcate conventional norms of personal conduct reveals the limitations of his talent in comparison with the genius of Shakespeare. Despite Heywood's moralistic intentions, however, *A Woman Killed with Kindness* is far from being an unambiguous work. In contrast to *Othello,* not only is Anne actually guilty of the adultery of which Desdemona is falsely accused, but Frankford, unlike Othello, succeeds in repressing the murderous violence aroused by his wife's betrayal. This self-restraint causes him to become an exemplary "instance" in a way opposite to the fallen Anne, but, in the central moral paradox of the play, proves to be a harsher punishment than any physical chastisement would have been. Thus, when Frankford declares to Anne

that he will "with usage / Of more humility torment thy soul / And kill
thee even with kindness" (xiii, 154–156), the reader is likely to be struck
less by his ostensible magnanimity than by his actual cruelty.[17]

Heywood rings additional changes on the paradox of his title in the
subplot, which concerns the financial collapse of Sir Charles Mountford,
and his attempt to save himself by prostituting his sister, Susan, to his
enemy, Sir Francis Acton. Unlike the main plot, the subplot ends happily
when Acton's lust is transformed into love and he agrees to marry Susan.
But though the outcome is fortunate, the conduct of the male characters
in the subplot is no less equivocal than in the main plot. Acton's decision
to ransom Mountford is in reality a bribe to gain the capitulation of Susan;
he unfolds his plans in a soliloquy: "Well, I will fasten such a kindness on
her / As shall o'ercome her hate and conquer it" (ix.66–67). By acceding
to Acton's scheme, Mountford, too, betrays a spiritual depravity equal to
that of Wendoll. In urging Susan to yield to Acton, he confesses, "His
kindness like a burden hath surcharged me, / And under his good deeds I
stooping go" (xiv. 63–64).[18] Acton's sudden conversion to genuine love
and his reconciliation with Mountford, though demanded by the exigencies of plot, do little to alleviate one's uneasy feeling that these two have
not been held accountable for their actions and that Acton's initial "kindness," like that of Frankford, carries with it an onerous "surcharge" of
cruelty or desire for mastery over the object of his affections.

Although Anne's address to the audience does provide an official statement of morality, Heywood's dramatic practice is thus far more complex
than this speech alone would indicate. Indeed, the finest thing in *A
Woman Killed with Kindness* is arguably the extended portrayal of the
adulterous affair between Anne and Wendoll. Both Anne and Wendoll are
shown struggling with temptation, then involuntarily yielding to it,
repeating the offense, and finally repenting upon being discovered by
Frankford. Because we experience both the sweets of their sin and their

17. In his Introduction, Van Fossen argues that Frankford's "apparent vindictiveness"
in this speech "must be seen in a seventeenth-century light" (p. xlv). But even when the
harshness of the traditional punishment for adultery is allowed for, a twentieth-century
awareness of the ambivalance in Frankford's attitude seems entirely appropriate.

18. The links between the two plots of *A Woman Killed with Kindness* are explored in
Freda L. Townsend, "The Artistry of Thomas Heywood's Double Plots," *PQ*, XXV
(1946), 97–119.

moral conflicts, we find it impossible to condemn the lovers completely. Anne, like Beatrice in *The Changeling,* becomes "the deed's creature," who cannot escape from the consequences of a course of action which she herself has set into motion. "Well, you plead custom," she tells Wendoll when he solicits her for a second time. "Once o'er shoes, we are straight o'er head in sin" (xi.111,114). Wendoll possesses something of the satanic quality of De Flores and Iago, and, like theirs, his predicament is presented to a large extent from within. Near the end of the play, when he comes upon the dying Anne, who is on her way to seek forgiveness from Frankford, he is moved to express his remorse: "I'll do my best good will / To work a cure on her whom I did kill" (xvi.98–99). But she brands him "The Devil" (xvi.108) and refuses to allow him to approach her. Wendoll's virtuous resolution gives a final twist to the play's title, for it aligns him with Frankford, Acton, and Mountford in his ambivalent fusion of tenderness and cruelty. Despite the limitations imposed by Heywood's didacticism, in the subtlety of his psychological exploration of jealousy and sexual guilt his achievement bears comparison with that of Shakespeare in *Othello.*[19]

Concerning the structure of *A Woman Killed with Kindness,* R. W. Van Fossen has observed, "The play opens with a wedding. It closes with a wedding that is also a funeral."[20] Shakespeare has modified the *novella* from Giraldi Cinthio's *Hecathommithi* that is his principal source for *Othello* to make his own play conform to the same pattern. Whereas in Cinthio the illicit marriage of the Moor and his Venetian bride is mentioned only in passing, Shakespeare conspicuously begins *Othello* on the night of the marriage of his interracial couple. In addition to beginning on the wedding night of Othello and Desdemona, the play parallels *A Woman Killed with Kindness* by concluding with what Michel Grivelet has called a "mariage restauré dans la mort."[21] Although the motif of love consummated in death is by no means confined to these two dramas, that it is

19. In *Elizabethan Revenge Tragedy 1587-1642* (1940; repr. Gloucester, Mass., 1959), Fredson Bowers remarks that in *A Woman Killed with Kindness* "Heywood had first put into dramatic form . . . the punishment which arises from the erring characters' consciousness of their guilt in place of the punishment of exterior physical revenge" (p. 225).

20. *A Woman Killed with Kindness,* ed. Van Fossen, p. xli.

21. Grivelet, *Thomas Heywood et le drame domestique Elisabéthain,* p. 306.

put to similar uses by Shakespeare and Heywood contributes to the un-
canny effect produced by reading *A Woman Killed with Kindness* as a
subtext of *Othello*.

When Anne is on her deathbed, after having starved herself as penance
for adultery, Frankford finally forgives her with the words, "And with
this kiss I wed thee once again" (xvii.117). Frankford's line corresponds to
the extraordinary couplet that is Othello's last speech in his play: "I kiss'd
thee ere I kill'd thee. No way but this, / Killing myself, to die upon a
kiss" (V.ii.358–359). Even the use of alliteration to collapse the opposites
of "killed" and "kindness" in Heywood's title is mirrored here, except
that Shakespeare employs chiasmus to heighten the effect of his own more
powerful antinomy of "kiss'd" and "kill'd." The conflation of Desdemona's marriage bed with her deathbed, the transformation of her
wedding sheets into her winding sheet, finds an analogue also in Frankford's lament after the death of Anne: "New marry'd and new widowed;
O, she's dead, / And a cold grave must be our nuptial bed" (xvii.123–
124). Desdemona's last words, moreover, are "Commend me to my kind
lord. O, farewell!" (V.ii.125), and Robert Heilman has pertinently won-
dered "whether the repetition of *kind* and *kindness* in *Othello* might not
have been felt as an allusion to Heywood's play." [22]

A Woman Killed with Kindness explores the sexual foundation of marriage, but especially in its subplot it does not neglect the economic
realities of domestic life; and in this respect, too, it provides an important
complement to *Othello*. Despite the happy ending brought about by
Acton's decision to marry Susan, the drama implicitly criticizes Mountford for the wasteful living that leads to his downfall. "I am now enforc'd
to follow husbandry, / And you to milk; and do we not live well" (vii.3–
4), says the impoverished aristocrat to his sister as he is on the point of
losing to his creditor, the scheming and upwardly mobile Shafton, "This
virgin title never yet deflower'd / By any unthrift of the Mountfords' line"
(vii.23–24). When Susan appeals to an elderly relative for financial assist-
ance, he answers sternly, "You say my nephew is in great distress— /Who
brought it to him but his own lewd life? / . . . / This is no world in
which to pity men" (ix.1–2,5). The notions of "unthrift" and "husbandry" receive a different emphasis elsewhere in the play when, as

22. Heilman, *Magic in the Web,* p. 284.

Nicholas approaches to warn Frankford of his wife's adultery, the latter interjects:

> Now, Nichlas, you want money,
> And unthrift-like would eat into your wages
> Ere you have earn'd it. Here's, sir, half a crown;
> Play the good husband, and away to supper.
>
> (viii. 27–30)

Although Frankford makes a characteristic mistake in his perception of Nicholas's reasons for wishing to speak to him, the passage is indicative of Heywood's condemnation of "unthrift" and his fusion (as in the previous metaphor of the "deflowering" of a "virgin title") of economic and sexual aspects of what it means to "Play the good husband." It is noteworthy that this very phrase appears in *The Taming of the Shrew* when old Vincentio denounces his son Lucentio's prodigality: "While I play the good husband at home, my son and my servant spend all at the university" (IV.v.68–70). In addition to reinforcing the thematic links between *A Woman Killed with Kindness* and *The Taming of the Shrew,* this direct verbal echo increases the probability that Heywood's title is indeed derived from Shakespeare's comedy.

The bourgeois values espoused by *A Woman Killed with Kindness* are announced in the Prologue, where Heywood advises the audience to "Look for no glorious state, our Muse is bent / Upon a barren subject, a bare scene" (ll. 13–14). In the first soliloquy following his marriage, Frankford likewise proclaims the virtues of moderation: "How happy am I amongst other men / That in my mean estate embrace content" (iv. 1–2). To the extent that Othello exceeds the "mean estate" of Frankford, *Othello* is more than a typical domestic drama. But like *A Woman Killed with Kindness, Othello* depicts "no world in which to pity men," and Shakespeare resembles Heywood in anatomizing the economic as well as sexual implications of "husbandry." Iago's repeated admonitions to Roderigo to "Put money in thy purse" and "Make all the money thou canst" (I. iii. 339, 354) define his role as chief "husband"—in the sense of "economist"—in the play.[23] His choice of imagery in insisting on the

23. See Heilman, "Iago as Economist," in *Magic in the Web,* pp. 73–85.

malleability of human nature, "Our bodies are our gardens, to the which our wills are gardeners" (I.iii.329–330), may likewise be understood as a literalization of the "husbandry" metaphor. The worldly practicality and retentiveness of Iago are contrasted with the "unthrift" and extravagance of Othello. Othello acknowledges his own carelessness when, in his suicide speech, he refers to himself as "one whose hand / (Like the base Indian) threw a pearl away / Richer than all his tribe" (V.ii.346–348). Othello's simile stresses the unnecessary wastefulness of his conduct, and his downfall does follow the pattern of domestic drama in showing the vulnerability of an aristocratic figure to the machinations of his bourgeois antagonist.

The affinity between *Othello* and *A Woman Killed with Kindness* is to a large extent explicable in terms of the common literary genealogy of both plays. As Shakespeare derived his inspiration from Cinthio, so Heywood found both his plots for *A Woman Killed with Kindness* in Italian *novelle,* as translated by Painter in his popular collection of stories from various writers, *The Palace of Pleasure.*[24] Heywood's innovation, as Van Fossen has observed, was to combine the Italianate plots with the "middle-class English setting" familiar from such earlier domestic tragedies as *Arden of Feversham* and *A Warning for Fair Women,* "and, concomitant with this setting, the realistic treatment of everyday life and domestic activity that contributes so much to the success of his play."[25] *Othello,* in keeping with its "glorious state," is set not in England but in Venice and Cyprus; but the play nonetheless shares with *A Woman Killed with Kindness*—and with Shakespeare's early comedies—a "realistic treatment of everyday life and domestic activity" that lends it a distinctively English quality.

In addition to blending English and Italian elements, both *Othello* and *A Woman Killed with Kindness* reveal the influence of medieval morality plays. H. H. Adams has argued that English domestic tragedy is an outgrowth of the homiletic tradition of fifteenth-century morality plays, where the action follows the outline of "sin, the intervention of Providence, and divine mercy," and in which "the plain citizen . . . first

24. The exact sources of the main plot of *A Woman Killed with Kindness* remain a matter of some controversy. See the discussion of Van Fossen in pp. xvii–xxvii of his edition.
25. *A Woman Killed with Kindness,* ed. Van Fossen, p. xxvi.

became recognized as a character suitable for serious drama." [26] Though certainly no "plain citizen," Othello differs from the heroes of Shakespeare's other major tragedies in not being of royal birth. Bernard Spivack has demonstrated the degree to which *Othello* partakes of the morality-play tradition, and Iago must be seen as the culminating example of the Vice figure on the English stage. [27] To recognize the medieval heritage shared by these plays is a needed complement to an emphasis upon their domestic themes, for only in the minds of some modern critics is realism incompatible with allegory.

Their common ancestry in medieval morality plays helps to explain a further unexpected similarity between *Othello* and *A Woman Killed with Kindness*. Drawing upon Cinthio, Shakespeare exploits the polarity of whiteness and blackness, as well as the related dichotomy of angel and devil, in his descriptions of various characters. Othello, when he has been convinced of Desdemona's unchastity, says that "Her name, that was as fresh / As Dian's visage, is now begrim'd and black / As mine own face" (III.iii.386–388); in the final scene, when Othello confesses that Desdemona's dying attempt to absolve him of her murder is false, Emilia exclaims: "O, the more angel she, / And you the blacker devil!" (V.ii.130–131). Although it lacks the interracial theme, *A Woman Killed with Kindness* nonetheless employs much the same sort of imagery. During the celebrated "card-playing scene," when Anne proposes that the assembled company "play at saint," Frankford mutters in an aside, "My saint's turn'd devil" (viii.150–151). Subsequently, as the repentant Anne is traveling to seek forgiveness from her husband, she says to herself: "But when my tears have wash'd my black soul white, / Sweet Saviour, to Thy hands I yield my sprite" (xvi.106–107); upon being approached by Wendoll, she calls out:

> My coach! This sin that with an angel's face
> Courted mine honour till he sought my wrack
> In my repentant eyes seems ugly black.
>
> (xvi.109–111)

26. Henry Hitch Adams, *English Domestic or Homiletic Tragedy* (New York, 1943), p. 55.

27. See Bernard Spivack, *Shakespeare and the Allegory of Evil: The History of a Metaphor in Relation to His Major Villains* (New York, 1958).

These polarities of blackness and whiteness and devil and angel in *A Woman Killed with Kindness* represent vestiges of the morality-play tradition. The theme of interracial marriage in *Othello* is thus in part an elaboration upon the contrast between inner spiritual reality and outward appearance also explored by Heywood.

In both *Othello* and *A Woman Killed with Kindness* the central situation is a triangular one. The pivotal triangle of *Othello,* though there are others, is that formed by Othello, Desdemona, and Iago; Frankford and Anne in *A Woman Killed with Kindness* evidently correspond to Othello and Desdemona, but both Nicholas and Wendoll embody aspects of Iago. (As the object of Frankford's jealousy, Wendoll is more nearly equivalent to Cassio, but in his intimacy with Frankford and his satanic quality he resembles Iago.) The importance of this triangular structure is that it points up how, in both dramas, the primary focus on romantic, heterosexual love is balanced by that on homosexual, male friendship. As Van Fossen has remarked, Wendoll's scruples do not hinge on the immorality of seducing Anne; rather, "his real concern is for the violation of his friendship with Frankford, who has been both friend and benefactor." [28] From a psychological standpoint, indeed, Wendoll's bond to Frankford provides the hidden motivation for his attraction to Anne, as well as for her capitulation. Upon Wendoll's arrival in Frankford's household, the latter somewhat mysteriously announces that he has "preferr'd him to a second place / In my opinion and best regard" (iv.34–35). When Frankford is forced to depart on business, Anne tells Wendoll, he leaves instructions that his friend "be a present Frankford in his absence" (vi.79). In seducing Anne, Wendoll is, as it were, only taking Frankford's invitation literally—that is, acting out his role as Frankford's double. *A Woman Killed with Kindness* may be a domestic drama, but its "middle-class English setting" does not exempt it from the oedipal configurations exhibited by the more notorious adulterous triangles of medieval romance—Mark, Isolde, and Tristan or Arthur, Guinevere, and Lancelot. The conflict between homosexuality and heterosexuality figures prominently also in the tragedy of Othello, who, when he receives Iago's pledge at the close

---

28. *A Woman Killed with Kindness*, ed. Van Fossen, p. xxxii. See also Louis B. Wright, "The Male-friendship Cult in Thomas Heywood's Plays," *MLN,* XLII (1927), 510–514.

of the "temptation scene," "I am your own for ever" (III.iii.479), appears to be married as much to his male betrayer as he is to Desdemona.

A final parallel between *Othello* and *A Woman Killed with Kindness* remains to be noted. Beginning with Rymer, one of the charges most frequently leveled against Shakespeare's artistry in *Othello* concerns the implausibility of the time scheme in the play—the fact that Othello and Desdemona have been married too briefly to lend credence to Iago's insinuations of a long-standing love affair between Desdemona and Cassio. It is at least a coincidence that *A Woman Killed with Kindness* is liable to a similar objection.[29] Although the play proceeds without obvious interruption from the opening wedding scene, in scene xiii, after Frankford confronts Anne with her infidelity, two children are suddenly produced by Heywood to heighten the pathos of Anne's guilt and repentance. However one explains the relation between the "double time" of *Othello* and *A Woman Killed with Kindness,* evidently neither Shakespeare nor Heywood hesitated to sacrifice chronological plausibility to heighten the effectiveness of his drama on the stage.

That the convergences I have documented between these two dramas are many and striking can, I think, hardly be doubted. Nor is the similarity between *Othello* and *A Woman Killed with Kindness* solely a discovery of recent criticism. In the subsequent history of Jacobean tragedy, the legacies of these works by Shakespeare and Heywood are intimately intertwined. Such plays as Marston's *The Malcontent,* Webster's *The White Devil,* Middleton and Rowley's *The Changeling,* and Ford's *'Tis Pity She's a Whore* and *Love's Sacrifice* all show their authors' acquaintance with either *A Woman Killed with Kindness* or *Othello* or both.[30] Accustomed as we are to

29. See Cook, "*A Woman Killed with Kindness*: An Unshakespearian Tragedy," p. 372.

30. Grivelet, in *Thomas Heywood et le drame domestique Elisabéthain,* suggests a view of Marston as an "anti-Heywood" (p. 297) and argues that the character of Duke Pietro in *The Malcontent* constitutes "la réplique burlesque de Frankford" (p. 299); he further notes that the last words of Isabella in *The White Devil,* "Unkindness do thy office, poor heart break, / Those are the killing griefs which dare not speak" (II.i.276–277), "semblent faire subtilement écho à ceux qui résument le destin d'Anne Frankford" (p. 308). The character of De Flores in *The Changeling* is evidently modeled on that of Iago, just as the passage in *Love's Sacrifice* in which D'Avolos arouses the jealousy of the Duke is derived from the "temptation scene" in *Othello.* One of the most interesting examples of the combined influence of *A Woman Killed with Kindness* and *Othello* is to be found in *'Tis Pity She's a*

studying and teaching Shakespeare's plays as a self-contained canon, it is salutary to be reminded that his works belong to traditions and genres— including domestic drama—also practiced by his contemporaries. At the same time, it should enhance our appreciation of *A Woman Killed with Kindness* to see Heywood's achievement as the same in kind, if not in degree, as that of Shakespeare.

Perhaps the most remarkable instance of a play indebted to both *Othello* and *A Woman Killed with Kindness,* moreover, is Heywood's own *The English Traveller,* where, in reworking his successful formula for domestic tragedy of some twenty years earlier, he simultaneously came under the spell of Shakespeare's greater creation. The imprint of *Othello* on *The English Traveller* is unmistakable in the scene where the Iago-like Delavil attempts to persuade Old Geraldine that the latter's son is having an affair with the wife of Old Wincott. Delavil insinuates, "For my part / How can I love the person of your son, / And not his reputation?" and further adds of the suspected couple, "yet in my conscience / I think them truly honest" (III.i, pp. 195–196).[31] Inasmuch as "honest" appears in both *A Woman Killed with Kindness* and *Othello,* it is fittingly circular that this same word should be reiterated by Delavil in the course of the scene, where the response of Old Geraldine implicitly casts him in the role of Othello (though it is not his wife whose chastity is impugned): "You have, sir /Possessed me with such strange fancies—" (III.i, p.195). In 1624, contemporaneously with *The English Traveller,* Heywood published

---

Whore, where, though Ford has drawn most extensively from *Romeo and Juliet,* conspicuous traces of *Othello* are present in the scene of Giovanni's murder of Annabella—"To save thy fame and kill thee in a kiss" (V.v.84), he vows—and of *A Woman Killed with Kindness* in the declaration of the Iago-like Vasques, "As sure as I am an honest man, he will go near to kill my lady with unkindness" (IV.iii.185–187). These references do not exhaust the influence of *A Woman Killed with Kindness* and *Othello* on the drama of their time, but do suffice to indicate its extent. For further discussion of Heywood's influence, see Grivelet, *Thomas Heywood et le drame domestique Elisabéthain,* pp. 294–316; and Alwine Winkler, *Thomas Heywood's "A Woman Killed with Kindness" und das Ehebruchsdrama seiner Zeit* (Borna-Leipzig, 1915).

31. Quotations from *The English Traveller* are from *Thomas Heywood,* ed. A. Wilson Verity, The Mermaid Series (New York, n.d.), with act, scene, and page numbers included parenthetically in the text. See the useful discussion of *The English Traveller* in Stilling, *Love and Death in Renaissance Tragedy,* pp. 183–194.

a lengthy prose treatise on women, *Gunaikeion,* in which the attitude expressed toward the punishment of adultery recalls that of *A Woman Killed with Kindness*:

The errours . . . and vices of the wife are either to be corrected, or indured. . . . But much is that inhumane rashness to be auoided by which men haue undertooke to be their owne justicers, and haue mingled the pollution of their bdes [*sic*] with the blood of the delinquents. . . . Besides, such as will not be reformed by counsell are by the Lawes to be punished.[32]

Although there is no reference in *Gunaikeion* to *Othello,* it is tempting to speculate that here, as in *The English Traveller,* there is a recollection of Shakespeare's play in Heywood's indictment of that "inhumane rashness . . . by which men haue undertooke to be their owne justicers."

But if the analogies between *Othello* and *A Woman Killed with Kindness* were recognized by contemporary dramatists, what of the additional possibility that one play constitutes a direct source for the other? The available historical evidence may be briefly summarized. We know from Henslowe's diary that *A Woman Killed with Kindness* was first performed by Worcester's Men in March 1602/3, though the first extant edition dates from a presumably unauthorized printing in 1607.[33] *Othello* is known to have been produced at court on 1 November 1604.[34] Although it is impossible to determine whether this performance was a premiere, *Othello* is customarily dated 1604; and the interval of more than eighteen months between the established dates of production thus makes it highly probable that *Othello* is the later play, and that any conceivable indebtedness must be on the part of Shakespeare rather than Heywood.

By 1604, *A Woman Killed with Kindness* was sufficiently popular to be the subject of familar allusion. A passage from *The Blacke Booke,* ascribed

32. Thomas Heywood, *Gunaikeion: or, Nine Bookes of Various History Concerninge Women; Inscribed by the Names of the Nine Muses* (London, 1624), pp. 178–179. The relevance of this passage from *Gunaikeion* to *A Woman Killed with Kindness* was first remarked by Grivelet, *Thomas Heywood et le drame domestique Elisabéthain,* p. 84.

33. See *Henslowe's Diary,* ed. R. A. Foakes and R. T. Rickert (Cambridge, Eng., 1961), pp. 223–225; and the information on dating supplied by Van Fossen on pp. xvi-xvii and lxiv-lxix of his edition of *A Woman Killed with Kindness.*

34. See *The Riverside Shakespeare,* ed. Evans, p. 54.

to Middleton, refers to the play while explaining how a wife may cuckold her husband:

And being set out of the shop, with her man afore her, to quench the jealousy of her husband, she, by thy instructions, shall turn the honest, simple fellow off at the next turning, and give him leave to see *The Merry Devil of Edmonton,* or *A Woman Killed with Kindness,* when his mistress is going herself, to the same murder.[35]

In addition to the widespread popularity of *A Woman Killed with Kindness,* what we have seen of the anticipation of Heywood's title in *The Taming of the Shrew* would give Shakespeare a particular reason to take interest in a play which alluded so conspicuously to his own work. Although there was no printed edition of *A Woman Killed with Kindness* before the writing of *Othello,* and it is unlikely that Shakespeare would have had access to one of the few manuscript copies of a work by an author belonging to a rival company, it is entirely conceivable to suppose that he could have become familiar with Heywood's play in the same way as did most of his fellow Londoners—by seeing it performed in the theater.[36] The period of less than two years between the appearance of Heywood's play and its presumed assimilation into *Othello,* furthermore, would conform to what we know of Shakespeare's habitual practice of making topical allusions and imitating the works of other writers in his own dramas.[37]

Whether or not the numerous echoes and parallels between *A Woman Killed with Kindness* and *Othello* are the result of specific indebtedness, they justify us in speaking of Heywood's play as a subtext of Shakespeare's. There is no decisive argument against the hypothesis that Shakespeare was directly influenced by Heywood, and a good deal of both circumstantial and textual evidence in support of it. I accordingly conclude that *A Woman Killed with Kindness* should be considered a probable source as well as an analogue for *Othello.*

35. Quoted in *A Woman Killed with Kindness,* ed. Van Fossen, p. lix.

36. I am grateful to Professor Bernard Beckerman for clarification of this point.

37. I am indebted both to John Wands and to James Bednarz, "Imitations of Spenser in *A Midsummer Night's Dream,*" on the questions of imitation and topical allusion in Shakespeare.

The Crafty Enchaunter:
Ironic Satires and Jonson's
Every Man Out of His Humour

FRANK KERINS

Inchauntment, *Ned* hath ravished my sence
In a Poetick vaine circumference.
Yet thus I hope, (God shield I now should lie)
Many more fooles, and most more wise then I.[1]

W HEN JOHN MARSTON introduced "*SATYRA NOVA*" in the second edition of his *Scourge of Villanie* he provided us with a gloss for reading both his own satires and the works of a number of his contemporaries. We have unfortunately become accustomed to viewing Marston's excesses and incongruities as those of an overwrought moralist or a borderline psychotic. Perhaps we might discover more about the nature of Elizabethan satire by seeking out an ironic basis in Marston's satiric art—the kind of irony that appears to be embodied in the final lines of "*SATYRA NOVA*," lines which form the epigraph of this essay. In this verse epistle to Everard Guilpin, Marston displays a much more measured

---

1. John Marston, "*SATYRA NOVA*," ll. 81–84, in *The Poems of John Marston*, ed. Arnold Davenport (Liverpool, 1961), p. 166. All quotations from Marston are from this edition. The i/j and u/v forms have been silently modernized in all Elizabethan citations.

and rational tone than in the frenzied satires that precede it in *The Scourge of Villanie*. Rather than the shrill ravings of his satiric persona, "W. Kinsayder," here we are presented with an authorial voice—one that can address a friend and fellow poet and look ironically on the psychological degeneration of the satirist Marston himself had created. This bifurcated satiric plot—a progression from Juvenalian indignation, through a mad "Inchauntment" with its own successes, finally culminating in a realization of the commonality of human frailty—is, I will suggest, the very cornerstone of the volumes of verse satire that emerged from the Inns of Court in the final years of the sixteenth century.

It is easy, however, to dismiss these satires as an embarrassing anomaly, an evolutionary dead end in the development of satire. Like Neanderthal Man, Elizabethan satire can be seen as crude, misshapen, and lacking in that rational and moral balance so evident in both the Romans and their eighteenth-century adaptors. But if we are to understand the influence that contemporary satire exerted on Ben Jonson's "Comicall Satyres," we must remove our Roman and neoclassical spectacles and view these plays in the light of Elizabethan satiric conventions. One fact unique to the satires of the late 1590s is that these works appeared not singly but in complete volumes. If the satiric persona is to be treated as an ironic figure, as I have suggested he is in Marston, might not the entire volume of satires reveal a carefully articulated plot concerning the satirist's own changing relationship to the world he confronts? Although the limitations of this paper preclude a thorough study of the structure of Elizabethan satiric volumes, a useful purpose can be served by comparing those few satiric poems that function as ironic commentaries on these volumes with the dramatic structure of Jonson's earliest "Comicall Satyre."

Jonson produced *Every Man Out of His Humour* in the months immediately following the June 1599 Bishops' ban on the publication of verse satire. By calling his play a "Comicall Satyre," Jonson clearly intended to exploit the contemporary furor over verse satire and to encourage into the theater the very audience for whom the satires had been written. Ever since Oscar Campbell's pioneering study we have been aware that many of the same abuses and satiric targets familiar from the poems reappear with little modification in the "Comicall Satyres." [2] In a

2. Oscar James Campbell, *Comicall Satyre and Shakespeare's Troilus and Cressida* (San Marino, Calif. 1938).

recent rebuttal, however, L. A. Beaurline denies the relevance of contemporary verse satire and suggests that we approach the plays with a view toward Jonson's sense of the harmonizing dramatic structure, a structure revealing itself most forcefully through "a compelling movement to an overwhelming conclusion." [3] Insofar as Beaurline's concern is for the progressive unfolding of these plays his corrective is useful, but his casual dismissal of Jonson's own term, "Comical Satyre," is altogether misleading. A number of Elizabethan satires familiar to Jonson were structured precisely along the lines that Beaurline discovers in Jonson's plays. By comparing these verse satires with the structure of Jonson's comedy we can see just how closely Jonson imitates Elizabethan satiric form.

During the time he was writing these innovative comedies Jonson's relationship with satirists like Marston and Guilpin was a close one. Many years later Jonson remarked to Drummond that he had been involved in numerous arguments with Marston and "wrote his Poetaster on him." [4] From this statement some have asumed that Jonson had always scorned Marston and his work. In 1599, however, the year of both *"SATYRA NOVA"* and *Every Man Out of His Humour,* there appeared a commendatory poem that seems to view the pair as friends and equals:

> *Epig.* 11 *Ad Jo: Marston & Ben: Johnson.*
> *Marston,* thy Muse enharbours *Horace* vaine,
> Then some *Augustus* give thee *Horace* merit,
> And thine embuskin'd *Johnson* doth retaine
> So rich a stile, and wondrous gallant spirit;
> That if to praise your Muses I desired,
> My Muse would muse. Such wittes must be admired. [5]

The poet who wrote these lines, John Weever, turned against Marston in 1601, but significantly he included both Jonson and Guilpin in his censure—labeling them collectively as "The VAYNE-GLORIOUS, / The

3. L. A. Beaurline, *Jonson and Elizabethan Comedy* (San Marino, Calif. 1978), p. 105.

4. Ben Jonson, *Conversations with Drummond,* in Ben Jonson, *Works,* ed. C. H. Herford and P. and E. Simpson (Oxford, 1925-1952), I, 140. All quotations from Jonson will be to this edition, cited in the text as *H & S.*

5. John Weever, *Epigrammes* (1599), quoted in A. Davenport, ed., *The Whipper Pamphlets* (1601), 2 vols. (Liverpool, 1951), I, viii.

Satyrist, Epigrammatist, and Humorist" and addressing them ironically as "Most worthy Triumviri." [6] It is clear, both in the 1599 commendation and the 1601 censure, that Weever saw Jonson not as a radically original dramatist but rather as the "embuskin'd" representative of the "Triumviri" of innovative satiric poets.

I

Certainly the most neglected of this "Triumviri" is Everard Guilpin. Many twentieth-century critics seem to agree with C. S. Lewis in dismissing Guilpin as "beneath criticism." [7] In his own age, however, no less than John Donne praised his wit and allowed him access to his own unpublished *Satyre* I. [8] Guilpin's *Skialetheia / or / A Shadowe of Truth* [9] appeared in 1598 containing epigrams and satires that imitated, parodied, and deftly played against much of the contemporary literary scene. D. Allen Carroll, in his recent edition, notes that in Guilpin "Words are slippery, duplicitous, masking in one signification only to function underneath toward a different, more significant end." [10] When Guilpin opens his "Satire V" with a blatant twelve-line imitation of Donne's *Satyre* I, critics question whether Guilpin is honoring Donne or plagiarizing him. [11] The pun in the poem's final line seems, however, to resolve the question: "Now let us home, I'me sure tis supper time, / The horne hath blowne, have done my merry rime." Guilpin's persona always plays the student poet imitating others—sometimes good-naturedly as here but often with a savage irony lurking beneath the surface.

6. (John Weever), *The Whipping of the Satyre*, in *Whipper Pamphlets*, I, 3. Davenport conclusively identifies the three in his "Introduction," v-viii.

7. C. S. Lewis, *English Literature in the Sixteenth Century Excluding Drama* (Oxford, 1954), p. 475.

8. See Donne's "To Mr. E. G.," in *John Donne: The Satires, Epigrams and Verse Letters*, ed. W. Milgate (Oxford, 1967), p. 64 with the editor's commentary, pp. 116–117, and pp. 216–217.

9. Everard Guilpin, *Skialetheia or A Shadowe of Truth*, in *Certaine Epigrams and Satyres*, ed. D. Allen Carroll (Chapel Hill, N.C., 1974). All quotations from Guilpin are from this edition.

10. Carroll, "Introduction" to *Skialetheia*, p. 22.

11. A. Alvarez, *The School of Donne* (New York, 1967), p. 147.

The most important poem for an understanding of Guilpin is his
"Satire I"—a poem that both explains Guilpin's own satiric method and
provides a close analogue for the climax of *Every Man Out of His Humour*.
"Satire I" begins with a persona dressed in the cloak of the Roman satirists
blatantly imitating the opening lines of Juvenal's first satire:

> Shall I still mych in silence and give ayme,
> To other wits which make court to bright fame?
> A schoole boy still, shall I lend eare to other,
> And myne owne private Muses musick smother?
>
> (ll. 1–4)

The ostensible pose is one of fierce indignation, an irrespressible attack on
"this sinne leapered age" (l. 5). The satirist views a world: "Where vertue,
like a common gossop shieldes / Vice with her name, and her defects
ore-guilds" (ll. 9-10). While the targets of Juvenal's first satire were greed
and extravagance,[12] Guilpin's focus throughout "Satire I" is hypocrisy in
all its forms. The vices this satirist attacks are not those gross enormities
that outraged Juvenal but rather the more subtle vices of the modern age,
vices masked by a semblance of virtue. The great irony of "Satire I,"
however, is the progressive realization that Guilpin's champion of virtue
is himself a hypocrite, hiding his own villainy beneath the cloak of
self-righteous indignation. The satirist's pretensions are finally exploded
in a climactic passage:

> Oh that the whip of fooles, great *Aretine*,
> Whose words were squibs, and crackers every line,
> Liv'd in our dayes, to scourge these hypocrites,
> . . . .
> Oh how the varges from his blacke pen wrung,
> Would sauce the *Idiome* of the English tongue,
> Give it a new touch, livelier Dialect
> To heare this two-neckt goose, this falshood checkt.
>   Me thinks I see the pie-bald whoresone tremble
> To heare of *Aretine*: he doth dissemble,
> There is no trust to be had to his quaking,
> To him once more, and rouse him from his shaking

12. Gilbert Highet, *Juvenal the Satirist* (1954; repr. New York, 1961), p. 246.

Feaver of fained feare, hold whip and cord,
Muse, play the Beadle, a lash at every word:
No, no, let be, he's a true cosener still,
And like the Cramp-fish darts, even throgh my quil
His slie insinuating poysonous juice,
And doth the same into my Spirit infuse.

(ll. 143–162)

What had begun as an imitation of the high-minded persona of Juvenal now ends with an invocation to one of the most ambiguous satirists of the age. In addition to his reputation as a satirist "Aretino was famous—or infamous—in England in the late sixteenth and early seventeenth centuries for his works of pornography, perhaps the first of their kind in Christendom." [13] Apparently this satirist sees no real differences between Juvenal and Aretino, viewing them both as appropriate models. Indeed, the sordid reputation of Aretino provides a sharply ironic commentary on Guilpin's irate champion of virtue. In these lines Guilpin completes the satiric structure through a pattern of iterative imagery which perfectly realizes the double perspective of his satiric plot. His satirist invokes the image of Aretino and muses on how he, if still alive, would have dealt with the hypocrisy now rampant in England. The harsh style of Aretino is described as "varges from his blacke pen wrung." "*Varges*" or verjuice, as Carroll points out (p. 165), "is the acid juice 'wrung' from crab apples, formed into a liquor, and used for cooking or medicinal purposes (*OED*)." This verjuice would spice the tongue (both of the English language and audience) in order to sharpen the sensitivity of the society toward all forms of hypocrisy. Guilpin, however, explodes his assertive satirist by developing the verjuice image into one of "slie insinuating poysonous juice" which both "darts, even throgh my quil" . . . "And doth the same into my Spirit infuse." The sharp juice with which he enlivens the morality of the world is also the venomous hypocrisy of a satirist who claims to be morally pure. The satirist must finally become self-conscious and realize his own hypocrisy:

13. Saad El-Gabalawy, "Aretino's Pornography and English Renaissance Satire," *HAB*, XXVIII (1977), 9.

> Me thinks already I applaud my selfe,
> For nettle-stinging thus this fayery elfe:
> And though my conscience sayes I merit not
> Such deere reward, dissembling yet (God wot)
> I hunt for praise, and doe the same expect:
> Hence (crafty enchaunter) welcome base neglect,
> Scoffes make me know my selfe, I must not erre,
> *Better a wretch then a dissembler.*
>
> (ll. 163–170)

These lines give us the clearest explication of Guilpin's satiric perspective. As the satiric plot develops it bifurcates into an attack on two concentric circles of dissimulation: the world in general swollen with an immense array of hypocrites; and *the satirist himself* who, unaware of his own participation in this fallen world, swells in indignation and pride as he lashes out at the sins of others. As the poem progresses, the two plots are increasingly contrasted by ironic iteration: the self-aggrandizement of the hypocrites is duplicated in the swelling anger of the narrator. At the climax of the satirist's indignation, he finally surfeits on his own villainy and is reduced to a startled awareness of his own sinful condition. In this act of recognition he is purged of all satiric venom through the banishment of his "crafty enchaunter," hypocrisy: "Scoffes make me know my selfe, I must not erre, / *Better a wretch then a dissembler.*"

The "crafty enchaunter" is a ubiquitous theme in the satires of Guilpin and Marston. When Marston tells Guilpin that "Inchauntment, *Ned* hath ravished my sence / In a Poetick vaine circumference," he reiterates Guilpin's theme that an excessively censorious attitude inflates one with pride and hypocrisy, creating a bloated, invenomed condition greatly in need of spiritual purgation. For Marston, as Guilpin, the arrogant moralist is ultimately a fool or madman. In censuring the world he ironically blinds himself to his own imperfections. In *"SATYRA NOVA"* Marston comments on the role of the satirist, a role he had been playing furiously throughout *The Scourge of Villanie*:

> Who'le scorne to sitte in ranke of foolery
> When I'le be maister of the company?
> For pre-thee *Ned,* I pre-thee gentle lad,
> Is he not frantique, foolish, bedlam mad,

That wastes his spright, that melts his very braine
In deepe designes, in wits darke gloomie straine?
That scourgeth great slaves with a dreadlesse fist,
Playing the rough part of a Satyrist?

(ll. 7–14)

In Marston, the satirist is always a theatrical role—one that he assumes in order to deflate the pretensions of assertive satire.

In *The Scourge of Villanie,* this satirist is given the name "W. Kinsayder," and the "Proem" of Book I shows him invoking the psychologically disoriented state that will allow him to villify the world: here the satirist entreats "*Melancholy*" to enthrone herself within his "jocond" blood to distort the natural flow of his spirits and force his brain to "runne / A sadde pac'd course, untill my whips be done" (ll. 9–14). The frame of the entire volume is completed by the last satire, "*Humours,*" in which "Dull sprighted *Melancholy*" is banished in favor of "Cheeke dimpling laughter" (ll. 1–10). In "*SATYRA NOVA*" Marston specifically exorcizes the satiric "humor," that insidious enchanter as spiritually debilitating as it is self-flattering: "Out on this humour. From a sickly bed, / And from a moodie minde distempered, / I vomit foorth my love." (ll. 73–75). The satirist ends up "scorning the honour of a Poets state" (l. 76), finally aware that the wielding of the satiric scourge is itself a "humour," a psychological seduction that results in a "minde distempered" requiring purgation. Throughout his satires Marston had used the bombastically arrogant W. Kinsayder as a parody of Joseph Hall's Juvenalian satirist. Here in "*SATYRA NOVA*" his reply to Hall's censure of him is simple: "*Medice cura teipsum*" (Physician heal thyself). Yet Marston is never without some self-deflating comic irony. The diseased physician in his "sickly bed" is not here Joseph Hall, nor is he simply W. Kinsayder—he is finally Marston himself.

To Guilpin and Marston all who engage in assertive satire eventually become corrupted by the necessarily Olympian vantage point they assume—a perspective that denies the satirist's own humanity. Thus the self-conscious satirist, after purging the world of its vanities, must finally be purged himself of the overweening pride and hypocrisy that his satiric perspective had nourished. In this connection these Inns of Court ironists might well have seized on Joseph Hall's own fanciful etymology for satire—"*Sat irae*" ("full of ire").[14] In the process of writing satires, the satirist fills himself to repletion with immoderate passion—leading himself into a state of psychological and moral turmoil at least as grave as any of his victims. In Guilpin's "*Satyre Preludium*," the narrator, after having demonstrated a suspicious familiarity with nearly every variety of contemporary lascivious writing, abruptly pontificates:

> The Satyre onely and Epigramatist,
> (Concisde Epigrame, and sharpe Satyrist)
> Keepe diet from this surfet of excesse,
> Tempring themselves from such licenciousnes.
>
> (ll. 65–68)

Here Guilpin is certainly being ironic, for the "surfet of excesse" precisely describes the satirist's moral development through his writings. It is only through the recognition and elimination of his "crafty enchaunter" that the satirist's moral stability can be finally restored. In *The Scourge of Villanie* this point is reached in the final lines of "*SATYRA NOVA*." Once these vitriolic passions are banished, Marston's narrator is freed to invoke a new "jocond Muse" in the opening lines of "*Humours*," the final satire of *The Scourge of Villanie*:

> . . . come sporting meriment,
> Cheeke dimpling laughter, crowne my very soule
> With jouisance, whilst mirthfull jests controule
> The goutie humours of these pride-swolne dayes,
> Which I doe long untill my pen displaies.
> O I am great with mirth, some midwifrie,
> Or I shall breake my sides at vanitie.
>
> (ll. 6–12)

In this poem the attitude is one of bemused tolerance instead of irascible indignation. The same passion-driven creatures who had been scourged in the earlier satires reappear here as comical figures. In the midst of them is seen an angry satirist who is "naught but censure" (l. 110) finally di-

---

14. Joseph Hall, "De suis Satyris" (l. 1) from *Virgedemiae* (1597), in *The Poems of Joseph Hall*, ed. Arnold Davenport (Liverpool, 1949), p. 10. This etymology was later used by Weever in his 1600 *Faunus and Melliflora*, ed. A. Davenport (London, 1948), l. 1068.

minished to the level of a typical humourist—just one more character in a landscape of fools abounding with excessive, misdirected activity. Although Marston employs the idea of a progressive satiric humor throughout his works, he never fully explicates it as a structural concept. It required Ben Jonson's feel for the concrete dramatic image to refine this notion into an articulated theory of humours—a theory that more precisely defines the satirist's moral development than Marston is capable of explaining in his own satires.

II

During the years when these volumes of verse satire were being published, events in the theater were moving in a parallel direction. In 1597 George Chapman's *An Humourous Day's Mirth* burst upon the scene as one of the most popular plays of the season, especially among courtiers.[15] In 1598 another self-taught intellectual, Ben Jonson, followed in Chapman's footsteps with *Every Man In His Humour.* Thus by 1599 the Comedy of Humours had emerged as a theatrically successful vehicle for sporting with human follies. Although there was little new in the complex intrigues of either play, their popularity seems to derive from the playwrights' close observation of the contemporary scene, those eccentricities in fashion and manners which were becoming more and more apparent as increasing numbers of people sought to cultivate courtly mannerisms and the kinds of singularity that could distinguish one from the crowd. The Comedy of Humours could well be termed wit's descant upon contemporary affectation. Like the *Epigrammes* of Sir John Davies, these plays employed supremely witty protagonists who could exhibit the humours of their foolish companions with the easy grace of a languid quip. Chapman's Lemot is almost the personification of verbal dexterity in action, and Jonson's young gallants, Lorenzo Jr. and Prospero, combine Plautine traits with the casual elegance of the most sophisticated of courtiers. In these comedies Chapman and Jonson crafted a flattering mirror for the enjoyment of the courtly audience for whom they were written.

15. W. David Kay, "The Shaping of Ben Jonson's Career: A Reexamination of Facts and Problems," *MP*, LXVI-LXVII (1968–1970), 228.

By naming his next play *Every Man Out of His Humour,* Jonson enticed his audience (and more importantly the censors) into the false supposition that what he was offering them was another witty but basically innocuous example of the popular Comedy of Humours. But, by including the epithet, "A Comicall Satyre," Jonson intimated to the literati something of the direction this radically innovative play was to take. In this area, however, discretion was crucial, for only a few months before this play hit the boards there appeared the famous Order of Conflagration including a ban of future satiric publications. Having gained a public reputation as a "Humourist," Ben Jonson was ideally prepared in 1599 to exploit that reputation and extend the Comedy of Humours in a moral direction—in effect, creating a dramatic revitalization of contemporary verse satire.

When we compare the structure of *Every Man Out of His Humour* with that of any of Jonson's earlier plays, we find that its most notable departures are in its employment of ironic distancing devices—notably its use of Induction and Chorus. Although the Induction seems to be a bridge between the real world and the fictive world of the drama, its true function is to act as a buffer between these worlds, heightening our perception of the artificial nature of the dramatic action that is to ensue. In the Induction to each of Jonson's "Comicall Satyres," the characters invariably discuss the play *as* play and, in so doing, diminish our suspension of disbelief—shifting our focus from emotional involvement to critical detachment.[16] In all of the "Comicall Satyres" this technique is employed, but in *Every Man Out,* with the addition of a Chorus that frequently interrupts the action and an Epilogue in which all the Induction figures re-emerge to give their final comments, this technique is central. The basic action of *Every Man Out,* the donning of the scourger's mask, its final explosion, and the subsequent reappearance of the moralist newly restored to humanity, is a perfect dramatic representation of the ironic satires of Marston and Guilpin.

As the Induction of *Every Man Out* opens, we are immediately thrust into a situation of dramatic conflict. Two gentlemen, Cordatus and Mitis,

---

16. Lynn Humphrey Elliott, "Engagement and Detachment: The Function of the Induction in Ben Jonson's Plays," Ph.D. dissertation, University of California (Santa Barbara), 1972.

are attempting to mollify the angry outbursts of Asper, a moralist so
overwrought with indignation that he loses all sense of social decorum:

> But (with an armed, and resolved hand)
> Ile strip the ragged follies of the time,
> Naked, as at their birth:
> CORDATUS
> (Be not too bold.
> ASPER
> You trouble me) and with a whip of steele,
> Print wounding lashes in their iron ribs.
>
> (Ind., ll. 16–21)

Right from the outset the dramatic contrast between Asper's indignation
and the civility of his companions isolates him as a creature of excess.
Cordatus's little interjection, "Be not too bold," effectively defuses the
growing power of Asper's rhetoric, reminding us that this satirist is not
alone on a lectern but purportedly engaged in a conversation with friends.
If Asper were sent out by himself to deliver the Prologue, his rage would
be more effectively realized. But in the context of the Induction his
fulmination stands out as an excessive, inappropriate display of trucu-
lence. Instead of talking *to* Cordatus and Mitis, he talks *at* them. Indeed,
after his friend's interjection, the satirist doesn't even deign to begin a
new sentence. He merely brushes off the disturbance, finds his place, and
resumes his oration.

Critics have generally neglected the function of the Chorus in this play.
These gracious courtiers are, however, much more than a passive audience
for Asper's execrations. Their observations serve at every turn to counter-
point the histrionics of this continually indignant satirist. Asper, however, is not merely a burlesque of the satirist figure. In the "Character" of
Asper, added to the (1600) published edition, Jonson describes him as *"an
ingenious and free spirit, eager and constant in reproofe"* (*H & S* III: 423). There
is no hint of irony in these lines. In Asper, Jonson creates an idealized
image of the assertive Juvenalian satirist. One function of the Induction,
however, is to illustrate the deficiencies of this ideal once it is realized in a
sophisticated social environment. Through their admonitions, Cordatus
and Mitis demonstrate the futility of Asper's rage:

MITIS

Gentle Asper,
Containe your spirit in more stricter bounds,
And be not thus transported with the violence
Of your strong thoughts.

CORDATUS

Unlesse your breath had power
To melt the world, and mould it new againe,
It is in vaine, to spend it in these moods.

(Ind., ll. 45–51)

In this satirist-Chorus relationship of the Induction Jonson creates what seems to be a dramatic parallel to the bifurcated satire of Marston and Guilpin. But, by modifying the relationship of satirist and commentator, he shifts the tone of his work. Once Asper is cast in the role of ideal moralist, the heavy irony which permeates the verse satires is necessarily diminished. In its stead we find a more balanced dialectic setting the emotional idealism of Asper against the civilized pragmatism of the Chorus. In the Induction this dialectic is left unresolved. We need not choose between the perspectives of Asper and Cordatus since both viewpoints are integral to the play. Instead, we are invited to view the play from a detached, judicial vantage point and to consider the main theme of the Induction—the problem of the assertive satirist in contemporary society.

In the Induction the difficulties he will encounter in the real world are constantly being pointed out to Asper only to have him scorn all timidity. The subject of Humours is first introduced by Mitis who warns Asper of his own Humour—being "too peremptorie" (ll. 73–74). This enrages Asper to such a degree that he becomes confused and totally forgets the cause of his anger:

MITIS

I, I pray you proceede.

ASPER

Ha? what? what is't?

CORDATUS

For the abuse of Humour.

ASPER

O, I crave pardon, I had lost my thoughts.

(ll. 85–88)

After regaining his composure Asper launches into his famous lecture on "Humour" without once realizing that the character he describes is the mirror image of himself as he appears to others. Asper defines humour in man as that condition in which "one peculiar quality / Doth so possesse a man, that it doth draw / All his affects, his spirits, and his powers, / In their confluctions, all to runne one way" (ll. 105–108). The main problem with Asper's definition is that he discusses humour only in terms of its final solidified manifestation—the condition of moral immobility in which the higher faculties are incapacitated by that "one peculiar quality" which preordains all thoughts and actions. Although this final state of calcified humour is the topic of Asper's oration, none of the characters whom Asper intends to reform exhibits this fully realized condition. They all merely "affect a Humour" (l. 113), and Asper vows to scourge them in his play to show "the times deformitie / Anatomiz'd in every nerve, and sinnew" (ll. 120–121). Because these ape-humourists are not totally possessed by their humour, they retain the mental capacity to be shamed into a recognition of their own folly. In this play there is only one character who has reached the final state of solidified humour, and that character is Asper himself.[17] The very fact that Asper is the epitome of the satiric perspective renders him a fully developed humourist on the human level—totally possessed by venomous indignation:

> CORDATUS
> Why this is right *Furor Poeticus*!
> Kind gentlemen, we hope your patience
> Will yet conceive the best, or entertaine
> This supposition, that a mad-man speakes.
>
> (ll. 147–150)

In this address to the audience Cordatus emphasizes the ambiguous nature of the ideal satirist in the real world—both "the best" in terms of his necessary function and "a mad-man" in the eyes of society.

Because the satiric impulse is always vulnerable to charges of hypocrisy, Jonson realized that the satirist must be clearly distanced from his creator.

17. My analysis of the progressive development of humours is greatly indebted to Robert Shenk's illuminating study, "The Habits and Ben Jonson's Humours," *JMRS*, VIII (1978), 115–136.

In *Every Man Out*, Jonson accomplishes this ironic detachment in two stages; first, through the invention of Asper as the fictional embodiment of the satiric impulse, and then by having Asper create and play the role of Macilente, envious and backbiting, the epitome of the satirist as viewed through the eyes of the world. Once the character of Macilente is totally imbued with the humour of envy, he acquires the dramatic motivation necessary to release the vitriol of the assertive satirist. In the cloak of Macilente, Asper believes he can "prodigally spend my selfe, / And speake away my spirit into ayre" (ll. 204–205). By exposing to ridicule the humourous inclinations of his community, Asper hopes to exorcize his own satiric impulse. He sees humours as "more infectious then the pestilence" and thus will administer "pills to purge, / And make 'hem fit for faire societies" (ll. 174–176). By purging the vanities of society Asper hopes to form in his mind an image of a cleansed order of reality. The world created in his play becomes an image of his own state of being and the purification of this world causes, one would suspect, a purification of the satirist as well.

Although this process seems to possess great dramatic potential, Jonson defies our expectations in his depiction of the moral degeneration of Macilente in the play proper. Instead of releasing his "spirit into ayre," Macilente becomes progressively more embittered as each fool is driven out of his humour to gravitate to a center of moral order. To appreciate fully the failure of Asper's satiric plot we must view it in the context of the disquieting critique of satiric presumption expressed in the verse satires. The plot of *Every Man Out*, as envisioned by Asper, would be no more than a dramatized version of an unself-conscious satiric process—the expiation of one's own ire through the explosion of the pretensions of others. This plot, though dramatically coherent, would be morally repugnant to an audience sensitized to the basic questioning of satiric authority. Jonson, however, knew his Inns of Court audience, and through his friendship with many members he was undoubtedly sensitive to the question of satiric hypocrisy.

Near the end of the Induction Cordatus reminds Asper that "We must not beare this peremptorie saile, / But use our best endevours how to please" (ll. 197–198). Surprisingly, Asper agrees, promising Cordatus to "mixe with you in industrie" in order to please "attentive auditors" who "come to feed their understanding parts." This "mixe" will form the underlying structure of the play—a combination of the satiric impulse of Asper and the artistic discrimination of Cordatus. Although Asper is both "author" and chief actor of the play, the directorial responsibilities fall to Cordatus, the *"Moderator"* who knows *"the scope and drift"* of the play (Character, *H & S* III: 427). It is Cordatus who will focus attention on the real subject matter of the drama and illuminate the progress of the play's satiric plot. In the complementary functions of Asper and Cordatus, Jonson combines the moral imperative of satire with the artistic sophistication necessary to realize its vision in a complex, intensely self-conscious society.

Soon after Asper exits "To turne an actor, and a Humorist" (l. 214), we realize that his plot is not about to develop quite along the lines he had envisioned. First, there is a lengthy delay in waiting for the Prologue. When he finally does appear, however, the Prologue bluntly refuses to deliver his lines, surprising Cordatus who expects the play to follow the same course he had seen in rehearsal. The Prologue blithely announces that he has forgotten his lines and that in any case Cordatus had inadvertently promised to speak them for him. Right in the midst of this, a second complication develops when Carlo Buffone, a character from the play, impatiently struts forth to toast the audience and berate the Author. After mocking the notion that the Author could ever drive him out of his humour, Carlo leaves, ordering the audience to "seale up their lips" (l. 352)—a highly ironic foreshadowing of Carlo's own ignominious fate at the end of the play itself. Jonson ends the Induction with a flurry of spontaneous disruptions in order to prevent his commentator from relaxing into a position of confident foreknowledge concerning the events about to unfold. In *The Spanish Tragedy*, Kyd shows what happens to a choral commentator possessed of absolute prescience: Revenge spends most of that play either bored or asleep.[18] By introducing some uncertainty into the character of Cordatus, Jonson transforms him from a passive vehicle into an ideal spectator, the "attentive auditor," aware of satiric structure and attentive to the variations Jonson will work on his theme.

18. Charles A. Hallett, "Andrea, Andrugio and King Hamlet: The Ghost as Spirit of Revenge," *PQ*, LVI (1977), 46.

III

To complicate matters further, in the play proper we find not one but two satiric voices—Macilente, the primary envious intriguer, and Carlo Buffone, a *"scurrilous, and prophane Jester"* who *"with absurd* simile's *will transforme any person into deformity"* (Character, *H & S* III: 423). Oscar Campbell views Carlo as "a typical buffoon" who uses various "forms of linguistic license" to allow Jonson to distinguish "true satire from raillery and mere detraction." [19] In the play itself Buffone is constantly described in terms of his ability to ridicule men through his "adult'rate *simile's*" (*Ind.*, ll. 363–364). In this light I think we should view Carlo not as a mere detractor (just as Macilente is certainly not the voice of "true satire"), but rather as another familiar figure in Elizabethan satiric verse— the epigrammatic wit. In Guilpin's epigrams scurrilous puns and assorted wordplay are frequently employed to deflate ostensible satiric targets. On a deeper level, however, they often rebound on their narrator— demonstrating the narrator's own salaciousness and hypocrisy. Then when Guilpin's epigrammatist sets out to define every possible variety of "Gull" (here imitating Sir John Davies's "Of a Gull") he ends up with the highly ironic statement, "And to conclude, who selfe conceitedly, / Thinkes al men guls, ther's none more gull then he" (*"To Candidus.* 20"). With his brazen catalog of gulls, the epigrammatist finally defines himself as the greatest gull of all. In the final epigram of *Skialetheia,* Guilpin explains his ironic method. If the world be as coarse and as foolish as various epigrammatists have depicted it, the proper "Decorum" necessitates an appropriate narrator: Guilpin declares that his epigrams "keepe *Decorum* on a comick stage" by employing "a foule-mouth Jester." But despite this admission Guilpin ends the poem declaring "I care not what the world doth think, or say, / There lies a morall under my leane play" ("70," ll. 16–20). The irony the permeates Guilpin, Marston, and Jonson was lost on John Weever who declared that they

> Plotted three wayes to put the Divell downe;
> One should outrayle him by invective vaine,
> One all to flout him like a countrey clowne;

19. Campbell, p. 67.

And one in action, on a stage out-face,
And play upon him to his great disgrace.
(The Whipping, ll. 830–834)

Although Weever's analysis is naïve, his linking of the satiric railer and
the epigrammatic flouter with Jonson's dramatic plot reinforces our belief
that Carlo Buffone is an integral part of Jonson's satiric craftsmanship.
Although Carlo can see through all pretense, he lacks any grain of moral
sensibility. Thus he professes friendship to Sogliardo (a rich clown affect-
ing gentility) solely in order to mold him into a ludicrous courtier. When
the knight, Puntarvolo, rebukes him for mocking his friend, Carlo scoffs
at the very idea of unfeigned friendship since none with "any opinion of
wit affect it" (IV.iii.113). Although Carlo spends much of the play
ridiculing courtiers, Jonson shows a profound sense of moral decorum by
refusing to allow Carlo himself into the environs of the court
(IV.viii.102–104). Carlo's proper arena is the world of the epigrams, the
ordinaries and taverns, and his discourse is little more than witty ribaldry.

In Act V, after a number of ape-humorists are shocked out of their
vanities by Macilente, a general melancholy overtakes the group, and they
resist the idea of attending the supper Carlo has had prepared for them.
Macilente, however, forces their compliance by reminding them of Carlo's
vicious wit: "our supper / at the Mitre must of necessitie hold to night, if
you love your / reputations" (V.iii.79–81). The key to Carlo's power lies
in this last phrase. Although none of these mannered fools thinks in moral
terms, each is terrified at the prospect of social ridicule. In the secularized
society the scalpel of wit is a necessary adjunct to the scourge of indignation. The Chorus underlines this fact by observing that it is "their feare of
CARLO" which "makes them / hold their meeting" (ll. 90–91).

As this scene makes clear, Carlo is himself crucial to the resolution of
the satiric plot. The effectiveness of Macilente is limited by his own
obsessive humour. Intensely malcontent, Macilente has become habituated to the belief that true merit has no effect in the real world. From this
perspective, all success is undeserved, and any who achieve it are, like
Sogliardo, mere "bull rushes" who "shoot up in a night to place, and
worship" (I.ii.162–163). The objectivity of the true moralist has long
since deserted the humourous Macilente: he is so possessed by envy of
others' success that any intimation of prosperity blinds him to all moral

considerations. The only character whose immorality is apparent to Macilente is Carlo Buffone—precisely because the latter lacks the prosperous social position which so distorts Macilente's perception. Though Macilente despises Carlo he needs his scurrilous wit to insure the success of his own envious designs. Thus Carlo is employed by Macilente first to bring Sogliardo to court in order to dishumour Saviolina and afterward to ridicule those ape-humourists whose follies have been exposed during their sojourn at court.

Actually, Macilente and Carlo Buffone have more similarities than differences in this play. Their symbolic union centers on the fact that neither is concerned with any moral effect of his actions on society. Macilente is so obsessed by envy that he dishumours others solely to obliterate them as objects of his obsession. Similarly, Carlo Buffone views civilized society as nothing but a façade hiding mankind's true bestiality. Unhindered by moral constraints, Carlo's licentious wit is given full range to reduce men to animals and to consume them through ridicule. In Carlo's discourse on the value of eating pork—since there is "nothing resembling man more than / a swine, it followes, nothing can be more nourishing" (V.v.69-70)—Jonson metaphorically underlines this obsessive dehumanization at the heart of Carlo's jests. Although Carlo literally and figuratively feeds himself at others' expense, his own humour prevents him from realizing that it is actually he, and not the objects of his ridicule, who is diminishing to the level of a beast. In the scenes at the Mitre in Act V, all of Carlo's actions intensify our developing appreciation that this wit, while superficially a *Circe*, transforming *others* into swine, is actually a *Grill*, the man who finds *himself* a swine and enjoys the state. In Act V, scene IV, after Macilente's exposure of a number of vain characters, the scene shifts to the Mitre Tavern wherein Carlo is envisioning the envy of Macilente and biding his own time by enacting a little puppet show with his drinking glasses. Both Carlo's description of Macilente here and his subsequent puppet show have symbolic value which further underscores an essential similarity between these two characters and intimates the ultimate result of their progressive satiric habituation.

When Carlo imagines Macilente's reaction to the mannered fools at court, he describes it as a process of "soking in their frothy / humours like a drie crust, till he has drunke 'hem all up" (V.iv.26–27). In these lines Carlo perfectly sums up the progress of Macilente's envy. The more examples of apparent social success that Macilente triumphantly deflates, the more he feeds his own habit and becomes calcified in his envious humour. Ironically, by freeing the fools from their affectations, Macilente isolates himself further and further from humanity. He becomes, in Carlo's image, a sponge drawing out the humours of others by incorporating them into his own fixed obsession—one that perverts his view of reality into an image of society ruled by the whirligig of Fortune—a world oblivious to true merit.

On one level Carlo's puppet play symbolizes a lack of a spiritual corrective for these perspectives of ambition and envy—an omission that results in the progressive self-destruction of the satiric personae of this play. Although Asper had promised to speak away his spirit into air, once the satiric spirit is released in society it takes on the tincture of corruption. Its two voices, the indignant moralist and the social wit, are vitiated by envy and cynicism. The dramatic characters representing these viewpoints begin to surfeit on follies and vice and swell to gigantic proportions. Neither Macilente nor Carlo can contain his satiric vein once it is opened. In his comical puppet play Carlo unintentionally demonstrates this process. Although this scene is often overlooked, the close attention paid by the Chorus, the repeated requests to "observe, observe him" (V.iv.68), show that Jonson wishes his audience to discover the symbolic meaning beneath this seeming farce.

The puppet play begins when Carlo takes two drinking mugs and uses them to impersonate a pair of affected courtiers pledging each other's health. As each toast is made, Carlo swills down the wine and refills the mugs. On one level, this stage business serves comically to get Carlo drunk in time for the return of his companions. On the symbolic level, however, Carlo demonstrates precisely what is occurring to the two satiric personae in the play. The satirists initiate intrigues that highlight the affectations of their victims just as Carlo concocts this little puppet show mocking courtly ceremony. As the puppets are put through their foolish paces, Carlo repeatedly drains the mugs—a symbolic restatement of the satirist's own absorption of the humours of his victims. With his puppets, Carlo quite literally re-enacts his metaphorical description of Macilente's plot: Carlo soaks in the "frothy humours" of his puppets "till he has drunke 'hem all up." By the end of the puppet show, Carlo is so thoroughly intoxicated that he loses all control over his puppets—and he is reduced to pleading with them to "respect your reputations" (V.iv.90). Finally, in his drunken rage, Carlo overturns everything on the table—an emblem of the self-destructiveness of the satiric humour.

IV

Every Man Out is the first work that Jonson deemed worthy of publication. The scrupulous attention Jonson gave to the Quarto publication (1600) highlights a significant anomaly in the finished product. Instead of the Quarto ending with the final scene of the play, we find an unusual appendix in which is included a very different version of the play's closing scene. This version, Jonson informs us, had been the original resolution of the play—one which he was forced to alter because of opposition to depicting Queen Elizabeth on the public stage. As it now stands, the text of the play presents a revised ending which totally deletes all reference to the queen. But Jonson's strenuous defense of the original version makes it apparent that he felt it the natural culmination of his entire dramatic design. The Quarto's additions indicate an uneasiness about the revision and give witness to the kind of satiric resolution Jonson wishes for his play in its published edition.

In 1972, J. A. Bryant, Jr., analyzed the Quarto evidence and reconstructed Jonson's original conclusion—one which, Bryant argues, realizes the necessary purgation of the satirist much more fully than does the revised text.[20] In the revised ending, after Macilente has succeeded in embarrassing the fools out of their humours (or, in the case of Carlo, a jester impervious to ridicule, silencing by force), the envious intriguer looks around and suddenly declares:

> Why, here's a change! Now is my soule at peace.
> I am as emptie of all envie now,
> As they of merit to be envied at.
> My humour (like a flame) no longer lasts
> Then it hath stuffe to feed it.
>
> (V.xi.54–58)

20. J. A. Bryant, Jr., *The Compassionate Satirist* (Athens, Ga., 1972), pp. 24–31.

In this version Macilente's facile reformation lacks any dramatic validity and, in effect, denies the play's emphasis on the obsessive nature of humour. In fact the revision totally ignores the play's central moral issue, the question of the satirist's own obsession which blinds him to human merit, a theme first brought up in the Induction and developed throughout the entire play. This revised conclusion coarsens Jonson's satiric design by simply obliterating Macilente's own villainy and allowing him to end the play through the simple evaporation of his own presumptuous indignation.

Jonson's original version seems to have included at least one additional scene in which Macilente, surfeited in his humour by the deflation of all prosperous fools, brazenly enters the inner sanctum of the court:

> with a purpos'd resolution (his Soule as it were new drest in *Envie*) to maligne at any thing that should front him; when sodainly (against expectation, and all steele of his *Malice*) the verie wonder of her *Presence* strikes him to the earth dumbe, and astonisht.
>
> (Appendix X: Original Conclusion, *H & S* III: 603; italics reversed)

The image of Macilente's "Soule" "new drest in *Envie*" identifies his condition at the final stage in the calcification of his humour—Envy is now a "second Nature" to him, completely overwhelming his rational faculties. In Macilente's vice-induced madness, he can no longer be cured by any rational means. As Jonson explains, "*Macilente* being so strongly possest with Envie, . . . it must bee no sleight or common *Object,* that should effect so soddaine and straunge a cure upon him" (*H & S* III: 602; italics reversed). The purgation of Macilente's envy-encrusted soul requires the intervention of a quasi-spiritual agency—a spectacular vision of the richness of virtue incarnate. Macilente enters the court expecting to see Fortune doting on fools. Through the course of the play this predisposition has been solidified by the results of the intrigues he had perpetuated. To Macilente, worldly success is now the province of fools and knaves.

Although Macilente's intrigue-exposures are generally discussed in a moral context, we lose something of the play's dimensions if we ignore Macilente's own perception of his wit intrigues. Here for a moment we must separate the Asper from the Macilente. Asper, as idealized satirist, seeks to eliminate vice and folly: Macilente, as worldly man lacking preferment, seeks to undermine all prosperity. Thus in the dishumouring of Deliro, the Asper half of the satiric impulse acts morally in freeing the husband from his uxorious inclinations; but the Macilente half achieves its satisfaction in the humiliation of a prosperous merchant. Asper, the idealist, sees only vice and folly and is blind to the complexities of human existence. Macilente, the malcontent, views only the prosperity of others and is similarly blind to the world's moral dimensions. Thus in Macilente's eyes his intrigues only reinforce a belief in a fickle society in which fools are rewarded by riches. He enviously eyes the successful, humbles them, and gloats in their misery. Since all intrigues reveal some lack of merit in the prosperous, Macilente enters the court, the paragon of society, fully intending to malign all that he encounters therein. Also, under the cloak of Macilente, Asper himself enters the Presence. No less a humourist than his alter ego, Asper is equally habituated to a false vision—the satiric humour presuming the ubiquity of folly and vice. Macilente comes to malign the prosperous and Asper to reprove their moral laxity.

The final luminous vision of Queen Elizabeth, as the epitome of prosperity and the embodiment of virtue, becomes the ultimate realization of social and moral harmony. This overwhelming affirmation of concord, both spiritual and social, is the cathartic shock needed to dissolve the humour of Macilente and to restore his moral sensibility. Beaurline's discussion of the tradition of *admiratio* (admiration and wonder) is a useful context for this startling transformation of Macilente, [21] but *admiratio* is usually understood as the effect of a play on its audience. In Jonson, the effect is achieved primarily within the play itself and only by extension on its audience. Asper/Macilente is himself transfigured and reduced to humanity. This marvelous vision precipitates a shocked awareness of the critic's own imperfection causing him to sink to his knees in repentance and homage. The startling reduction of the envenomed social critic to a level of moral self-consciousness closely imitates, in dramatic terms, the climax of Guilpin's "Satire I." Jonson's use of the spectacular presence of

21. Beaurline, pp. 35–65.

the queen and his dramatic employment of *admiratio* demonstrate how brilliantly he translates the rhetorical effects of Guilpin by finding precise and effective dramatic analogues.

Jonson uses Queen Elizabeth as a powerful emblem of virtue closing a play concerned primarily with folly and vice. Her appearance is decorous not only in terms of the Macilente plot, but also as an effective counterbalance to the image of the world conjured up by the various satiric figures in the play. Asper, the angry satirist, sees only moral corruption ripening all around him; Macilente, Asper's manifestation in society, views fools achieving great prosperity; Carlo Buffone, Asper's image of the satiric wit, regards all men as beasts. In the main part of the play our only corrective to these distorted perceptions is the various comments of the Chorus. Although the interjections of Cordatus keep the audience attentive to the developing humours of the three satiric figures—characters who might otherwise be mistaken for authorial spokesmen—the mere revelation of satiric hypocrisy does not in itself realize an image of virtue and harmony in the world. The medium of drama, however, implies a movement toward clarification and reconciliation. Thus, the final, miraculous appearance of the queen has great dramatic validity as the powerful emblematic statement of a world of harmony and virtue—a world to which the characters of this play, newly purified, can finally return.

In the 1616 Folio, his last recension of the play, even without the symbolic use of the queen, Jonson does effect a resolution of his satiric dialectic. This is achieved by investing the final appearance of his satiric presenter with symbolic value. This version restores the Epilogue in which Asper comes forward in his own person but still cloaked in the garb of Macilente. This is an emblem toward which the entire play has been moving. Asper must ultimately see himself as in part Macilente: the assertive satirist must accept his own frailties in the world of men. As Bryant notes, "the etymological meaning of Asper's Latin name is 'without hope.'" [22] In a secularized society there is no hope for the indignant moralist blind to his own failings. Asper must therefore garb himself in humanity in order to have any hope of accomplishing the purification of his own soul and the community of man. In his final speech, Asper/

22. Bryant, p. 29.

Macilente declares himself "nothing so peremptorie as I was in the beginning" (V.xi.81–82). In his rejection of the peremptory humour Asper
finally banishes his "crafty enchaunter" and rejoins the human
community.

V

One might expect that this detailed anatomy of satiric presumption
would cast a long shadow over Jonson's next two "Comicall Satyres."
Surprisingly enough, this is hardly the case. The influence of the Guilpin/
Marston mode of satire diminishes rapidly in the later works. The Prologue of *Cynthia's Revels* (1600) proclaims that Jonson's Muse now "shunnes the print of any beaten path; / And proves new wayes to come to
learned eares" (ll. 10–11). And indeed the central movement of this play
becomes a process of discrimination to "define / What merit is" (ll. 16–
17). At one time critics tended to view the *Every Man* plays as companion
works, but I think we might learn more about Jonson's satiric development through a consideration of the first two "Comicall Satyres" as opposite and complementary approaches to the question of satiric authority.
Instead of an indignant Asper itching to scourge the world, in *C.R.* we
meet Crites, a satirist so reluctant to engage his satiric talent that he
spends half the play simply ignoring the "straw devices" (III.iii.6) of the
vicious courtiers, smugly pleased that by his passive disdain he "can thus
(with such a sweet neglect) / Plucke from them all the pleasure of their
malice" (ll. 38–39). In this play Jonson demonstrates the ethical
responsibility of a satirist to utilize his art for the betterment of society.
Crite's "merit" is realized only after he rededicates himself to *Arete* ("active virtue") in Act III, scene iv, and fashions the masque of Act V—the
"rare device" which reveals both the ideal society and the vicious courtiers
who have conspired to debase it.

This movement away from an ironic conception of the satirist reaches
its logical conclusion in Jonson's 1601 *Poetaster*. In this play we are
presented with two contrasting images of the satiric persona. On the one
hand we have the ethical Horace, civilized, urbane, and secure of both his
place in society and his necessary function in the Commonwealth. On the
other hand, we have Crispinus, the "gent'man, parcell-*poet*" (III.iv.160),
a burlesque embodiment of the opportunistic role player. The latter's

comical self-aggrandizement from gallant through amorist to bombastic satirist climaxes in his attempt to degrade the proper function of satire through his calumny against Horace: *"taxing him, falsly, of* selfe-love, arrogancy, impudence, / rayling, filching by translation, &c."* (V.iii.231–232). By this point in his career Jonson could see that the self-limiting perspective of the ironists was not in itself a viable or sufficient method for the public mode of dramatic satire. In the arraignment of Crispinus Jonson circumscribed the boundaries of ironic satire and opened the frontier to the kinds of social satire that would culminate in his great satiric comedies of the next decade.

Bartholomew Fair
as Urban Arcadia:
Jonson Responds to Shakespeare

THOMAS CARTELLI

'Slid! here's Orpheus among the beasts, with his fiddle, and all! . . . And
Ceres selling her daughter's picture, in gingerwork!

T HE TITLE OF THIS ESSAY may seem rather fanciful to those who are
suspicious of all attempts at yoking together such mighty opposites
as Jonson and Shakespeare, much less such traditionally opposed words as
"urban" and "Arcadia."[1] The title is, however, meant to provoke the kind
of interest that has, in the past, been frequently lacking in our critical
response to the plays and polemics of Jonson: an interest in the fact that

---

1. Most of these attempts have been admirably concluded. Those which have broken
the ground for this one include: Robert Ornstein, "Shakespearian and Jonsonian Comedy,"
ShS, XXIII (1969), 43–46; Harry Levin, "Two Magian Comedies: *The Tempest* and *The
Alchemist,*" *ShS,* XXIII (1969), 47–58; Nancy Leonard, "Shakespeare and Jonson Again:
The Comic Forms," *RenD,* N.S. X (1979), 45–70; Anne Barton, *"The New Inn* and the
Problem of Jonson's Late Style," *ELR,* IX (1979), 395–418, and "Harking Back to
Elizabeth: Ben Jonson and Caroline Nostalgia," *ELH,* XLVIII (1981), 706–731. The
present essay may, in all due humility, be considered a companion piece to Levin's which is
primarily concerned with Shakespeare's response to Jonson; see "Magian Comedies," pp.
57–58.

Jonson (self-professed and professing classicist though he might have been) was both conscious of and responsive to the dominant dramatic concerns of his time, and was, therefore, quite capable of exploiting those concerns for his own peculiar ends. In reading Jonson, we are too often apt to take him at his word when he derides past and contemporary dramatic usage in favor of the decorum of his beloved ancients: to accept the Jonsonian letter without probing too deeply into the Jonsonian spirit or into the psychological and professional circumstances that inform his compulsive (and seemingly compulsory) polemics. In negotiating my own departure from the Jonsonian letter, I have found that in *Bartholomew Fair* Jonson demonstrates an active preoccupation with the relatively recent romances and earlier comedies of his master and nemesis, Shakespeare, that is not unrelated to a simultaneous preoccupation—well-documented by Jonas Barish and Leo Salingar, among others—with adapting his characteristic dramatic concerns to a form intended to ensure a less qualified measure of success than his previous productions seem to have enjoyed.[2] Robert Ornstein, Nancy Leonard, and, especially, Anne Barton have already taught us much about the interpenetration of what Leonard calls "the comic forms" of Shakespeare and Jonson.[3] But it is to other critical voices that the present approach to *Bartholomew Fair* is more heavily indebted: an approach that involves seeing the play as working off and within a quintessentially Shakespearean pastoral/romance pattern of withdrawal and return in order to effect dramatic ends that are both saturnalian and satiric in orientation.[4]

2. See Leo Salingar, "Crowd and Public in *Bartholomew Fair*," RenD, N.S. X (1979), 141–160, and Jonas A. Barish, "Jonson and the Loathèd Stage," in *A Celebration of Ben Jonson*, ed. William Blissett et al. (Toronto, 1973), pp. 27–53.

3. See note 1. Also see Anne Barton's forthcoming book on Jonson to be put out by Chatto & Windus, a glimpse of which was given in her address—entitled "Shakespeare and Jonson"—to the International Shakespeare Congress at Stratford-upon-Avon, 4 August 1981. Professor Barton has advised me that a revised version of her address will be published in the volume of selected Proceedings of the Congress.

4. Jonas Barish was, to my knowledge, the first scholar to associate *Bartholomew Fair* with Shakespeare's saturnalian comedy. He did so in the following passage from his early "*Bartholomew Fair* and Its Puppets," MLQ, XX (1959): "As in Shakespeare's 'saturnalian' comedy, pleasure, rather than learning or wisdom has become the touchstone" p. (15). This statement also appears in Barish, *Jonson and the Language of Prose Comedy* (New York, 1970), p. 236.

These critical voices belong to C. L. Barber and William Empson who have shaped so much of our present thinking about saturnalian comedy and the many versions of pastoral. Although Professor Barber did not (to my knowledge) specifically discuss Jonsonian satire in his many and varied critical pronouncements, he did discuss, if only in passing, the relation of satire—generically considered—to saturnalian comedy in the introductory chapter of *Shakespeare's Festive Comedy*:

Satirical comedy tends to deal with relations between social classes and aberrations in movements between them. Saturnalian comedy is satiric incidentally; its clarification comes with movement between poles of restraint and release in everybody's experience.[5]

The saturnalian pattern, as Barber defines it, the movement "through release to clarification," can, in other words, apply to satire when the subject of satire—"relations between social classes"—is sufficiently broadened to take up the question of the relations between men and women generally, independent of class distinctions. Empson strikes a kindred note in the opening pages of his essay on *The Beggar's Opera* when he asserts that pastoral "describes the lives of 'simple' low people to an audience of refined wealthy people, so as to make them think first 'this is true about everyone' and then 'this is specially true about us.' " In suggesting that this is exactly what *The Beggar's Opera* does, Empson appropriates what he terms Swift's "first conception" of the play and styles it "the pastoral method applied to Newgate."[6] The common element in Barber and Empson's approaches is the attempt to bridge conventional notions of genre differences—between saturnalian and satiric comedy on the one hand, pastoral and mock-pastoral on the other—in order to come to a more broadly based understanding of specific artistic achievement and its general application to the world outside it. Empson is especially keen on this point:

Clearly it is important for a nation with a strong class-system to have an art-form that not merely evades but breaks through it, that makes the classes feel part of a

5. C. L. Barber, *Shakespeare's Festive Comedy* (Princeton, N. J., 1972), p. 8.
6. William Empson, *Some Versions of Pastoral* (New York, 1960), pp. 185–186.

larger unity or simply at home with each other. This may be done in odd ways, and as well by mockery as admiration.[7]

Barber comes to a similar conclusion in describing the over-all effect of saturnalian comedy: "Behind the laughter at the butts there is always a sense of solidarity about pleasure, a communion embracing the merrymakers in the play and the audience, who have gone on holiday in going to a comedy."[8] In each instance, the movement of the respective art form is envisioned as a movement toward audience unification, premised on the theatrical dissolution of normative class differences: a process that makes it conceivable for a mockery of pastoral form to achieve the same ends as the idiom it denies and makes it possible for the social disruptions of satire to be healed by means of a saturnalian clarification that compels an audience to acknowledge its essential solidarity.[9]

Although neither Empson nor Barber had Jonson's *Bartholomew Fair* in mind in making his formulations, the play clearly provides a common meeting ground for their relative positions: a satire that is "festive" or saturnalian in orientation, a pastoral that is both urban and Arcadian in its approach to theatrical experience, that mocks and upholds its theatrical mode at one and the same time. Jonson, in fact, promises as much in his Induction: that is, "a new sufficient play called *Bartholomew Fair,* merry, and as full of noise as sport: made to delight all, and to offend none; provided they have either the wit or the honesty to think well of themselves" (Ind., ll. 79–85).[10] The play's fulfillment of its saturnalian promise has been convincingly established by Jonas Barish, John J. Enck, and Richard Levin, among others, who all discern in *Bartholomew Fair* a prevailing mood of benevolence and acceptance that represents a departure for Jonson from the more bitterly satiric spirit of most of his earlier

7. *Ibid.,* p. 189.

8. Barber, pp. 8-9.

9. As Empson, in his remarks on *The Beggar's Opera,* has it: "It is both mock-heroic and mock-pastoral, but these take Heroic and Pastoral for granted; they must be used as conventions and so as ways of feeling if they are even to be denied" (p. 185).

10. All quotations from the play refer to the Revels Plays edition, edited by E. A. Horseman (London, 1960).

productions.[11] What has not been noted is that the play's comparative benevolence is closely bound up with Jonson's ongoing attempt to "break through" and move beyond the "aberrations" that conventionally characterize the relations between social classes in purely satiric comedy; that the method employed by Jonson to effect this breakthrough into saturnalian clarification owes much to the methods employed by Shakespeare in his pastoral comedies (e.g., *A Midsummer Night's Dream* and *As You Like It*) and romances (especially *The Tempest*) to structure and organize his own breakthroughs; and that the play as a whole dramatizes Jonson's efforts at coming to terms with Shakespearean influence and his Shakespearean inheritance.[12]

The common pattern that informs Shakespeare's pastoral comedies and romances is (as has often been noted) the pattern of withdrawal and return which effectively grounds the saturnalian movement through release to clarification. Although Shakespeare's application of the pattern as an organizing principle differs greatly in each play, it usually involves the movement of a select group of characters (either sinful, as in *The Tempest,* or more sinned against than sinning, as in *Dream* and *As You Like It*) away from a commonly perceived real or first world of care and anxiety into a green or golden world which is not completely care-less, but which is sufficiently removed from the real world to give its guests time and space in which to work out their problems, hostilities, and anxieties. Once these problems are satisfactorily resolved, the characters willingly (indeed, eagerly) return to their first worlds, changed to greater and lesser degrees

11. See the chapters devoted to *Bartholomew Fair* in Barish, *Language of Prose Comedy,* pp. 187–239, and Enck, *Jonson and the Comic Truth* (Madison, Wis., 1966), pp. 189–208. See also Barish, "Feasting and Judging in Jonsonian Comedy," *RenD,* N.S. V (1972), 3–36, and Richard Levin, "The Structure of *Bartholomew Fair,*" *PMLA,* LXXX (1965), 172–179.

12. The latter point has its analogue in Barton's "*The New Inn* and the Problem of Jonson's Late Style." Barton, however, contends that Jonson "seems at last to have come to terms with Shakespearean comedy and with popular dramatic forms that he had earlier despised," not with the writing of *Bartholomew Fair,* but "In the plays written after *Bartholomew Fair*" (p. 417), mainly with *The New Inn* which "carries the situation of *As You Like It* and *The Winter's Tale* to the breaking point" (p. 401). In short, I see Jonson beginning to work out what Barton elsewhere calls his "subtle rapprochement" with Shakespeare (stimulated by his "Elizabethan nostalgia") much earlier, as a direct response to Shakespeare's retirement from the stage.

from what they were originally. As applied by Jonson, the pattern reveals only a few, but a crucial few differences. The play is structured around the movement of a collection of characters away from a first world of pretension, prejudice, and stupidity into a second, rather gray world (embodied by the Smithfield Fair) that is not without corruptions of its own, but which accepts them as common human imperfections and gives them free rein.[13] The gray world of Smithfield is, in short, green enough to be relatively free of the first world's pretensions and prejudices; abundant in experience of what the flesh is heir to, the natives of Smithfield judge not lest they be judged in a fallen world that accepts its fall graciously.[14] Intensified involvement with these denizens of the social underworld ultimately brings the visitants into intimate contact with their own imperfections and compels most of them to acknowledge their previously denied citizenship in the commonwealth of human folly.[15] Once this collective recognition is achieved, the Fair-proper—like Arden, the forest outside Athens, and Prospero's isle—is effectively left behind, having been imaginatively annexed to the first world of reality by the fair-goers themselves who, when last we see them, are planning to "ha' the rest o' the play at home" (V.vi.117–118).

   Although this summary clearly oversimplifies both Shakespeare's and Jonson's variations on the withdrawal/return paradigm, it sufficiently illustrates the nature of Jonson's dramatic debt to Shakespeare and the nature of his divergence from him. Like Shakespeare, Jonson is very aware that all is not golden in the pastoral second world, whether that world be located in the forest of Arden or the Smithfield Fair. What Douglas Cole has said about Shakespearean pastoral can, in this respect, apply as well to Jonson's appropriation of the pastoral mode: "For all its idyllic possibili-

   13. For the best appraisal to date of the play's plot, see Richard Levin's previously cited "The Structure of *Bartholomew Fair*."
   14. For similar estimates of Jonson's attitude toward judgment in the play, see Barish, *Prose Comedy*, p. 236, and "Feasting and Judging," pp. 28–30. For an opposing point of view, see Douglas Duncan, *Bartholomew Fair and the Lucianic Tradition* (Cambridge, Eng., 1979), who contends that Jonson's "probing of the censorious mentality results in [his] most morally complex play, rightly compared with *Measure for Measure* as a comic parable on the text, 'Judge not that ye be not judged' " (p. 205).
   15. See Duncan's association of *Bartholomew Fair* with *The Praise of Folly* in *Lucianic Tradition*, p. 212.

ties, pastoral is still this side of paradise." [16] On the other hand, Jonson chooses to take precisely what is not golden in Shakespeare—as exemplified by the "rough weather" of Arden, the "pangs" that accompany the "sweet sounds" of Prospero's isle—as his primary focus of dramatic interest in *Bartholomew Fair,* as his analogue to the most positive aspects of the Shakespearean greenworld. Jonson chooses, in other words, to move his version of Arcadia even farther away from Paradise than Shakespeare's Arden, into a plainly "fallen" urban setting in which the fools and knaves who populate the borders of Shakespeare's invention are more the rule than the exception. Whereas Shakespeare takes his characters on a kind of therapeutic vacation halfway out of this world in order to make them whole, Jonson rubs the faces of his characters in the dirt of this-worldly experience in order to relieve them of their pretensions and unnaturalness, to make them, if not whole, at least a bit more acclimated to "things as they are." [17] The novel approach taken by Jonson toward what is usually identified as a peculiarly Shakespearean dramatic design is, moreover, neither accidental nor gratuitous. Rather, in *Bartholomew Fair* Jonson seems to have attempted to place the composite Shakespearean greenworld and all that it implies about Shakespeare's approach to dramatic art in critical juxtaposition with the gray-on-gray confines of an urban version of the pastoral Arcadia, in part to burlesque dramatic usages which he considered silly and outmoded (nay, "mouldy"); in part to demonstrate the resilience and staying power of his own "potent art" in the face of what he construed to be "real-world" concerns; and in part to pay a dramatic debt to Shakespeare that he could not consciously pay in any other way.

Jonson's intentions are, I believe, discernible in his ambitious Induction to the play where he attempts to dissociate his production from confusion with rival theatrical styles and, in so doing, to clear out a theatrical space for himself that is uniquely his own. The Induction begins, curiously enough, with an indirect jibe against exactly the kind of literal-mindedness that initially seems to inform "the author's" own di-

16. Douglas Cole, "Shakespearean Pastoral," *RenD,* N.S. V (1972), p. 216.

17. Cf. Eugene M. Waith, "Things as They Are and the World of Absolutes in Jonson's Plays and Masques," in *The Elizabethan Theatre IV,* ed. G. R. Hibbard (London, 1974), pp. 106–126. Also see Alvin Kernan's comparative discussion of *Bartholomew Fair* and *The Tempest* in *The Revels History of Drama in English,* vol. III, ed. J. Leeds Barroll et al. (London, 1975), p. 458.

atribe against Shakespeare in the contract portion of the Induction. The opinionated Stagekeeper assumes the role of defender-of-reality which Jonson usually reserves for himself when he inveighs against the playwright's apparent misrepresentation of the Smithfield Fair:

> When't comes to the Fair once, you were e'en as good go to Virginia for anything there is of Smithfield. He has not hit the humours, he does not know 'em; he has not convers'd with the Bartholomew-birds, as they say; he has ne'er a sword and buckler man in his Fair, nor a little Davy, to take toll o' the bawds there, as in my time, . . .
>
> (Ind., ll. 10–15)

I call attention to this passage because it should remind the reader (as it probably served to remind its contemporary audience) that Jonson is, from the outset, quite conscious that his playworld version of the Smithfield Fair has a stronger basis in fantasy than fact; that it is, in other words, no less fictional, no less play-full, than the forest of Arden. Like Shakespeare, Jonson is aware that his green (rather, gray) world is a never-never-land of the dramatic imagination, "a fantasy accommodated 'to delight all' who can 'think well of themselves'. . . . a deliberate construct, demanding audience collaboration." [18] Indeed, by working within a pastoral/romance structural pattern that could be easily associated with Shakespeare, Jonson implicitly calls attention to the superficial resemblances between what he is doing and what Shakespeare has done. But he does so that he might better demonstrate that *his* distortion of reality—his "version" of pastoral, if you will—constitutes a more valid mode of dramatic representation than Shakespeare's: one that subverts and, in subverting, "corrects" Shakespeare's purportedly artless flights of fancy. In short, Jonson promises to present, if not "reality" itself, at least a theatrical facsimile which, however distorted, essentially remains faithful to its model or source: "Instead of a little Davy, to take toll o' the bawds, / the author doth promise a strutting Horse-courser, with / a leer Drunkard, two or three to attend him, in as good / equipage as you could wish" (Ind., ll. 119–122).

---

18. Gabriele Bernhard Jackson, "Structural Interplay in Ben Jonson's Drama," in *Two Renaissance Mythmakers,* ed. Alvin Kernan (Baltimore, 1977), p. 139.

Jonson's argument on behalf of the fictitiousness of his dramatic re-
creation of the Smithfield Fair does not, in other words, preclude a
concurrent argument against the factitiousness of popular theatrical
styles, especially those which, in his opinion, encourage audiences to
remain stultified in their judgments, or present completely fanciful imitations of nature. His critique of the "constant" judgment of those who
"will swear [that] *Jeronimo* and *Andronicus* are the best plays yet" (Ind., ll.
107–108) is, for instance, motivated by his desire to have his audience set
its sights exclusively on the present, on the here and now of a play that
promises a marked departure from the primitivism of the past. Jonson's
insistence on displacing his audience's groundedness can probably be
attributed to his understandable anxiety about being judged by the same
standards which had consigned many of his earlier productions to the
limbo of underapplauded excellence. In order to disarm his audience of
the expectations his earlier plays may have encouraged, Jonson attempts
to fashion a reciprocal agreement with the audience, the terms of which
involve his coming closer to its standards if it comes closer to his own: "It
is further covenanted, . . . that / how great soever the expectations be,
no person here is to / expect more than he knows, or better ware than a
Fair / will afford . . ." (Ind., ll. 114–117). Jonson's intentions extend as
well to exponents of more recent theatrical styles whom he accuses of
demonstrating the same disregard for "Nature" as did the earlier pur-
veyors of bombast, but with whom he promises to conform if conformity
ultimately proves necessary:[19]

> . . . If there be never a
> servant-monster i' the Fair, who can help it? he says; nor a nest of antics? He is
> loth to make Nature afraid in his plays, like those that beget *Tales, Tempests,* and
> such like drolleries, to mix his head with other men's heels; let the concupiscence
> of jigs and dances reign as strong as it will amongst you: yet if the puppets will
> please anybody, they shall be entreated to come in.
>
> (Ind., ll. 128–135)

In offering this rather unguarded critique of Shakespeare's recent productions, Jonson superficially reveals what we have come to recognize as

19. See Joel H. Kaplan, "Dramatic and Moral Energy in Ben Jonson's *Bartholomew
Fair,*" *RenD*, N. S. III (1970), 155.

the characteristic blind spot in his estimate of his elder competitor. I say "superficially" because in this instance the attitude Jonson adopts toward Shakespeare seems more strategic than felt. As Harry Levin has noted, while "the attack on *The Winter's Tale* and *The Tempest* is fairly overt" and apparently consistent with Jonson's insistence on the primacy of art over nature, "The paradox is that Jonson, for once, was criticizing Shakespeare from the standpoint of nature rather than art."[20] Given the paradoxical nature of Jonson's critique of Shakespeare, I think it safe to assume that pronouncements such as this one and the infamous "Shakespeare wanted art" later recorded by Drummond of Hawthornden can be considered rather advanced symptoms of a massive case of Bloom's anxiety of influence.[21]

Although my own reasoning might seem paradoxical to some, I see Jonson trying to claim a place for himself here that had recently been vacated by Shakespeare; and I see him staking his claim by subtly reversing his own critical categories in response to the changed nature of his position *vis-à-vis* the recently retired master of the stage. The point is that Jonson was not so muddleminded that he was incapable of distinguishing between what Shakespeare discerned as fact and what Shakespeare presented as fantasy; indeed, as we have seen, he goes to great lengths in the first part of the Induction to relieve his audience of just such an affliction in regard to his own play. But he was *strategically* obtuse enough to misread Shakespeare (and to do so in public) for his own immediate ends,

---

20. Harry Levin, p. 49.

21. In *The Anxiety of Influence* (New York, 1973), Harold Bloom contends that Jonson had "no anxiety as to imitation" (p. 27) and thus fails to register a most interesting case-study in the politics of influence. Indeed, Jonson's chronic imitation of his Roman masters conceivably served as a defensive buffer against the competing influence of his contemporaries upon his work, and constituted a complex strategy by which he might maintain distinction in his ongoing battle for recognition. As Anne Barton has recently observed, "During the 1590's, Jonson developed a distinctive poetic and, more particularly, a comic mode by reacting against a loosely defined Elizabethan norm" (in "Harking Back to Elizabeth," p. 720). When he came to compose *Bartholomew Fair,* Jonson seems to have revised his strategy in order to exploit some of the same influences he had earlier "reacted against." He began, as Barton writes, "to use selected Elizabethan authors, Marlowe, Sidney, and Shakespeare, in the way he had long been accustomed to use Horace, Virgil, Seneca, or Quintilian: as guides to right ways of thinking and feeling" (p. 724).

those ends being the displacement of what it pleases him to call in another context (the 1612 Preface to *The Alchemist*) an "art that is afraid of nature" by an art that presumes to give nature its due.[22] Jonson was, moreover, sufficiently astute to recognize (also in public) that, in attempting to avoid mixing "his head with other men's heels," in trying to go beyond Shakespeare into dramatic territory Shakespeare had mined so well, he might well be engaging in self-defeating activity of a peculiarly ironic variety. And it is this recognition that informs the grudging concession which closes off his apparent blast against Shakespeare, "yet if the puppets will please anybody, they shall be entreated to come in."

What we have here is a Jonson of two interrelated states of mind: a Jonson who needs to clear out theatrical space for himself and needs, therefore, to make semi-arbitrary and self-serving distinctions between himself and the man he will later call his "Beloved Master"; and a Jonson who (however grudgingly) is finally willing to give the "grounded judgement" of the audience what it wants and who must, therefore, make some of the same concessions to popular taste for which he chides Shakespeare.[23] The Induction as a whole suggests that Jonson intended to fulfill his artistic needs and desires by offering his public something in the way of a "naturalized" version of the two Shakespearean romances to which he alludes: a play populated by fictions drawn from the inner city of reality, rather than from the far reaches of the imagination or the latest animal show, "A wise Justice of Peace *meditant,* instead of a juggler with an ape" (Ind., ll. 125–126). To do so, Jonson needed to have his audience retrospectively consider Shakespeare's dramatic usage in *The Winter's Tale* and *The Tempest* as akin to Epicure Mammon's attempts to "naturize nature" against the "infections" of reality in *The Alchemist*. In the exchange Jonson found it necessary to adopt as his own Perdita's rather naïve perspective

22. See Ornstein, pp. 45-46, who presents two opposed conceptions of Jonson's attitude toward the "natural"; see also George Hibbard, "Ben Jonson and Human Nature," in *A Celebration of Ben Jonson,* pp. 55–82.

23. The "two Jonsons" I portray should not be confused with the "Two Ben Jonsons" George Parfitt describes in his recent *Ben Jonson: Public Poet and Private Man* (London, 1976), pp. 14–35. For an excellent revision of the traditional attitude taken by scholars toward Jonson's poetic tribute to Shakespeare, see T. J. B. Spencer, "Ben Jonson on his beloved, The Author Mr. William Shakespeare," in *The Elizabethan Theatre IV,* pp. 22–40.

toward the allowable commerce between nature and art—especially her
opposition to "grafting," which she considers equivalent to the making of
monsters out of nature—in his ongoing battle against Shakespeare/
Polixenes.[24] He thus counters what he seems to have needed to portray as
an art "naturized" beyond the pale of Nature itself with an art that is
completely attuned to and representative of the nature that is human.
Although one may quarrel with Jonson's (and my own) distinctions, it is
this kind of logic that appears to have informed Jonson's substitution of
the Smithfield Fair—as the repository of infinite human variety—for
Shakespeare's superficially more "natural" greenworlds.

The long and the short of Jonson's aproach to his play is, to return to
Empson, the pastoral method applied to Smithfield. In order to effect his
public displacement of Shakespeare's unnatural naturalism—what Anne
Barton has called Shakespeare's "ruralization of cities"—Jonson develops a
dramatic strategy specifically geared toward the urbanization of experience; he attempts, in other words, to exploit what he perceives to be
Shakespeare's weaknesses by playing to his own characteristic strengths.[25]
In the play proper, Jonson's repeated allusions to Shakespeare's comedies
and romances constitute strong and purposive "counterblasts" to
Shakespeare's own most characteristic concerns. An especially illuminating example of just such an allusion is provided in the play's second act
when two Bartholomew-birds, Leatherhead and Joan Trash, are debating
the relative merits of Joan's wares:

LEATHER

Sit farther with your ginger-
bread progeny there, and hinder not the prospect of my shop, or I'll ha' it
proclaim'd i' the Fair, what stuff they are made on.

TRASH

Why, what stuff are they made on, Brother Leatherhead? Nothing but what's
wholesome, I assure you.

24. My argument here owes much to Harry Levin's comparative dicussion of these three
plays in "Two Magian Comedies," pp. 47-50. See also Alvin Kernan's note to II.i.64 of
The Alchemist in his edition of that play (New Haven, Conn., 1974) where he suggests that
"by 'naturized' Mammon means not a lesser form of nature but a more intensive 'super-
nature', nature 'firked up in its center' . . ." (p. 209).

25. The remark attributed to Professor Barton was made in the course of her address,
"Shakespeare and Jonson," at the International Shakespeare Congress; see note 3.

LEATHER

Yes, stale bread, rotten eggs, musty ginger, and dead honey, you know.

(II.ii.3–10)

What Jonson's characters and, by extension, Jonson himself are alluding to here is, of course, Prospero's "We are such stuff as dreams are made on" speech from the fourth act of *The Tempest*: a speech which, in our own time, is more often identified with Shakespeare's prevailing attitude toward artistic creation than with the immediate context of the play in which it appears. Jonson, however, seems to be equally aware of both creator and context in making the allusion. By summoning up remembrance of the immediate occasion of Prospero's remarks (that is, the conceivably grotesque Revels that now are ended) in the immediate context of his own remarks about servant-monsters in the Induction, Jonson tacitly compels his audience to compare Shakespeare's inflation of "airy nothings" with his own leveling of material reality to the standard of "Nothing but what's wholesome." [26] Prospero's impressive but tendentious masque of Juno and Ceres—a masque which, we may recall, is didactically devoted to the rather puritanical rooting out of premarital sexual impulses—is effectively brought down to earth and displaced by a stand of gingerbread which, appropriately, includes (as we later learn from Quarlous) a "gingerwork" of "Ceres selling her daughter's picture" (II.v.10–11). I use the word "displaced" because Jonson's motivation here—as throughout *Bartholomew Fair*—is not so much to bring Shakespeare down as to raise himself up to Shakespeare's level, to balance Shakespeare's preoccupation with the stuff of dreams by overasserting the priority of the stuff of reality, which, after all, may be as corrupt as Leatherhead suggests.

The fertility of this allusion to *The Tempest* should imply that there is more than may at first meet the eye in Jonson's seemingly parodic "quotes" from Shakespeare which range from his virtual theft of the Autolycus episode in *The Winter's Tale* to his puppet-play burlesque of the Pyramus and Thisbe play-within-a-play in *A Midsummer Night's Dream*.

---

26. As Harry Levin has it: "Jonson, who well knew how insubstantial a pageant could be, would hardly have accepted Prospero's masque as a paradigm of reality. Rather, it was what he had meant by antics that 'runne away from Nature'—modes of escape no less evanescent, to him, than the wish-dreams of Sir Epicure" (p. 56).

Perhaps the most sustained allusions to Shakespeare in the play are the assumption by Adam Overdo of a stance toward the rooting out of enormity that is curiously consistent with Prospero's attitude toward the rooting out of errant sexuality and evil in the Masque and Judgment scenes, and the transformation of character Overdo undergoes which echoes Prospero's coming to terms with "the rarer action" that is mercy, rather than vengeance. Overdo's movement away from the "cloud-cover" that hides him and his "black book" (Jonson's version of the book Prospero "drowns"?) in Act II, scene i, and toward the evenhanded resolve initiated by his assumption of responsibility for the fate of Troubleall in Act IV, scene i, constitutes a direct dramatic re-enactment of Prospero's movement away from a cautious voyeurism to an equally cautious but active involvement in the affairs of men near the close of *The Tempest*: "I will be more tender hereafter. I see compassion / may become a Justice, though it be a weakness, I confess; / and nearer a vice, than a virtue" (IV. i. 77–79).[27]

In re-creating this Shakespearean situation, Jonson is not, however, paying uncritical tribute to Shakespearean standards of judgment. Rather, by having Overdo himself recognize that he is "but Adam, flesh and blood," Jonson presents us with a more humanly sympathetic character than the insistently imperious Prospero, who may drown his book and bury his wand but can hardly be accused of harboring the egalitarian impulses with which Jonson endows the humbled Overdo at the close of the play. Perhaps Jonson, in correcting what he might have perceived as the later Shakespeare's presumptuous grandstanding—that is, his attempt, through Prospero, to legislate from on high an acceptable reality out of the recalcitrant human material he had taken for his subject—is implicitly correcting an earlier Jonson's own presumption in setting himself up as an unanswerable critic of manners and morality. Shakespeare

27. Instead of seeing thematic consistency between *The Tempest* and Jonson's allusions to the earlier play, Jackson I. Cope argues that the symbolic "pattern is of a very different design in a world wherein the staff of quasi-omnipotence is carried by Overdo rather than Prospero," in "*Bartholomew Fair* as Blasphemy," *RenD*, VIII (1965), 135. I disagree. Although Overdo no doubt represents a "lower" species of character than the "potent" Prospero, his acknowledgment of Troubleall as his own creation is, for instance, quite consistent with a symbolic pattern in which Prospero acknowledges Caliban as "mine own." In short, Overdo operates in a lower but no less valid orbit than Prospero.

conveniently becomes, in this process of transference, a surrogate student of the teacher who succeeds him.

To expedite this exchange of roles, Jonson may have been compelled to sacrifice his own characteristic imperiousness, the moral and aesthetic elitism which had heretofore distinguished him from his comparatively more genial contemporary. That is, for Jonson to fill the place vacated by Shakespeare, he may have found it necessary to exploit some of the same popular stereotypes which, according to Leslie Fiedler, permitted Shakespeare—especially in his festive comedies—to connect in a nonalienating way with hs audiences.[28] Such a reading is, at least, consistent with the recent approaches taken toward the play by Douglas Duncan—who views *Bartholomew Fair* as an ironic "comedy of accommodation"—and George Parfitt—who contends that the closure of the play represents somewhat of a moral compromise for Jonson, "an acceptance of the norm" that constitutes a grudging submission to his own prevailing "sense of man as an animal beyond the reach of his moral art."[29] I am not, however, completely happy with the condescendingly moral persuasions brought to bear on the play by Parfitt and Duncan which seem too rooted in the puritanism with which Jonson was so at odds throughout much of his dramatic career.[30] Rather, I agree with Anne Barton who has recently suggested that "in *Bartholomew Fair* Jonson finally managed to get his entire world onstage at the same time" and that he "aimed here at an inclusiveness he never sought before."[31]

The real question seems to be, why now?, at this particular point in his dramatic career? And the answer appears to be profoundly tied to the retirement of Shakespeare, whose withdrawal from the stage gave Jonson his first real opportunity to write a play that did not have to suffer from

28. My reference to Fiedler is drawn from his contribution to a seminar on "Shakespeare and the Popular Tradition in Comedy" which convened on 4 April 1980 at the annual meeting of the Shakespeare Association of America in Cambridge, Massachusetts.

29. See Duncan, pp. 189–225, and Parfitt, pp. 83–85.

30. Duncan effectively falls into his own trap when he moralizes Jonson on the heels of his own judicious depiction of the evaluative habits of literary critics: ". . . most of us enjoy measuring fiction by more rigorous standards of morality than we normally apply in real life" (p. 3). On this count, see Barish's review of Alan Dessen's *Jonson's Moral Comedy* in *MP*, LXXI (1973), 80–84.

31. "Shakespeare and Jonson."

the occupational hazards of deviance, defiance, and just plain difference
that characterize all such oedipal rivalries in literature and life. In other
words, Jonson may well have been able to accept, in Fiedler's terms, the
"new stereotype of equalized relations" upon which the success of *Bartholomew Fair* as "Jonson's lone non-alienating play" is premised, because
for probably the first time in his career as a playwright his own professional relations had been sufficiently equalized to allow him to place his
own characteristic concerns in direct and responsive relationship with
those of his powerful adversary.[32]

Richard Levin's influential study of the structure of the play can be of
help to us here since we are now ready to return to our own starting
premises. In emphasizing the pivotal role played by the visitors to the Fair
in determining the structure and significance of the play as a whole, Levin
essentially describes (without naming it himself) the precise kind of
dramatic pattern we tend to associate with Shakespearean comedy and
romance:

The fair, . . . while it is the precipitating cause of much of the action, is not its
center; that place is occupied by the visitors, whose careers demarcate the main
stages of the plot: it begins when they decide to attend the fair, its central portion
follows them through their day at Smithfield, and it ends when they agree to
leave the fair and return, greatly changed, to their normal environment.[33]

The plot, as Levin describes it, recapitulates the movement from release to
clarification that characterizes Barber's conception of the saturnalian pattern. And it does so, as Empson might have it, not by simply focusing on
the private transformations of Levin's visitors to the Fair, but by bringing
these visitors into productive relationship both with themselves and with
the natives of the Fair-world itself: that is, by making the originally
separate classes of visitors and natives "feel part of a larger unity or simply
at home with each other."

What Jonson is ultimately after in *Bartholomew Fair* is profoundly akin
to what Shakespeare was after in plays as different as *The Tempest* and *As
You Like It*: namely, the establishment of a human community out of

32. See note 28.
33. Richard Levin, p. 173.

disparate groups of disparate individuals, what Leo Salingar calls "a crowd." [34] Jonson, moreover, attempts to bring this community about with as much awareness of the tenuousness of human relationships as Shakespeare brings to bear on his own productions. Just as Shakespeare is aware in *As You Like It* that some people—namely, Jaques—must remain forever alienated from the human community, and even more aware in *The Tempest* of the danger of committing oneself to cohabitation with un-regenerate members of that community (indeed, aware of the tenuousness of the very idea of community), so too does Jonson tread softly around the ragged edges of his social design. The likes of Troubleall, for instance, can never really be reintegrated into even a more enlightened form of the community that has maddened him. Nor are we encouraged to trust in the permanence of the reformations of Busy, Overdo, and Dame Pure-craft, least of all in the Iago-like vow of silence of Wasp. Littlewit's wit will probably continue to do violence to plays, and Cokes will surely never be more than a sophomore in the great college of experience.

But for Jonson, all this does not now seem to matter. His sense of community appears to be more closely allied to the question "what to make of a diminished thing" than to Prospero's quest to have fallen humanity conform to his ambitious designs. Having gained perspective from Shakespeare's own exertions in this mode, Jonson sets his sights on more modest goals and, hence, imposes fewer demands on human nature in *Bartholomew Fair*. His idea of community is effectively embodied by the ad hoc community-sentiment of the otherwise anarchic Bartholomew-birds when they collectively rush to the aid of the scalded Ursula in Act II, scene V, or share the "vapour of experience," among others, in Act IV, scene iv. [35] Jonson does not, in short, really ask us to imagine that the supper to which all the characters are invited at the close of the play will

34. Salingar, p. 143. His statement reads, "Although it is a holiday occasion, [the characters] are not a community but a crowd."

35. I completely endorse Barish's response to those scholars who consider the game of vapors "degrading" or "anti-social": "The vapors, . . . though they issue in quarrels, at the same time form a compelling reminder of the kinship between men" (*Prose Comedy*, p. 230). Indeed, the play as a whole could be considered an elaborate game of vapors in which Jonson expends his animosity against Shakespeare in order to establish his kinship with him.

establish a community that will last much longer than the first course, much less dessert. As Anne Barton has noted, the ending of the play "falls considerably short of the Shakespearean 'one feast', 'one house'." [36] But it does so *not*, as Barton suggests, because Jonson is unable to achieve a full-blown Shakespearean reconciliation, but because for Jonson a community that is really no more than a temporary communion is sufficient and, perhaps, all one can hope for in the urban Arcadia that is at once the Fair, London, and, most notably, the theater itself.

In lowering his demands on human nature in *Bartholomew Fair,* Jonson demonstrates a broadened appreciation of human nature in all its corrupt and hopelessly venal variety. And it is this, I believe, that serves to distinguish his achievement from Shakespeare's productions in the pastoral / romance mode, and makes more understandable the attitude toward those productions which Jonson assumes in the Induction. Whereas Shakespeare in his own versions of pastoral and romance often seems to need, as Robert Ornstein has noted, to smooth over the rough spots of his lower, comparatively vulgar characters and to need as well authority figures such as Theseus and Prospero to preside over the messiness of imperfect attempts at reconciliation, Jonson is, in *Bartholomew Fair,* more willing to allow human nature free-play and more interested in bringing authority down to the same level over which it presumes to preside.[37] Jonson's commitment to free-play eventuates, for instance, in the admittedly surprising but comparatively believable marriages of Winwife to Grace and Quarlous to Dame Purecraft ("believable" when compared, say, with the marriage of Oliver to Celia in *As You Like It,* or the forced marriage-arrangements at the end of the problem comedies). These marriages, moreover, attest further to the purposiveness of Jonson's appropriation of Shakespearean pastoral conventions.

Rather than rely, as Shakespeare often relies, on the instant alchemy of love-at-first-sight or on questionable moments of epiphanic revelation when spurned characters are seen as if for the first time, Jonson treats love much as he probably found it treated in the workaday world around him: as a practical matter, gone into with business acumen, common sense, and a marked measure of supremely human perversity. This is not to suggest

36. "Shakespeare and Jonson."
37. See Ornstein, p. 43.

that Jonson treats his love-matter in as cold and colorless a manner as some critics contend.[38] Although there is little in the way of romance of even the blandest sort in *Bartholomew Fair,* Jonson manages to negotiate the dissolution of two misbegotten bethrothals by giving the ladies in question ample opportunity to make rearrangements of their own with the help of their own inner dispositions and the kind of fantasy-fulfillment which indulgence in the Fair affords. Perhaps even more notable is the way in which disinterested observance of the Fair cedes to all-out indulgence when two of the only characters in the play who belong neither to the category of gull or native—namely, Winwife and Quarlous—also exploit the Fair's invitation to Arcadian pastime and do so in a self-consciously Arcadian way:

> GRACE
>   . . . You shall
> write, either of you, here, a word, or a name, what you like best; but of two, nor three syllables at most: and the next person that comes this way (because destiny has a high hand in business of this nature) I'll demand, which of the two words he or she doth approve; and according to that sentence, fix my resolution, and affection, without change. . . .
>   QUARLOUS
> These conditions are very courteous. Well, my word is out of the *Arcadia,* then: 'Argalus.'
>   WINWIFE
> And mine out of the play, 'Palemon.'
>
>   (IV.iii.48–54; 67–69)

Although Anne Barton has contended that "Jonson disapproved of romance literature" and that in Jonson's *Everyman Out of His Humour* "characters who are halfwits read the *Arcadia,*" hence, that Winwife and Quarlous virtually "damn themselves" by choosing the roles they do, it seems clear from the context of the exchange that Jonson is doing no more with Sidney and "romance literature" generally than demonstrating how they can be gainfully employed in a sophisticated form of play.[39] That the

---

38. Jackson I. Cope, for instance, in his discussion of the quasi-legalistic chicanery that informs the marital disposition of Grace; see *"Bartholomew Fair* as Blasphemy," pp. 137–140.

39. *"Shakespeare and Jonson."*

otherwise worldly and cynical likes of Quarlous and Winwife choose this particular way of participating in the Fair appears, moreover, to validate Jonson's attempt in the play to portray a dramatic world cross-fertilized by both green and gray world concerns. For her part, Grace—whom Barish describes as "disengaged to the end, poised, judicious, and slightly inhuman"—in choosing how she wishes to be wooed, demonstrates a similar sense of playful release from the constraints of absolute predictability.[40] Her first and motivating desire—as commonsensical as one could wish—is to be freed at all costs from her contract with the despicably foolish Cokes. But she is not so prosaic as to enter into another contract without at least enjoying a mating game with men who obviously attract her and with whom, we assume, she has something in common.

The point is that, had he wished, Jonson could have written a mock-pastoral satire that might have taken on Shakespeare, Sidney, and the Marlowe of *Hero and Leander* all at one shot. In the process, he could have sullied and dragged through the dirt every poetic standard and ideal regarding love, truth, and beauty that he considered beyond the pale of reality as it is constituted in this world. That he did *not* write such a play is, perhaps, a testament to the maturity that came to Jonson, not so much with age, as with the passage of sufficient time to allow him to deal constructively with his own anxieties about the achievement and influence of artists whom he may well have revered despite his comments to the contrary—"this side Idolatry."[41]

This is not to suggest that the parodic spirit does not also thrive in the rundown Arcadia that is Jonson's Smithfield. On the contrary, Jonson is clearly conscious (and makes us conscious as well) of the inadequacies of literary idealism and of the equally unacceptable vision of reality he attempts to uphold in its stead. His ironic reminder is embodied by the

40. Barish, *Prose Comedy,* p. 223.

41. Although Anne Barton reserves Shakespeare's pre-eminence in Jonson's writing for *The New Inn,* she makes the following provision about the active influence of the poets on Jonson's composition of *Bartholomew Fair* in "Jonson's Late Style": "In *Epicoene,* the degradation and decline of the present age had been measured through reference to the classical past. *Bartholomew Fair* subsequently, with its memories of Chaucer and Sidney and of Marlowe's *Hero & Leander,* altered the touchstone. It was English literature, especially the non-dramatic work of the early Elizabethan period, which sat in final judgement upon the debased activities of the Fair" (pp. 417–418).

madman, Troubleall, who makes Grace's marital decision for her and then unwittingly plays Bottom to Dame Purecraft's Titania when the Puritan matron decides that her mate must be mad or no mate at all. Jonson carries his subversion of pastoral romance alliances one step further in his Bankside burlesque of Marlowe's *Hero and Leander* and reduces as well the legendary friendship of Damon and Pythias (a reference, perhaps, to our own two noble kinsmen, Argalus and Palemon?) to absurd proportions.[42] But Jonson's interest in parody is easily exhausted and ultimately mastered by more constructive concerns. In a manner that is analogous to his over-all treatment of Sidney and Shakespeare in the course of the play, once Jonson has successfully deflated the romance-idylls of love and friendship, he turns his attention to bridging the differences between his opposing characters in order to make them, again in Empson's words, "feel part of a larger unity or simply at home with one another." Not insignificantly, he employs to this end the puppets' defense of profanity and confutation of Busy: that is, a dramatic medium which, like the overarching version of pastoral that frames it, both mocks and upholds itself at one and the same time. In the process, Jonson transforms what starts out as a parodic impulse into wholesale acceptance of the same kind of theatrical extravagance which inspired his earlier diatribe against Shakespeare: "Let it go on. For I am changed, and will become a be-/holder with you" (V.v.109–110), say the confuted Busy and a reconstructed Jonson in the same surprisingly acquiescent voice.

Associating Jonson with Busy, as well as with the vituperative Wasp and the rooter-out-of-enormities, Overdo, has become a predictable way for critics to respond to the dramatic reversals that occupy the closing movement of the play. I do not, however, think the associations should be underplayed, much less summarily discarded simply because they are easy to make. If Jonson was perceptive enough to see (as many others have seen) a Shakespeare in Prospero, he may well have been sufficiently astute to recognize (and expose) various images of himself in the trio of mystified demystifiers who define themselves in opposition to the puppet-monsters of invention embodied by the Fair and its unregenerate inhabitants. Similarly predictable, though no less crucial, is the notion that Jonson, in reforming this trio—or, if "reforming" be deemed too strong a word, in

42. See Barish, *Prose Comedy,* pp. 233–234.

driving these characters out of their respective "humours," through release into varying forms of clarification—may well be reforming himself
as well: the "old" Jonson who, like the old Adam, sees enormity in every
stone and pebble of human imperfection. At the very least, Jonson comes
into a clarification of his own about the saturnalian potential of satire and
the theatrical measures—puppets and all—a playwright may need to take
to make his representations of reality both applicable and accessible to the
workaday world around him.

This clarification is effectively acted out in the oft-noted benevolence of
the play's closure which, in reconciling "butts" with "merrymakers" in
the solidarity of pleasure, pays an obvious debt to the festive endings of
Shakespeare's comedies and the redemptive endings of his romances. It is
here that the mock-pastoral impulse, which probably started Jonson down
this road in the first place, demonstrates its complete consistency with the
very idiom it intends to subvert. When Quarlous suggests that the
characters "drown the memory of all enormity" in Overdo's biggest wine
bowl (a backhanded reference to the gracious waters of Lethe if there ever
was one), mockery and acceptance are conjoined in a formula for
reconciliation that has its closest analogues in Shakespeare's own artful
attempts to drown "the critical faculty at large" in a warm bath of
fellow-feeling.[43] In effecting this conjunction, Jonson shapes a response to
Shakespeare that is at once a declaration of independence from and a living
memorial to the influence of his rival and master. Purged for the present
of his competitive envy of Shakespeare and of the defensive contempt for
his public that envy inspired, Jonson is free, at the close of the play, to
endorse Overdo's Horatian maxim as his own standard for satiric art: "for
correction, not destruction, building up, not tearing down."

43. Cf. Duncan's moralized estimate of Quarlous's gesture from which the quoted
phrase has been taken (p. 211).

Jonson's The New Inn *and Plato's Myth of the Hermaphrodite*

PATRICK CHENEY

CRITICS HAVE AGREED unanimously that Jonson's *The New Inn* examines Platonic or neo-Platonic love. As yet, however, no one has examined the significance of Jonson's reference to the myth of the hermaphrodite that Plato developed in the *Symposium*. In Act III, during the Court of Love, the protagonist Lovel attempts to define love as "Desire of vnion with the thing beloued," which prompts his companion, Lord Beaufort, to say:

> Then I haue read somewhere, that man and woman
> Were, in the first creation, both one piece,
> And being cleft asunder, euer since,
> Loue was an appetite to be reioyn'd.[1]

Lovel recalls, "It is a fable of Plato's, in his Banquet, / And vtter'd, there, by Aristophanes" (III.ii.86–87). The Host of the Inn concludes the dis-

---

1. *The New Inn*, III.ii.75 and 79–82. All quotations are from *Ben Jonson*, ed. C. H. Herford and P. and E. Simpson (Oxford, 1938), VI, except for one quotation from *Discoveries* in vol. VIII. Future citations will be included in the text.

cussion by saying, "'Twas well remembred here, and to good vse" (l. 88).

Taking the Host's cue, we may wonder why the myth is "well remembred here, and to good vse." A study of the relation between the play and the myth shows that they have three primary features in common: the same general theme (identity—fundamentally based on human love); the same basic plot structure (the separation of lovers and their search for reunion); and the same general motif (in the myth, that of hermaphroditism; in the play, the corresponding dramatic device of disguise). We may tentatively speculate that the myth is well remembered here and to good use because Jonson is identifying the mythical core of his comedy.

Although critics have agreed that *The New Inn* examines Platonic or neo-Platonic love, they remain divided over the exact nature of Jonson's treatment. Early critics, following the lead of Edward B. Partridge, tended to see the play ironically. According to Larry Champion, Jonson parodies Platonic love in general and the neo-Platonic love cult at the English court of Queen Henrietta Maria specifically.[2] Attempting to refute this ironic reading, Richard Levin has suggested that if Jonson had wanted to parody neo-Platonic love he would have mentioned this in one of his defenses; for Levin, *The New Inn* is just a "bad" play.[3] Recently, critics have been more sympathetic. In an important essay, Anne Barton has denied both that the play is bad and that it satirizes romance and Platonic love. For Barton, Jonson has constructed a kind of Platonic romance—"his most impressive and memorable lament for the age of Elizabeth and for the dramatist who was best in it. . . . Shakespeare— with some help from Sidney, Spenser, Lyly, Kyd, and Donne—presides over *The New Inn*."[4]

---

2. Larry Champion, *Ben Jonson's "Dotages": A Reconsideration of the Late Plays* (Lexington, Ky., 1967), p. 81. For Partridge's ironic reading, see *The Broken Compass: A Study of the Major Comedies of Ben Jonson* (London, 1958), pp. 189–205. For subsequent ironic readings, see C. G. Thayer, *Ben Jonson: Studies in the Plays* (Norman, Okla., 1963), pp. 198–232; Robert E. Knoll, *Ben Jonson's Plays: An Introduction* (Lincoln, Neb., 1964), pp. 181-190; and Claude J. Summers and Ted-Larry Pebworth, *Ben Jonson* (Boston, 1979), pp. 103–107.

3. "The New *New Inn* and the Proliferation of Good Bad Drama," *EIC*, XXII (1972), 41–47.

4. "*The New Inn* and the Problem of Jonson's Late Style," *ELR*, IX (1979), 417–418. Although Barton is not explicit about linking Platonism with romance, as I am, she does discuss the two together (pp. 408–409). For an anticipation of Barton's romantic reading,

Presently, I should like to qualify Barton's argument in two ways. First, the romantic elements she identifies coexist with elements from Jonson's usual "humour" comedy, creating what I would call a "humour romance." [5] Second, *The New Inn* looks back not merely to the Elizabethan age in general, but to a specific symbol at the center of Elizabethan literature: the hermaphrodite as a symbol of love. Accordingly, Jonson in *The New Inn* is focusing his new hybrid form of comedy on a particular myth, that of the Platonic hermaphrodite. Significantly, Jonson's interpretation of the myth resembles the neo-Platonic interpretation of it found in Spenser, Donne, and Shakespeare. Jonson's nostalgic use of the myth suggests that he is identifying it not simply as the mythical core of his own comedy, but as the mythical core of the Renaissance comic tradition as a whole. When seen in this light, *The New Inn* becomes both a comedy and a commentary *on* comedy.

The tale that Aristophanes tells in the *Symposium* was famous in the Renaissance. Originally, says the great classical comic poet, there were three kinds of human beings, each with a double nature: man, woman, and the hermaphrodite (who is both man and woman). Because mankind grew corrupt through pride, however, Zeus grew angry and divided each kind in two. As a result, those beings previously male now seek a male mate, those previously female seek a female mate, and those previously hermaphrodites seek the half they are missing. Aristophanes concludes:

So you see, gentlemen, how far back we can trace our innate love for one another, and how this love is always trying to redintegrate our former nature, to make two into one, and to bridge the gulf between one human being and another.[6]

---

see L. A. Beaurline, *Jonson and Elizabethan Comedy: Essays in Dramatic Rhetoric* (San Marino, Calif., 1978), pp. 257–274.

5. For a similar but undeveloped view, see Alexander Leggatt, *Ben Jonson: His Vision and His Art* (London and New York, 1981), pp. 35–44. In noting that Jonson balances romance with irony, Leggatt echoes the suggestion of Douglas Duncan, "A Guide to *The New Inn*," *EIC*, XX (1970), 321, that "Jonson would appear to have aimed at a . . . serio-comic balance." Though Duncan disagrees with Partridge's strictly ironic reading, both Levin and Barton have placed Duncan in the ironic camp. As such, his argument remains enigmatic, and the nature of the "balance" remains largely unexplored.

6. *Symposium*, 191d, trans. Michael Joyce, in *The Complete Dialogues of Plato*, ed. Edith Hamilton and Huntington Cairns (Princeton, N.J., 1961). Future citations will be included in the text.

For Aristophanes, the myth of the hermaphrodite is primarily an allegory of human love, revealing the fundamental principle of "two into one" as the basis of human love. Man had an original identity that was sexual in nature, in which he was complete within himself because he combined the masculine and feminine forces of creation. But because of his own pride he jeopardized that completeness, and subsequently was divided into two parts. His loss of sexual wholeness leads him to search for his original form. "The happiness of the whole human race," says Aristophanes, "is to be found in the consummation of our love, and in the healing of our dissevered nature by finding each his proper mate" (193c).

Although the myth is an allegory treating human love as the basis of personal identity, there is the hint that the myth has a further significance—one that becomes important for Renaissance commentators. "The purely sexual pleasures," says Aristophanes,

could hardly account for the huge delight [lovers] take in one another's company. The fact is that both their souls are longing for a something else . . . , which they can only give an inkling of in cryptic sayings and prophetic riddles.

(192d)

Although focusing on a physical union that Socrates will transcend in his later speech, Aristophanes' myth conceals the truth that man's happiness depends on his union with his "proper mate" and on this union having both a sexual and a spiritual dimension (the "something else" that man cannot name). The myth, that is, has two primary meanings, each closely related. Accordingly, each meaning becomes the basis for a tradition of commentary on the myth leading into Jonson's time: man's original hermaphroditic nature reveals, first, that he must reunite with a beloved through love to recover his wholeness, and, second, that he must have two parts to his own nature, physical and spiritual, to attain that wholeness.

Not surprisingly, Italian neo-Platonists like Ficino and Pico emphasized the latter of the two meanings. Ficino, for example, in his commentary on the *Symposium* suggests that man's original hermaphroditic nature means that man is "equipped with two lights, one natural and the other supernatural." [7] Man's division of his wholeness resulted when the

7. *Commentary on Plato's "Symposium,"* speech 4, chap. 2, trans. Sears R. Jayne (Columbia, Mo., 1944), p. 155. See also pp. 158–159. Future citations will be included in the text.

soul "used only one of its two lights [the natural or physical] and neglected the other" [the supernatural or spiritual], which led man into
"sensuality and lust." However, through maturation and learning, the
mind can "recover its divine light. This kind of appetite and desire is true
love" (speech 4, chap. 5, p. 159). In Ficino's neo-Platonic interpretation,
the myth is no longer an allegory of human love; rather, it is an allegory of
an earthly creature who aims to recover his former divine nature through
heavenly love.

Ficino's commentary allowed Pico in the *Heptaplus* to syncretize the
Platonic myth with the neo-Platonic commentary of Philo and Origen on
the story of Adam in Genesis 1:27 ("male and female created he them"),
so that Pico concluded "God created . . . man male and female":

It was commonly the practice of the ancients . . . to designate by the terms *male*
and *female* these two powers in the same substance, one of which is engaged in
contemplation while the other rules the body.[8]

Pico, like Ficino, has both biblical and classical authority to envision man
as a great hermaphrodite, whose masculine nature signifies his spiritual
essence and whose feminine nature signifies his physical body. The fact
that the Aristophanic man had its biblical counterpart in the
hermaphroditic Adam suggests, in part, why the Platonic myth became
acceptable to English Renaissance writers.[9]

In Elizabethan England, the concept of "two into one," which could be
interpreted either sexually (as with Aristophanes) or metaphysically (as
with Ficino), becomes an important expression for neo-Platonists like
Donne and Spenser. Donne, for example, as a religious poet, followed

8. *Heptaplus*, II.vi, in *Pico della Mirandola: On the Dignity of Man, On Being and One,
Heptaplus*, trans. Charles Glenn Wallis, Paul J. Miller, and Douglas Carmichael (In-
dianapolis, 1965), p. 104.

9. Sir Thomas Browne, in *Pseudodoxia Epidemica*, III.vi, in *The Works of Sir Thomas
Browne*, ed. Geoffrey Keynes (Chicago, 1964), II, 215, synthesizes the Platonic and
Christian or neo-Platonic myths when he adopts their authority for believing in "Man the
Hermaphrodite" (see also Keynes, II, 196). In *Religio Medici*, I.34 (Keynes, I, 44–45),
Browne shifts metaphors only slightly when he speaks of man as "that great and true
Amphibium" who lives in "divided and distinguished worlds": man is that "amphibious
piece betweene a corporall and spirituall essence, that middle frame that links those two
together, and makes good the method of God and nature."

Ficino in using the hermaphrodite as a symbol of the double nature of
man. In "To Mr. Tilman after he had taken orders," Mr. Tilman becomes
a "blest Hermaphrodite" who combines in his person "Both these": the
heavenly father and the earthly mother—spirit and body.[10] As a love
poet, however, Donne followed Aristophanes in using the hermaphrodite
as a symbol of the union between man and his "proper mate," with the
more explicit notion that the love is both physical and spiritual—as in
such familiar examples as "The Extasie," "The Dissolution," and "A
Valediction: forbidding mourning." Similarly, Spenser in his love poetry
used the hermaphrodite as a symbol of two souls becoming one—
especially within the context of married love. In the original ending to
Book III of *The Faerie Queene,* for example, Amoret joins Scudamour in an
embrace to form a "faire Hermaphrodite": "So seemd those two, as
growne together quite."[11] This hermaphroditic union represents the
"unfolding" of the great hermaphrodite, Venus, who in Book IV is por-
trayed as "Both male and female, both under one name: / She syre and
mother is her selfe alone" (x.41). The hermaphroditic Venus uniting
Scudamour with Amoret in a hermaphroditic embrace becomes an
emblem of a love that is both physical and spiritual.

In the area of Elizabethan drama, Shakespeare treated the theme of
hermaphroditic love in a more comic vein. In *Twelfth Night,* which Jonson
evidently had in mind while writing *The New Inn,* Viola dons the disguise
of a male page, and at the end, when her twin brother, Sebastian, appears,
the Duke Orsino says, "One face, one voice, one habit, and two persons."[12] Sebastian himself tells Olivia, the lover of the "page" Viola:
"You are betroth'd both to a maid and man" (l. 263). The comical
confusion of sexual identity is resolved when Sebastian unites with Olivia,
and Viola unites with the Duke. Significantly, by the end of the play,
Viola has functioned as a male to Olivia and as a female to the Duke; as

10. *The Poems of John Donne,* ed. Sir Herbert Grierson (London, 1912).

11. *The Faerie Queene,* III.xii.46 (original ending), in *The Poetical Works of Edmund
Spenser,* ed. Ernest De Sélincourt and J. C. Smith (London, 1909), vol. I. Future citations
will be included in the text. Although Spenser reveals that his figure derives from the
Ovidian myth of Salmacis and Hermaphroditus, rather than from Plato, he does retain a
symbolic meaning common to both myths during the period.

12. *Twelfth Night,* V.i.216, in *The Riverside Shakespeare,* ed. G. Blakemore Evans et al.
(Boston, 1974). Future citations will be included in the text.

with the hermaphroditic Venus in Spenser, she embodies a spirit of love responsible for uniting couples in marriage, thus creating for them a complete human identity.[13]

In Shakespeare, as in Jonson and other dramatists of the period, comedy takes as its central theme human identity. According to Northrop Frye,

> The most common form of identity . . . is the form achieved by marriage, in which two souls become one. . . . The discovery of sexual identity occurs when the heroine returns to her normal female garments, but sexual identity is a more deep-seated theme in comedy than it looks. The center of the comic drive toward identity is an erotic drive, and the spirit of comedy is often represented by an Eros figure who brings about the comic conclusion but is in himself sexually self-contained, being in a sense both male and female.[14]

He cites the hermaphroditic Viola, Puck, and Ariel as examples of this hermaphroditic Eros figure functioning as a force of union, and we could add Spenser's Venus as well. This Eros figure uniting couples in love is suggestive of a view of love that is both physical and spiritual. Significantly, Frye's association of this figure with the spirit of comedy implies

---

13. The two traditions of the hermaphrodite—one as a symbol of the union of male and female, the other as a symbol of the union within man of the spirit and the body—conveniently come together in John Cleveland's "Upon an Hermaphrodite":

> Adam, till his rib was lost,
> Had the sexes thus engrossed.
> When Providence our Sire did cleave
> And out of Adam carved Eve,
> Then did man 'bout wedlock treat,
> To make his body up complete.
> Thus matrimony speaks but thee
> In a grave solemnity.
> For man and wife make but one right
> Canonical hermaphrodite.

(In *Poems of John Cleveland*, 9–18, ed. J. M. Berdan [New Haven, Conn., 1911].) For Cleveland, the hermaphroditic union of male and female recovers the original hermaphroditic nature of man.

14. *A Natural Perspective: The Development of Shakespearean Comedy and Romance* (New York, 1965), p. 82.

that comedy is about the hermaphroditic union of male and female in a love that is both physical and spiritual.[15]

Frye's subsequent delineation of the three main "phases" of the comic plot reinforces his emphasis on the hermaphroditic nature of human love as central to comedy. The first phase consists of a parental figure imposing a harsh law on a comic society. The second consists of the confusion created by this law, generally causing a temporary loss of sexual identity. And the third consists of the discovery of man's true identity and the reunion of the separated lovers.[16] In a general way, the comic plot moves from a state of separation and confusion to a state of recognition and reunion. As Frye points out, sexual disguise becomes an important motif in this plot.[17] A female disguised as a male tends to symbolize the confusion about sexual identity that most of the play is concerned with, whereas the female taking off her disguise tends to symbolize a recognition about the true nature of human identity: the female's consequent reunion with her lover tends to symbolize the true hermaphroditic nature of human love, the means by which man attains his original wholeness.

From this, we can note three primary features that Renaissance comedy has in common with the Platonic myth of the hermaphrodite. Both take identity as their central theme—an identity that combines spiritual with physical love. Both present a three-phase plot structure, beginning with a harsh law that dissolves an original wholeness and causes a loss of identity, moving on to a period of confusion, and finally resolving with recognition, in which the separated parts realize who they really are and reunite blissfully. And both use a corresponding motif to represent their theme and plot: in the myth, hermaphroditism; in the drama, disguise.

Frye's discussion clearly anatomizes the nature of comedy in a way that is revealing for Jonson's *The New Inn*—especially if we recall that Frye is

15. One of the fullest treatments of the hermaphroditic spirit of love, functioning as the spirit of comedy, occurs in Dekker and Middleton's *The Roaring Girl*. See Patrick Cheney, "Moll Cutpurse as Hermaphrodite in Dekker and Middleton's *The Roaring Girl*," forthcoming in *Ren&R*. A play like *The Roaring Girl* reveals both the widespread recurrence of the hermaphrodite as a figure embodying the nature of love in the drama of the period and the conventional use of this figure embodying the nature of comedy.

16. *A Natural Perspective*, pp. 73 ff.

17. *Ibid.*, pp. 83 ff.

anatomizing "Shakespearean comedy and romance," and that *The New Inn,* as Barton has argued, is a comedy looking back nostalgically to Shakespeare. However, Frye does not directly link his discussion of comedy and its central theme of hermaphroditic love with the Platonic myth of the hermaphrodite in the *Symposium.* I hope to suggest that Jonson in *The New Inn* does. Thus, whereas Frye delineates the basic idea, Jonson identifies the mythical source of the idea—and shapes his comedy accordingly. It is in this sense that *The New Inn* becomes both a comedy and a commentary on comedy.

As in Plato's myth of the hermaphrodite, in Jonson's *The New Inn* the central theme is the relation between love and human identity, as the play's central episode, the Court of Love, reveals. One of the protagonists of the play, Lovel, seems to equate the action of the play (that is, life itself) with love—an action that the end of the play fully applauds:

> There is no life on earth, but being in loue!
> There are no studies, no delights, no businesse,
> No entercourse, or trade of sense, or soule,
> But what is loue!
>
> (I.vi.84–87)

The play takes place in the New Inn, at the "sign" of the Light Heart. With its two levels (upstairs and downstairs), the Inn becomes a kind of Spenserian allegory of the human heart, with its two kinds of love, physical and spiritual. As in Ficino's commentary on Plato's myth of the hermaphrodite, Jonson's play treats the hermaphroditic theme of "two lights" in a single "heart." Unlike in Ficino, however, the play will push toward a view of love as a hermaphroditic union between male and female in a love that is both physical and spiritual. Essentially, Jonson adapts the myth in the manner of Spenser and Donne, with the addition that he adapts this Elizabethan interpretation of the myth to the conventions of his own humour comedy. This adaptation is what makes *The New Inn* a "humour romance."[18]

18. Richard Peterson, in "Imitation and Praise in Ben Jonson's Poems," *ELR,* X (1980), 265–299, argues that imitation of classical writers stands at the center of Jonson's choice of content, method of treating materials, and view of life. For Jonson, says Peter-

In the play, life at the New Inn is quickly revealed to be the life of love. And the Host of the New Inn, Goodstock, becomes a representation of the life of love that man leads. Seven years before the play opens, the Host has lived as Lord Frampul with his wife and their two daughters, Frances and Laetitia. However, discontented with his wife and family life in general, Lord Frampul leaves home. Separated from his beloved ones, he repents of his pride and returns home, only to find that his wife has departed also, taking Laetitia with her. Consequently, Lord Frampul sets out to find them. When the play opens, he is disguised as the Host of the New Inn, having failed so far in his quest for reunion. (In actuality, his wife lives with him in the Inn, together with Laetitia, but husband and wife are both in disguise and do not recognize each other.) The action, in other words, has begun when the Host imposed a kind of "law" on his family, and most of the rest of the play will deal with the consequent separation and confusion, as the opening conversation between the Host and Lovel suggests:

> HOST
> A strange division of a familie!
> LOVEL
> And scattered, as i'the great confusion!
>
> (I.v.75–76)

Like the Aristophanic man that Jonson refers to in Act III, the Host and his wife were "both one piece," but "being cleft asunder, euer since, / [their] Loue [is] an appetite to be reioyn'd." The Host's past drive toward independence has led to separation and ultimately to loneliness; he has denied the hermaphroditic love that the play is concerned with. At the end of the play he lovingly realizes that his selfishness has been "the cause of all the trouble" (V.v.92). But, here at the beginning, he remains

son, knowledge of classical writers provides the foundation for great art. The poet's materials are not "sources" in the usual sense of the word; they are *signs* that a work's originality, organization, and continuing life depend on suggestive links to the great writers of antiquity. But Jonson does not merely imitate, adds Peterson; rather, Jonson gathers in a "source," then transforms it, creating an enhanced whole—"turne[s] all into Honey," to use Jonson's metaphor for this technique in the *Discoveries* (VIII, 2477–2478). What Peterson says about Jonson's use of classical sources in the poems seems to me equally applicable to Jonson's use of Plato's *Symposium* in *The New Inn*.

isolated from the true union that is to become so central to his own identity.

The Host and his wife are not the only characters living in a state of separation. Lovel himself is separated from his beloved, Frances, who has just arrived at the New Inn as the play opens. Lovel is separated from Frances because his charge, Lord Beaufort, has declared his own love for her, and Lovel nobly refuses to interfere with Beaufort's chance of happiness. Because Lovel refuses to let Frances know his feelings, he becomes "as a man neglected" (I.vi.112); though he has "desire enough," he has "no successe" (I.vi.101–102). According to Lovel, "my passion / [will] Burne me to cinders" (I.vi.158–159)—consume him in grief through his impossible predicament. Like the Host, Lovel is isolated from the hermaphroditic union that could make him happy. Similarly, Frances herself is separated, not merely from her destined husband, Lovel, but also from her present suitors, because she is "of so bent a phant'sie, / As she thinks nought a happinesse, but to haue / A multitude of seruants" (I.v.51–53); she is a "Lady, that professeth still / To loue no soule, or body, but for endes, / Which are her sports" (I.vi.54–56). Moreover, as her name reveals, she is a "frampull lady, / One was runne mad with pride, wild with selfe-loue" (V.ii.29–30). As with Lovel, Frances's separation from the object of her desire is largely self-imposed; she is "as cock-brain'd as ere [her] father was" (I.v.66): her self-love denies the hermaphroditic union she is destined for. Finally, from the perspective of the play's end, Lord Beaufort is separated from his destined bride, Laetitia; and Frances's chambermaid, the wise Pru, is separated from her destined husband, Lord Latimer.

This state of separation, in which all of the main characters find themselves at the beginning of the play, manifests itself in a loss of wholeness or identity. When the Host asks Lovel if his name is "Loue-ill or Louewell," Lovel is forced to admit, "I doe not know't my selfe" (I.vi.95–96). Working from the tradition in which a name identifies the essence of its object, Jonson reveals in Lovel a man who does not know who he really is; and, because of the name itself, Jonson reveals that Lovel's problem with identity results from confusion about the true nature of love. Later on, Lovel exclaims in his great thwarted passion, "I remember not where I haue bin, / Or what I am" (IV.iv.260–261). Appropriately, his mate Frances makes a similar remark about herself, after she has genuinely

fallen in love with Lovel but remains separated from him: "I know not
wher I am, or no" (V.ii.55). As in the *Symposium,* the separation of man
from his "proper mate" takes complete identity away.

This loss of identity or wholeness Jonson presents as a lost bodily
completeness, consisting of an imbalance among the conventional four
"humours." Hence, the man who has lost his identity takes on the quality
of one of the humours. The Host begins the play by declaring that he will

> maintayne the Rebus 'gainst all humors,
> And all complexions i' the body of Man.
>
> (I.i.9–10)

What he insists on is maintaining a "light heart," which becomes simultaneously the heart of love within man and the "sign" or "Rebus" of the
Inn itself, in an attempt to prevent a separation of the humours that
would cause an imbalance. In alchemy, the hermaphrodite is also called
the "rebis," representing "the apex of transmutation," the point at which
two natures (male and female) meet.[19] Hence, the New Inn at the "sign"
of the Light Heart is a hermaphroditic rebus (or sign or symbol) in which
male and female meet to create the required wholeness. The Inn as a
symbol of the human heart is to become a kind of alembic turning all to
gold.

Not surprisingly, the Host objects to Lovel's "melancholique" humour
(I.v.116), which, of course, becomes an agent of separation. "Be merry,"
says the Host to Lovel,

> and drinke Sherry; that's my pösie!
> For I shall neuer ioy i'my light heart,
> So long as I conceiue a sullen ghest.
>
> (I.ii.29–31)

In his condemnation of Lovel's melancholy and in his insistence on joviality, the Host declares himself to be sanguine; he is the "Humerous Host"

---

19. See Edgar Wind, *Pagan Mysteries in the Renaissance,* rev. and enl. ed. (New York,
1968), p. 214. Jonson, of course, as *The Alchemist* alone makes clear, was entirely familiar
with alchemical terminology and symbolism. As we shall see, Jonson picks alchemical
symbolism back up in *The New Inn* and applies it even more directly to the theme of love.

(I.ii.32). "I must ha' iouiall guests" (I.i.22), he tells Lovel's servant, Ferret; and shortly afterward he expresses the idea to Lovel himself: "Be iouiall first, and drinke, and dance, and drinke" (I.ii.14). For the Host, sanguineness becomes the agent of union that his Inn *signifies*. Similarly, Frances is phlegmatic, in her refusal to love; she is such, "As, out of humour, will returne no loue" (I.vi.152). She is the appropriate match for Lovel at this point because her humour also functions as an agent of separation. Finally, Lady Frampul, disguised as the old Irish Nurse, is choleric:

> a poore silly foole,
> But an impertinent, and sedulous one,
> As euer was: will vexe you on all occasions.
>
> (II.ii.35–37)

In turn, she is the appropriate match for her husband at this point, because, as with Lovel's melancholy and Frances' phlegm, her choler functions as an agent of separation.

The only figures who seem free from a particular humour—that is, who do not suffer from a psychological imbalance due to a problem with love—are the wise Pru and the Host's servant, Fly, "the Inflamer of the reckonings" at the Inn ("Persons of the Play," l. 57). At the end of the play, Lord Latimer says of Pru that "she is a dowry / So all-sufficient in her vertue and manners, / That fortune cannot adde to her" (V.v.143–145). And, similarly, Fly is said to be "A Creature of all liquors, all complexions" (II.iv.13). As we shall see, the reason Pru and Fly have no particular humour is that they function as spirits of love bringing other couples together—city-comedy correlates of Venus and Cupid, and companions of Ariel, Puck, and Viola.

The loss of sexual wholeness that takes as its psychological form a particular humour takes as its physical form a particular disguise. Essentially, everyone in the play (again, except Pru and Fly) tries to hide his humour behind a mask. The Host, beneath his joviality, is really Lord Frampul, a man who has lost his family. The Host's joviality is revealed as a disguise as soon as he begins conversing with Lovel in Act I; after the Host has exploded in ridicule, first at Lovel, then at the world, Lovel says: "Yo'are tart, mine host, and talke aboue your seasoning, / Ore what you seeme" (I.iii.89-90). And, as the Host himself says at the end, revealing that his humour has been absent of joviality all along, he has "coffin'd [him] selfe alive, in a poore hostlery, / In pennance of my wrongs done" (V.v.105–106). Similarly, Lovel has disguised himself from being recognized as the lover of Frances; as we see later, the true nature of love (and Lovel) is not melancholic and private, but jovial and social. Lady Frampul, in turn, is disguised as the choleric old Nurse, blind in one eye and an alcoholic, but she uses her disguise to order the life of Laetitia with the care of a mother hen. If anything, the Host's wife is really melancholic:

> the mother . . . lost her selfe.
> A fond weake woman, went away in a melancholy.
>
> (I.v.69–70)

Laetitia herself is disguised as her "son" Frank (the masculine name of her eldest daughter, Frances), unknown to the Host, who generously educates the "boy" in Latin. And finally, Frances disguises her true self by avoiding any close relationship with a male lover: "(Though she be very honest) yet she venters / Vpon these precipices, that would make her / Not seeme so" (I.v.54–56). In a sense, disguise becomes the physical form of a humour, a manifestation of one's unbalanced character as a result of having been separated from an original wholeness. Importantly, too, the humours the characters suffer from (melancholy, choler, phlegm) are all agents of separation, not union.

Although people come to the New Inn masking their true identity, the Inn becomes, like Prospero's magic island, a place of wondrous transformation, in which people come "out of their humour" and out of their disguise. The agent of transformation becomes love, which in the *Symposium* had been seen as a magical or alchemical power.[20] When revealing her new feeling for Lovel, Frances says:

> How am I changed! By what alchimy
> Of loue, or language, am I thus translated!

20. In the *Symposium,* 203d, trans. Joyce, Plato calls Love a magician or alchemist: "an adept in sorcery, enchantment, and seduction." Plato's linking of love and magic becomes particularly important for Ficino, with his interest in magic (see speech 6, chap. 10, trans. Jayne, pp. 199–200), and, indeed, for Renaissance neo-Platonism in general.

His tongue tip't with the Philosophers stone,
And that hath touch'd me th[o]rough euery vaine!
I feel that transmutation o' my blood,
As I were quite become another creature.

(III.ii.171–176)

However excessive Frances's claim may appear, it expresses a common neo-Platonic notion of love as a magical power that transforms all to gold (especially prominent in Spenser, Donne, and Shakespeare). Frances's lover, Lovel, will join her in being "Transcendent to the Melancholy" (II.vi.234) he feels, once he is received favorably by her. "It glads my light Heart," says the Host, "To see you rouz'd thus from a sleepy humor, / Of drouzy, accidentall melancholy" (III.ii.264–266). And Lord Beaufort, originally the lover of Frances, undergoes a "change" as well (II.vi.245) during the Court of Love, falling for Laetitia. Jonson's use of the humour convention in alliance with the Shakespearean convention of transformation is an important indicator of Jonson's attempt to blend his conventional humour comedy with Shakespearean romance.[21]

Whereas Pru is responsible for changing both Frances and Lovel (through her scheming), Fly is responsible for changing the status of Beaufort and Laetitia (by overseeing their marriage). Pru and Fly become agents of love, a civic Venus and Cupid. As "Queene Regent of Loue" (III.ii.17), during the Court of Love, Pru resembles Spenser's Venus in the Temple of Venus episode of *The Faerie Queene* (IV.x). There are even hints that Pru is hermaphroditic: wearing a mysterious gown, which conceals the fact that she is both maid and queen (Spenser's Venus wears a mysterious veil to conceal her hermaphroditic nature), she is called a "she-Traian" (II.vi.133), complete with two sides to her personality: "sweet Pru, smooth Pru, / Soft, debonaire, and amiable Pru, / May doe as well as rough, and rigid Pru" (II.vi.224-226). Moreover, as judge in

---

21. See Barton, "*The New Inn* and the Problem of Jonson's Late Style," p. 399: "In this play, . . . Jonson admitted the possibility that people may actually learn from experience, that they can metamorphose themselves and change. They do so here not through the specious means of linguistic alchemy, as practised by Face and Subtle, but fundamentally and—in both senses of the phrase—for good. This premise, absolutely central to Shakespearean comedy, Jonson had resisted for most of his dramatic career. But it lies at the very heart of *The New Inn.*"

the Court, she bears resemblance to the figure of Justice whom Ficino correlates with the hermaphrodite in his commentary on the Platonic myth (speech 4, chap. 2, pp. 156 and 160). Similarly, Fly is called the "bird" of the Inn, and is even thought of as the "Bird" of Pru (II.v.29–30). As his name reveals, he becomes a winged creature of love, the "bird o' the Heart" (V.v.1), a dove of both Venus and her son Cupid. As such, he becomes the proper heir of the New Inn at the sign of the Light Heart (V.v.126–127). If the Host, together with his family, represents the life of love that man leads, Pru and Fly represent the spirit of a wise and just love linking couples together. Jonson's splitting of the Eros figure into a male and a female is suggestive of the hermaphroditic nature of love—and represents a significant innovation from *The Tempest,* in which Shakespeare had used the masculine spirit Ariel disguised as a nymph to unite Ferdinand and Miranda (I.ii).

Because love is the magical agent of transformation, responsible for bringing man out of his humour and out of his disguise, the central episode in the play is the Court of Love. What the episode does is delineate thematically what the play is all about. With Pru presiding as queen, Lovel in the first session must define "what loue is" (III.ii.59), in order to receive a kiss from Frances. Then, in the second session, he must define "what true valour is" (IV.iv.26), in order to receive his second kiss.

In his first speech, Lovel defines love as "Desire of vnion with the thing beloued" (III.ii.75). The definition is Platonic in the common sense of the word, so that the union he speaks of is entirely spiritual: "Loue is a spirituall coupling of two soules" (III.ii.105). The "end of loue," he says,

> is, to haue two made one
> In will, and in affection, that the mindes
> Be first inoculated, not the bodies.
>
> (III.ii.152–154)

Lovel's Platonism comes from Aristophanes' speech in the *Symposium,* not from the speech of Socrates, which emphasizes the transcendence of earthly love to a heavenly love that contemplates the absolute form of beauty. That is, the idea of love that informs the play comes from that part of the dialogue containing the myth of the hermaphrodite. The play's Platonism is less Socratic, more Aristophanic. But Lovel's speech is not entirely true to Aristophanes' speech either; rather, it is a neo-Platonic interpretation of that speech. For, whereas Aristophanes had emphasized the physical union of lovers, Lovel emphasizes their spiritual union. In a sense, Lovel interprets Aristophanes in the light of Socrates.

Importantly, Lovel's direct allusion to the *Symposium* leads Lord Beaufort to refer actually to the Platonic myth. Jonson here links the conventional Elizabethan neo-Platonic view of love as "two into one" with Aristophanes' speech. This is not merely appropriate; it is poetic decorum: for Aristophanes' speech is the source of the idea. If Spenser, or Donne, or Shakespeare has failed to acknowledge his debt to Plato, Jonson, the scholar poet, will ensure that he does not. And that is why the reference to the myth is so important. Jonson becomes a kind of dramatic mythographer, a stage Natale Conti: he instructs the audience in the mythical origin of comedy and in its archetypal pattern of narrative and meaning. Thus, in *The New Inn* Jonson uses the Platonic myth of the hermaphrodite to comment on the nature of comedy.[22] Though the myth of the hermaphrodite is of subordinate importance in the *Symposium* itself, Ficino gave it importance coordinate with the central speech of Socrates, so that subsequent writers picked it up as a key symbol of love. Jonson simply ensures that we are aware of that shift.

While Jonson has Lovel defining love in strictly "Platonic" or spiritual terms, he has Beaufort redefining it in "Ovidian" or physical terms.

---

22. Jonson's *mythographical* technique for commenting on the nature of comedy complements his *metaphorical* technique, documented by Harriett Hawkins in "The Idea of a Theater in Jonson's *The New Inn*" (*RenD*, IX [1966], 205–226). According to Hawkins, "From the beginning to the end, Jonson stresses the fact that his play, through almost outrageous 'feigning,' can teach the audience significant truths about various kinds of illusion within both the world of the theater and the 'theater of the world' " (p. 206). For Jonson's metaphorical correlation between the action in the play and drama, see, in particular, the Host's comment,

> I imagine all the world's a Play;
> The state, and mens affaires, all passages
> Of life, to spring new scenes, come in, goe out,
> And shift, and vanish; and if I haue got
> A seat, to sit at ease here, i' mine Inne,
> To see the Comedy . . .
>
> (I.iii.128–137)

During Lovel's "philosophical feast" (III.ii.125), Beaufort is reaching for his "banquet o' sense" (III.ii.126)—Laetitia, who appears in a double disguise as the boy Frank redisguised as the girl "Laetitia" (and played by a boy actor!). The juxtaposition of Plato's philosophical feast with Ovid's banquet of sense should remind us not merely that Plato and Ovid had different views about love, but also that Plato and Ovid were the two great mythmakers of the hermaphrodite: both were writers who saw love as hermaphroditic in nature. Rather than satirizing Platonic love here, Jonson is presenting a view of love combining Plato and Ovid, spirit and sense, the soul and the body, much as we have seen in the neo-Platonic interpretation of the Platonic myth and in the poetry of Spenser and Donne, as well as in a play such as *The Tempest,* in which love between man and woman means a total union of body and soul. Man's true identity consists of his hermaphroditic union with the "proper mate" in a love that is both physical and spiritual.[23]

In the second session of the Court of Love, we are told that love begets true valor (IV.iv.27–28). True valor itself, says Lovel, is action performed out of sound reason and guided by mature judgment (IV.iv.38 ff.). For Jonson, love is not merely a personal passion expressed within the human heart; it is a social action that is expressed within society and that combines reason with passion. As in the neo-Platonism of Spenser, love is a wise and truthful force serving as the basis of virtuous action in the world. The man who combines love with wisdom in his breast is the man capable of true valor; but the man who has passion without reason is the man who

---

23. According to Sir Kenelm Digby, in *Private Memoirs,* ed. H. Nicolas (London, 1827), p. 9, love is that "infinite blessed state wherein the almighty God reigneth, by uniting two persons, two souls, two wills, in one; which by breathing together produce a divine love; and then their bodies may justly strive to perpetuate that essence by succession, whose durance in themselves is limited" (quoted in Barton, "*The New Inn* and the Problem of Jonson's Late Style," p. 409). Robert Ellrodt, in *Neoplatonism in the Poetry of Spenser* (Geneva, 1960), has traced this kind of neo-Platonism (found in Spenser but not in Ficino, Pico, Benivieni, and Castiglione) to the philosophies of M'ario Equicola, Leone Ebreo, and Louis Le Roy. "In Italian courtly circles and in the language of fashion, married love and Platonic love indeed were usually contrasted. . . . The originality of Spenser's philosophy of love lies in the association of Platonic idealism with an acceptance of bodily union" (p. 146). Jonson's neo-Platonism in *The New Inn* belongs to this Spenserian kind of neo-Platonism.

falls into "angry valor." If Lovel himself, by the end of the play, comes closest to embodying the ideal of a physical and spiritual love leading to true valor, Nick and Pinnacia Stuff come to embody physical love without spiritual affection, while Sir Glorious Tipto embodies "angry valor."

Nick and Pinnacia embody physical love in its worst form. As the tailor to Frances, Nick has access to Pru's gown. Customarily, Nick likes to dress his wife up in a client's dress, then throw her on the bed and make love to her. Although Nick and Pinnacia "ha' beene coupled now seuen yeares" (IV.iii.56), what they disguise is their marriage itself: Pinnacia pretends she is a lady, while Nick pretends he is her servant. This "fine species, / Of fornicating with a mans owne wife" (IV.iii.76–77) thus denies the true spirit of love that the comedy is concerned with. Their hermaphroditic "coupling" is a perversion of the hermaphroditic union symbolized at the end of the play by the other couples.

Similarly, Sir Glorious embodies angry valor, a parody of Lovel's true valor. Tipto is a colonel in the army, and tries to organize the servants in the lower part of the Inn into a working militia—an attempt that proves unsuccessful. The crew abuses the sacred liquid of the Inn, wine, and ends up in a ridiculously drunken and rowdy state. As a result, they reenact the battle between the Centaurs and the Lapithes, with Sir Glorious and Hodge Huffle representing the chief opposing forces. Significantly, the fight breaks out over who will court Pinnacia—over human love. The entire crew fights ignobly, being guided by mere passion, not reason: the wine of love has transformed them, as in the story of Circe, into "half-beasts" (IV.ii.101). Tipto becomes the incarnation of a beast—the man who has given up his god-given gift of reason to participate in angry valor: "what a glorious beast our Tipto shew'd" (IV.iii.4). As such, he parodies Love himself in Aristophanes' speech in the *Symposium*: "therefore it is our duty one and all to inspire our friends with reverence and piety, for so we may ensure our safety and attain that blessed union by enlisting in the army of Love and marching beneath his banners" (193b). Appropriately, Tipto denies the hermaphroditic nature of love when he accuses Fly of wanting to "diuide the thanks with me . . . share in my glories" (II.vi.41).

The play thus moves toward revealing true and false love and valor for what they are. Nick and Pinnacia are disrobed and expelled from the Inn, as is Sir Glorious: they are found guilty of treason to the Court of Love, within the sign of the Light Heart. Similarly, the main characters are revealed for what they are. The key to this latter recognition, importantly, is the hermaphroditic Laetitia/Frank/"Laetitia," who functions as a kind of Epicoene, an embodiment of the sexual confusion most everyone is suffering from; Pru calls her "Lady-No-body" (II.ii.55).[24] The figure responsible for the recognition is the bird of the Inn, Fly, who has secretly arranged the marriage between Beaufort and the disguised "Laetitia," and who has then informed the Host of the comical marriage. The Host, believing Laetitia to be Frank, a "counterfeit mirth, and a clip'd Lady" (V.iv.48), tells Beaufort: "See whom you ha' married, / Your hosts sonne, and a boy" (V.iv.45–46). A servant adds, "A boy, a boy; my Lord has married a boy" (V.iv.49).

The phase of sexual confusion and separation among lovers ends when the old Irish Nurse enters, having learned that her daughter has been married "in a stable, / And sold vnto a husband" (V.v.8–9). Speaking in plain English, "Quite like another creature" (V.v.27), she reveals her true nature, as well as that of her daughter. The Host reveals himself to be Lord Frampul, and reunites with his wife; he gives his daughter Frances to Lovel, and blesses the marriage of his other daughter, Laetitia, to Lord Beaufort. And Lord Latimer, who has been masking his feelings for Pru all along, reveals his desire to marry her. As with Shakespeare's last plays, *The New Inn* ends on a note of reconciliation, celebration, love, and marriage—with the Host presiding:

> Best goe to bed,
> And dreame it ouer all. Let's all goe sleepe,
> Each with his Turtle.
>
> (V.v.122–124)

Lovel, revealing his transformation, adds: "light vs all to bed" (V.v.151). The light he speaks of is that from the human heart, the magical force of

24. See Partridge, *The Broken Compass,* p. 162, for a definition of *epicene* that is "central to *The Silent Woman*": "the abnormal no man's land (and no woman's land) between the normal male and the normal female." In this regard, the epicene is a kind of aberration of the hermaphrodite.

love directing man in his destiny to recover his original wholeness: "two Turtles, makes, / A heart with a light stuck in't, a light heart" (I.i. 16–17). The light, in other words, is the illumination of a wise and truthful love that is both physical and spiritual. The Host concludes the play by saying that tonight he will "woo afresh, / And like Mecaenas, hauing but one wife, / [he'll] marry her, euery houre of life, hereafter" (V.V.154–156).

In *Epicoene,* Jonson had formally satirized the Elizabethan love code of hermaphroditism, by making Epicoene the central figure embodying sexual confusion. Revealing the futility of such a romantic notion of love, Jonson transforms the traditional hero as lover into merely a lustful "Sir Amorous La Foole." If for the Jacobeans the great symbol of confusion about love had been the epicene, and if for the Elizabethans the great symbol of love itself had been the hermaphrodite, then in *The New Inn,* a Carolinian play turning toward an Elizabethan vision, Jonson adopts an Elizabethan symbol: the hermaphrodite as a figure of love embodying true identity.

As we have seen, Jonson appropriately structures his comedy around the theme, plot, and motif of the Platonic myth of the hermaphrodite. He even refers to the myth at a central point. The reference is not casual, but provides the informing idea for the play as a whole, suggesting that Jonson is identifying the mythical core for his comedy. And, because *The New Inn* looks back nostalgically to Shakespeare, Spenser, and the Elizabethans, Jonson's use of the myth may suggest that he is identifying the mythical core for the Renaissance comic tradition in general. Drama becomes more than entertainment and instruction about man and society; it becomes entertainment and instruction in the art of comedy. *The New Inn* is both a comedy and a commentary on comedy in the sense that, through the medium of the play, Jonson at the end of his career is surveying the entire expanse of Renaissance comedy. What he sees is that his own "humour" comedy shares with the romantic comedy of Shakespeare and the Elizabethans a common narrative pattern and, ultimately, a common vision of life. He sees, too, that all have their genesis in Plato's myth of the hermaphrodite in the *Symposium.* The myth is "well remembred here, and to good vse" because, in a sense, Jonson is putting his own play and Renaissance comedy into the context of the myth. In adapting the myth to his new hybrid form of comedy, "humour romance," Jonson is revealing not merely his gift for using a classical source magically to "turne all into Honey," as he says in the *Discoveries,* but also his gift for lending continuity to the entire range of the literary tradition.

Notes on Contributors

JAMES P. BEDNARZ, Assistant Professor of English at C. W. Post College of Long Island University, is currently engaged in a study of literary relations among eminent Elizabethan authors. His essay on "Ralegh in Spenser's Historical Allegory" appears in *Spenser Studies* IV.

THOMAS CARTELLI, Assistant Professor of English and Drama at Muhlenberg College in Allentown, Pa., is working on a book-length study of Marlowe and Shakespeare. He has recently published several articles on Shakespeare.

PATRICK CHENEY, Assistant Professor of English at The Pennsylvania State University, teaches courses in technical writing and literature. He has articles forthcoming in *English Language Notes* and *Studia Neophilologica* on Spenser's *Faerie Queene*, in *Renaissance and Reformation* on Dekker and Middleton's *The Roaring Girl*, and in *Milton Studies* on Milton's *Sonnet XXIII*.

FRANK KERINS, who is in the English Department of Fördham University, Bronx, N.Y., is currently writing a book on Elizabethan satire and Ben Jonson's plays.

RONALD L. MARTINEZ is Associate Professor of Italian at the University of Minnesota. He writes on trecento and Renaissance topics and is currently completing a study, in collaboration with Robert Durling, on Dante's *petrose*.

JOHN W. ROBINSON, Professor of English at the University of Nebraska-Lincoln, is the co-author of *English Theatrical Literature 1559-1900: A Bibliography*, and author of *Theatrical Street Ballads: Some Nineteenth-Century Street Ballads about the Theatre*. He has published many essays about the early English drama, most recently in *Leeds Studies in English* and *Comparative Drama*.

PETER L. RUDNYTSKY is Assistant Professor of English and Comparative Literature at Columbia University. He has published or has forthcoming articles in *Raritan, Texas Studies in Literature and Language, World Literature Today, American Imago, Erasmus of Rotterdam Society Yearbook,* and *Denver Quarterly*. A second essay on *Othello,* "The Purloined Handkerchief in *Othello,*" will appear in *The Psychoanalytic Study of Literature.* In 1983-1984, he will be a Mellon Faculty Fellow at Harvard, where he plans to complete a book on *Freud and the Myth of Oedipus.*